MANIFEST DESTINY

CHRIS DINGESS — WRITER

MATTHEW ROBERTS — PENCILLER & INKER

OWEN GIENI — COLORIST

PAT BROSSEAU — LETTERER

SEAN MACKIEWICZ — EDITOR

MATTHEW ROBERTS & OWEN GIENI
COVER ART

IMAGE COMICS, INC.
Robert Kirkman—Chief Operating Officer
Erik Larsen—Chief Financial Officer
Todd McFarlane—President
Marc Silvestri—Chief Executive Officer
Jim Valentino—Vice President

Eric Stephenson—Publisher / Chief Creative Officer
Corey Hart—Director of Sales
Jeff Boison—Director of Publishing Planning
 & Book Trade Sales
Chris Ross—Director of Digital Sales
Jeff Stang—Director of Specialty Sales
Kat Salazar—Director of PR & Marketing
Drew Gill—Art Director
Heather Doornink—Production Director
Nicole Lapalme—Controller

IMAGECOMICS.COM

MANIFEST DESTINY
CREATED BY
CHRIS DINGESS

SKYBOUND
For SKYBOUND ENTERTAINMENT

Robert Kirkman - Chairman
David Alpert - CEO
Sean Mackiewicz - SVP, Editor-In-Chief
Shawn Kirkham - SVP, Business Development
Brian Huntington - Online Editorial Director
June Alian - Publicity Director
Andres Juarez - Art Director
Jon Moisan - Editor
Arielle Basich - Associate Editor
Paul Shin - Business Development Coordinator
Johnny O'Dell - Social Media Manager
Dan Petersen - Director of Operations & Events

International inquiries: ag@sequentialrights.com
Licensing inquiries: contact@skybound.com

www.skybound.com

MANIFEST DESTINY, VOL. ONE: FLORA AND FAUNA. THIRD PRINTING. ISBN: 978-1-60706-982-9. PUBLISHED BY IMAGE COMICS, IN
OFFICE OF PUBLICATION: 2701 NW VAUGHN ST., STE. 780, PORTLAND, OR 97210. COPYRIGHT © 2018 SKYBOUND, LLC. ALL RIGHT
RESERVED. ORIGINALLY PUBLISHED IN SINGLE MAGAZINE FORMAT AS MANIFEST DESTINY #1-6. MANIFEST DESTINY™ (INCLUDIN
ALL PROMINENT CHARACTERS FEATURED HEREIN), ITS LOGO AND ALL CHARACTER LIKENESSES ARE TRADEMARKS OF SKYBOUN
LLC, UNLESS OTHERWISE NOTED. IMAGE COMICS® AND ITS LOGOS ARE REGISTERED TRADEMARKS AND COPYRIGHTS OF IMAG
COMICS, INC. ALL RIGHTS RESERVED. NO PART OF THIS PUBLICATION MAY BE REPRODUCED OR TRANSMITTED IN ANY FORM O
BY ANY MEANS (EXCEPT FOR SHORT EXCERPTS FOR REVIEW PURPOSES) WITHOUT THE EXPRESS WRITTEN PERMISSION OF IMAG
COMICS, INC. ALL NAMES, CHARACTERS, EVENTS AND LOCALES IN THIS PUBLICATION ARE ENTIRELY FICTIONAL. ANY RESEMBLAN
TO ACTUAL PERSONS (LIVING OR DEAD), EVENTS OR PLACES, WITHOUT SATIRIC INTENT, IS COINCIDENTAL. PRINTED IN THE U.S
FOR INFORMATION REGARDING THE CPSIA ON THIS PRINTED MATERIAL CALL: 203-595-3636 AND PROVIDE REFERENCE # RICH - 7995

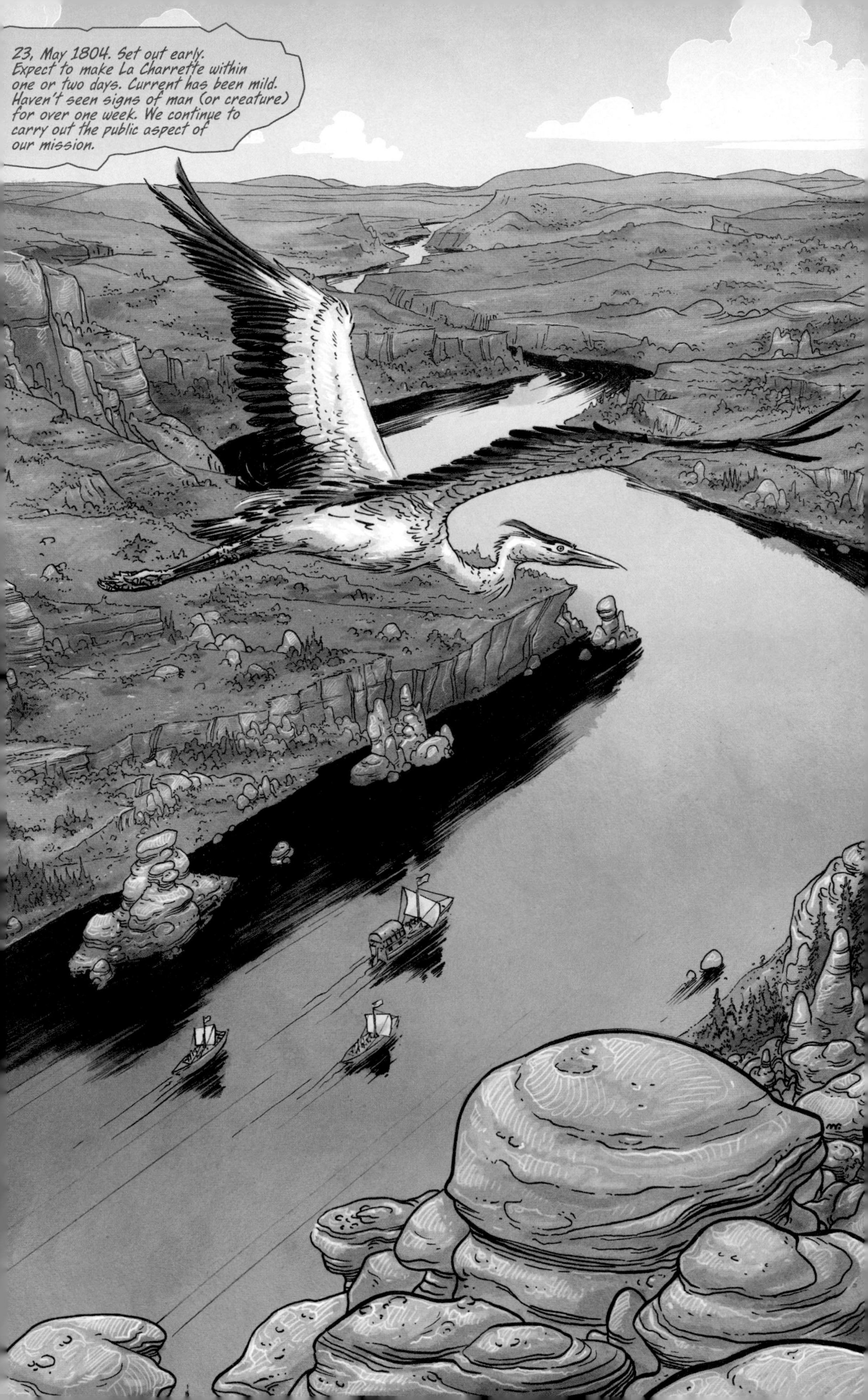
23, May 1804. Set out early. Expect to make La Charrette within one or two days. Current has been mild. Haven't seen signs of man (or creature) for over one week. We continue to carry out the public aspect of our mission.

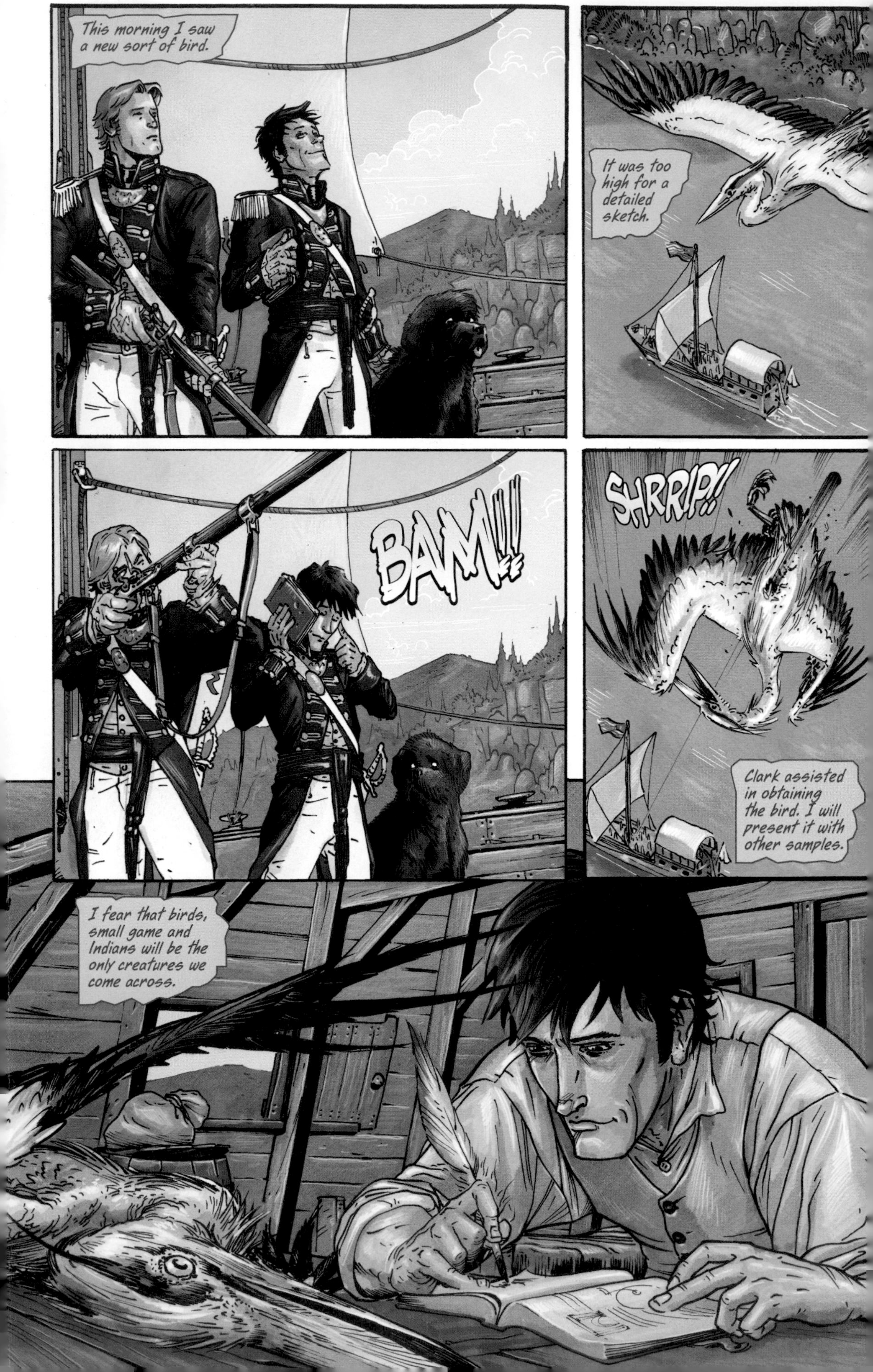
This morning I saw a new sort of bird.
It was too high for a detailed sketch.
BAM!!!
SHRRIP!!
Clark assisted in obtaining the bird. I will present it with other samples.
I fear that birds, small game and Indians will be the only creatures we come across.

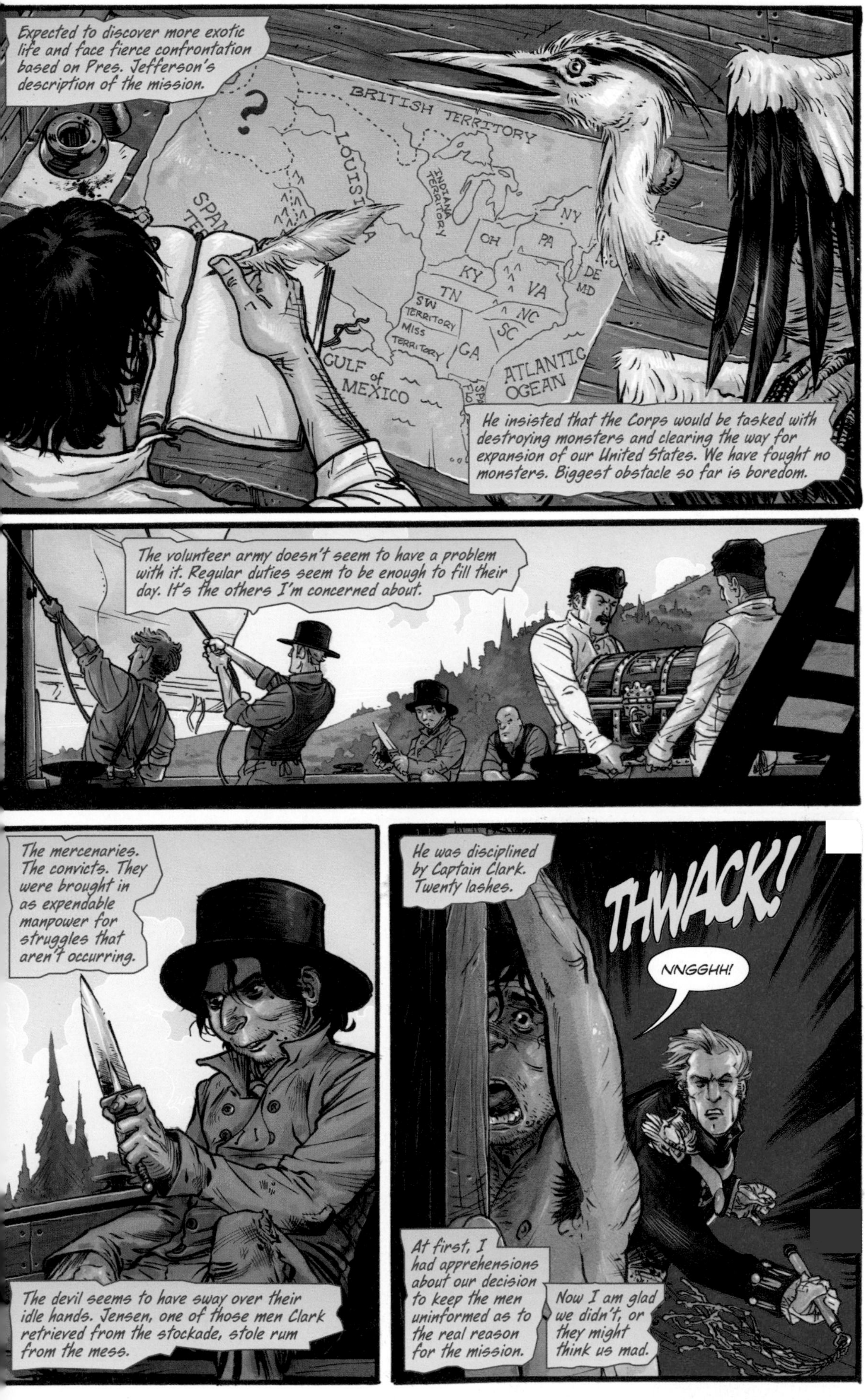
Expected to discover more exotic life and face fierce confrontation based on Pres. Jefferson's description of the mission.
BRITISH TERRITORY
INDIANA TERRITORY
NY
OH
PA
KY
DE
MD
VA
TN
NC
SC
SW TERRITORY
MISS TERRITORY
GA
GULF of MEXICO
ATLANTIC OCEAN
He insisted that the Corps would be tasked with destroying monsters and clearing the way for expansion of our United States. We have fought no monsters. Biggest obstacle so far is boredom.
The volunteer army doesn't seem to have a problem with it. Regular duties seem to be enough to fill their day. It's the others I'm concerned about.
The mercenaries. The convicts. They were brought in as expendable manpower for struggles that aren't occurring.
The devil seems to have sway over their idle hands. Jensen, one of those men Clark retrieved from the stockade, stole rum from the mess.
He was disciplined by Captain Clark. Twenty lashes.
THWACK!
NNGGHH!
At first, I had apprehensions about our decision to keep the men uninformed as to the real reason for the mission.
Now I am glad we didn't, or they might think us mad.

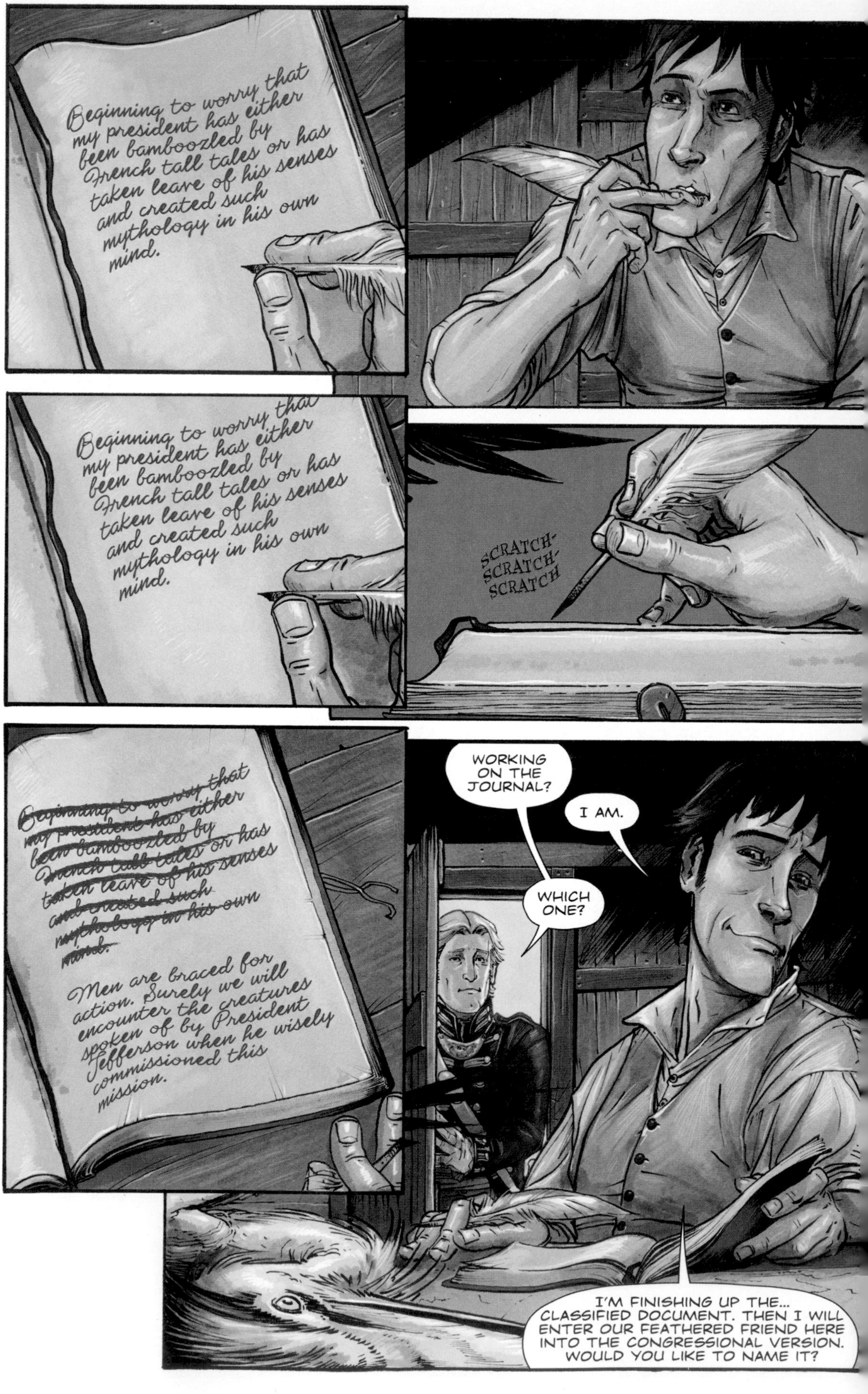
Beginning to worry that my president has either been bamboozled by French tall tales or has taken leave of his senses and created such mythology in his own mind.
Beginning to worry that my president has either been bamboozled by French tall tales or has taken leave of his senses and created such mythology in his own mind.
SCRATCH-SCRATCH-SCRATCH
~~Beginning to worry that my president has either been bamboozled by French tall tales or has taken leave of his senses and created such mythology in his own mind.~~
Men are braced for action. Surely we will encounter the creatures spoken of by President Jefferson when he wisely commissioned this mission.
WORKING ON THE JOURNAL?
I AM.
WHICH ONE?
I'M FINISHING UP THE... CLASSIFIED DOCUMENT. THEN I WILL ENTER OUR FEATHERED FRIEND HERE INTO THE CONGRESSIONAL VERSION. WOULD YOU LIKE TO NAME IT?

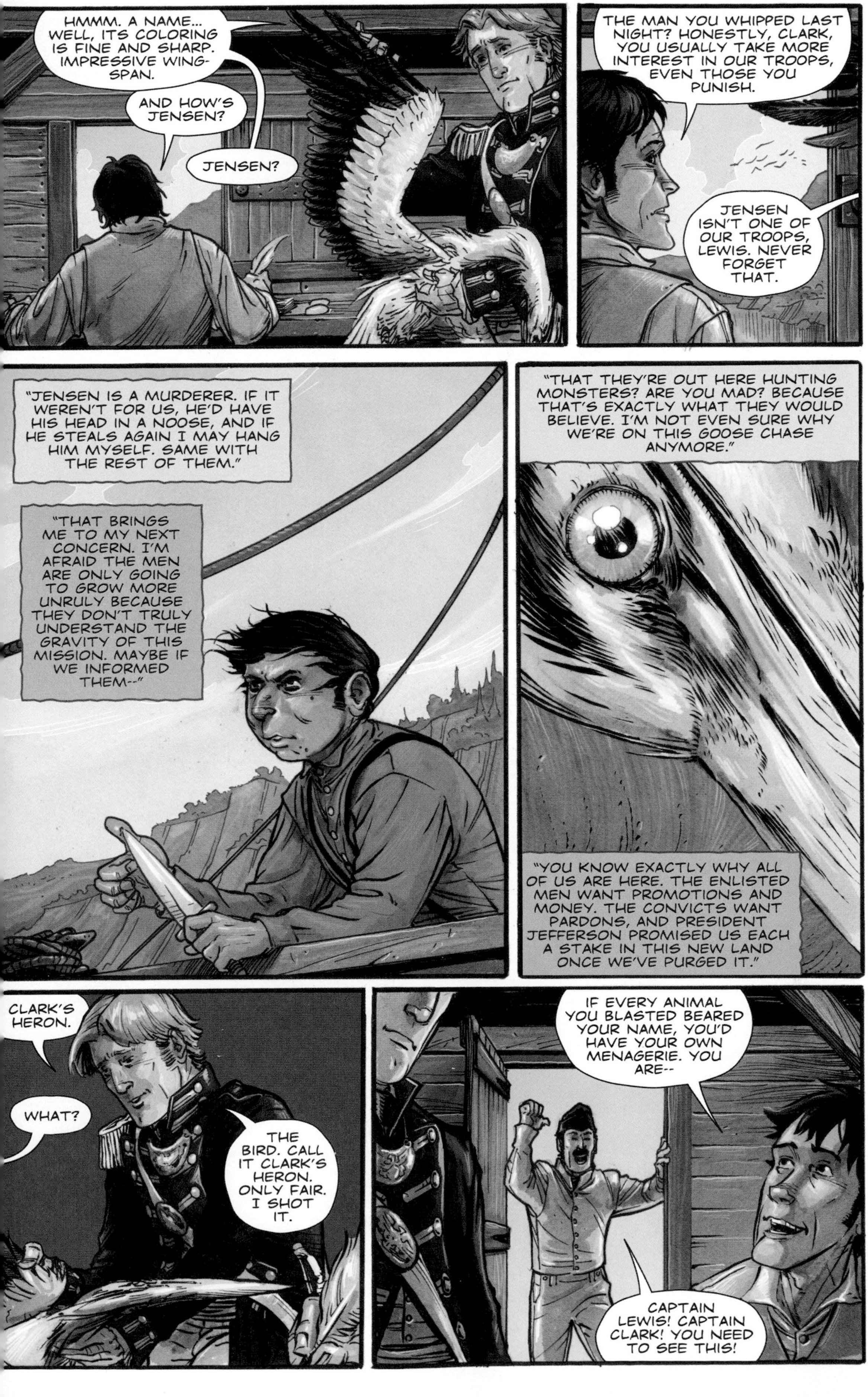
HMMM. A NAME... WELL, ITS COLORING IS FINE AND SHARP. IMPRESSIVE WING-SPAN.
AND HOW'S JENSEN?
JENSEN?
THE MAN YOU WHIPPED LAST NIGHT? HONESTLY, CLARK, YOU USUALLY TAKE MORE INTEREST IN OUR TROOPS, EVEN THOSE YOU PUNISH.
JENSEN ISN'T ONE OF OUR TROOPS, LEWIS. NEVER FORGET THAT.
"JENSEN IS A MURDERER. IF IT WEREN'T FOR US, HE'D HAVE HIS HEAD IN A NOOSE, AND IF HE STEALS AGAIN I MAY HANG HIM MYSELF. SAME WITH THE REST OF THEM."
"THAT BRINGS ME TO MY NEXT CONCERN. I'M AFRAID THE MEN ARE ONLY GOING TO GROW MORE UNRULY BECAUSE THEY DON'T TRULY UNDERSTAND THE GRAVITY OF THIS MISSION. MAYBE IF WE INFORMED THEM--"
"THAT THEY'RE OUT HERE HUNTING MONSTERS? ARE YOU MAD? BECAUSE THAT'S EXACTLY WHAT THEY WOULD BELIEVE. I'M NOT EVEN SURE WHY WE'RE ON THIS GOOSE CHASE ANYMORE."
"YOU KNOW EXACTLY WHY ALL OF US ARE HERE. THE ENLISTED MEN WANT PROMOTIONS AND MONEY. THE CONVICTS WANT PARDONS, AND PRESIDENT JEFFERSON PROMISED US EACH A STAKE IN THIS NEW LAND ONCE WE'VE PURGED IT."
CLARK'S HERON.
WHAT?
THE BIRD. CALL IT CLARK'S HERON. ONLY FAIR. I SHOT IT.
IF EVERY ANIMAL YOU BLASTED BEARED YOUR NAME, YOU'D HAVE YOUR OWN MENAGERIE. YOU ARE--
CAPTAIN LEWIS! CAPTAIN CLARK! YOU NEED TO SEE THIS!

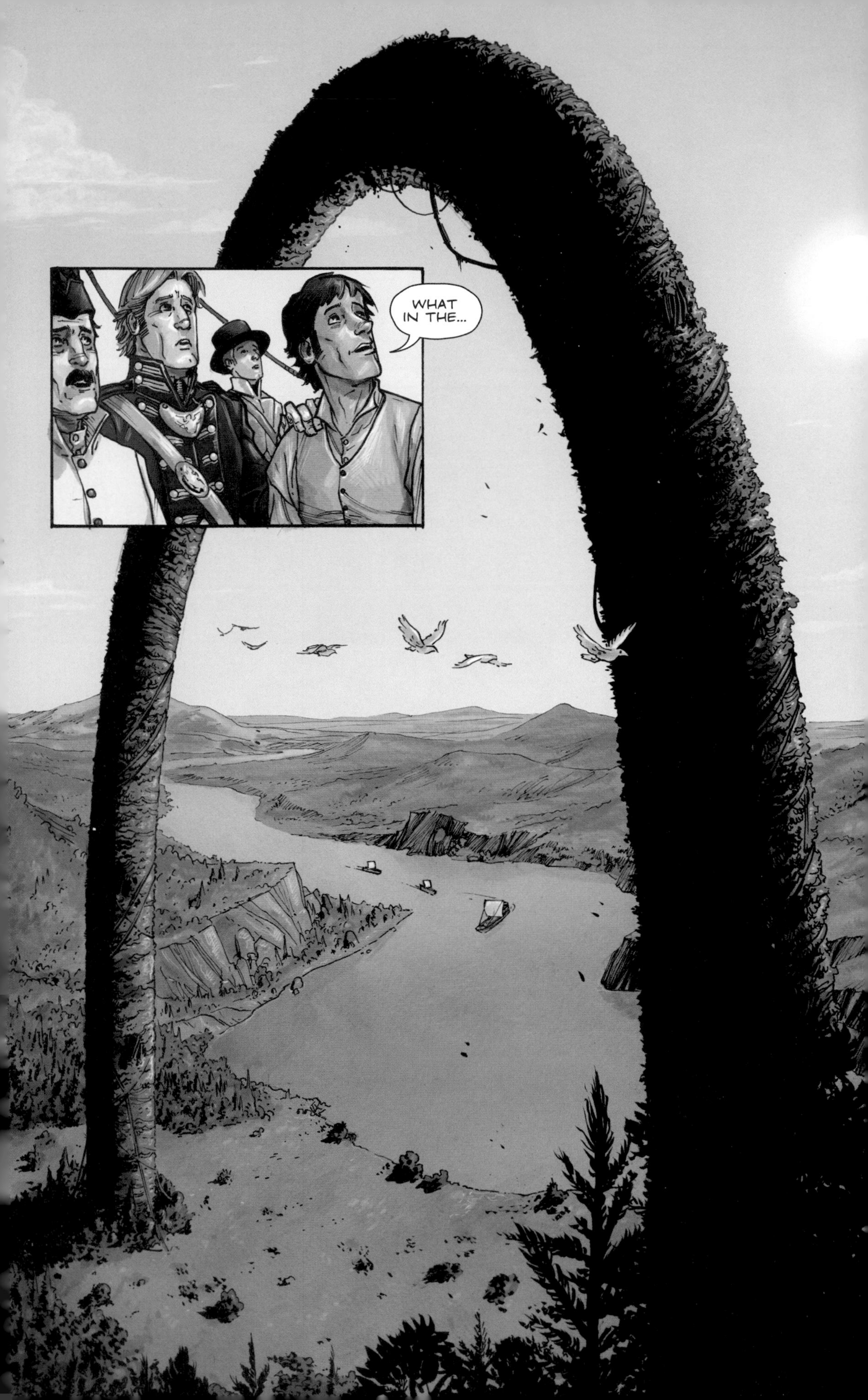
WHAT IN THE...

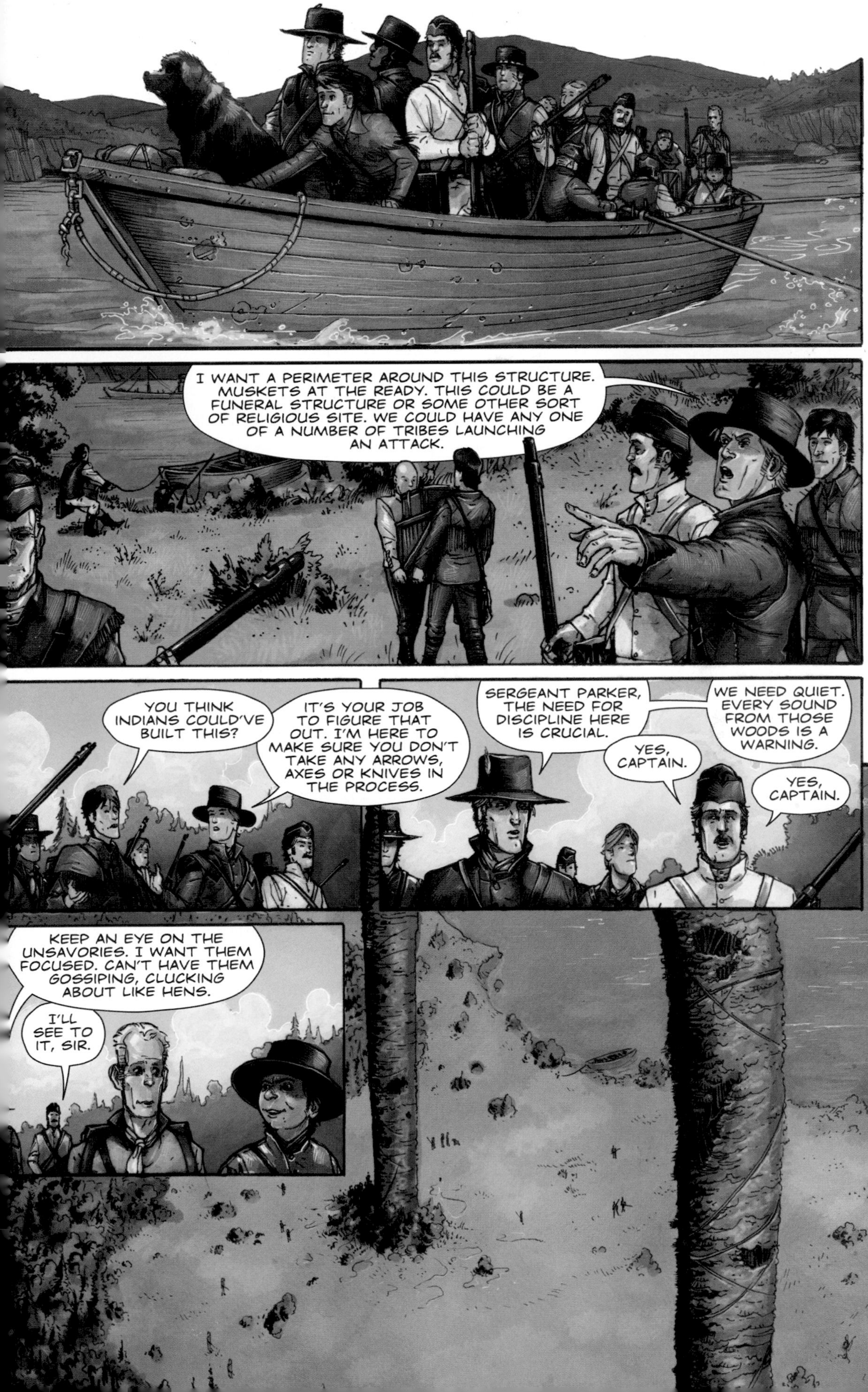
I WANT A PERIMETER AROUND THIS STRUCTURE. MUSKETS AT THE READY. THIS COULD BE A FUNERAL STRUCTURE OR SOME OTHER SORT OF RELIGIOUS SITE. WE COULD HAVE ANY ONE OF A NUMBER OF TRIBES LAUNCHING AN ATTACK.
YOU THINK INDIANS COULD'VE BUILT THIS?
IT'S YOUR JOB TO FIGURE THAT OUT. I'M HERE TO MAKE SURE YOU DON'T TAKE ANY ARROWS, AXES OR KNIVES IN THE PROCESS.
SERGEANT PARKER, THE NEED FOR DISCIPLINE HERE IS CRUCIAL.
WE NEED QUIET. EVERY SOUND FROM THOSE WOODS IS A WARNING.
YES, CAPTAIN.
YES, CAPTAIN.
KEEP AN EYE ON THE UNSAVORIES. I WANT THEM FOCUSED. CAN'T HAVE THEM GOSSIPING, CLUCKING ABOUT LIKE HENS.
I'LL SEE TO IT, SIR.

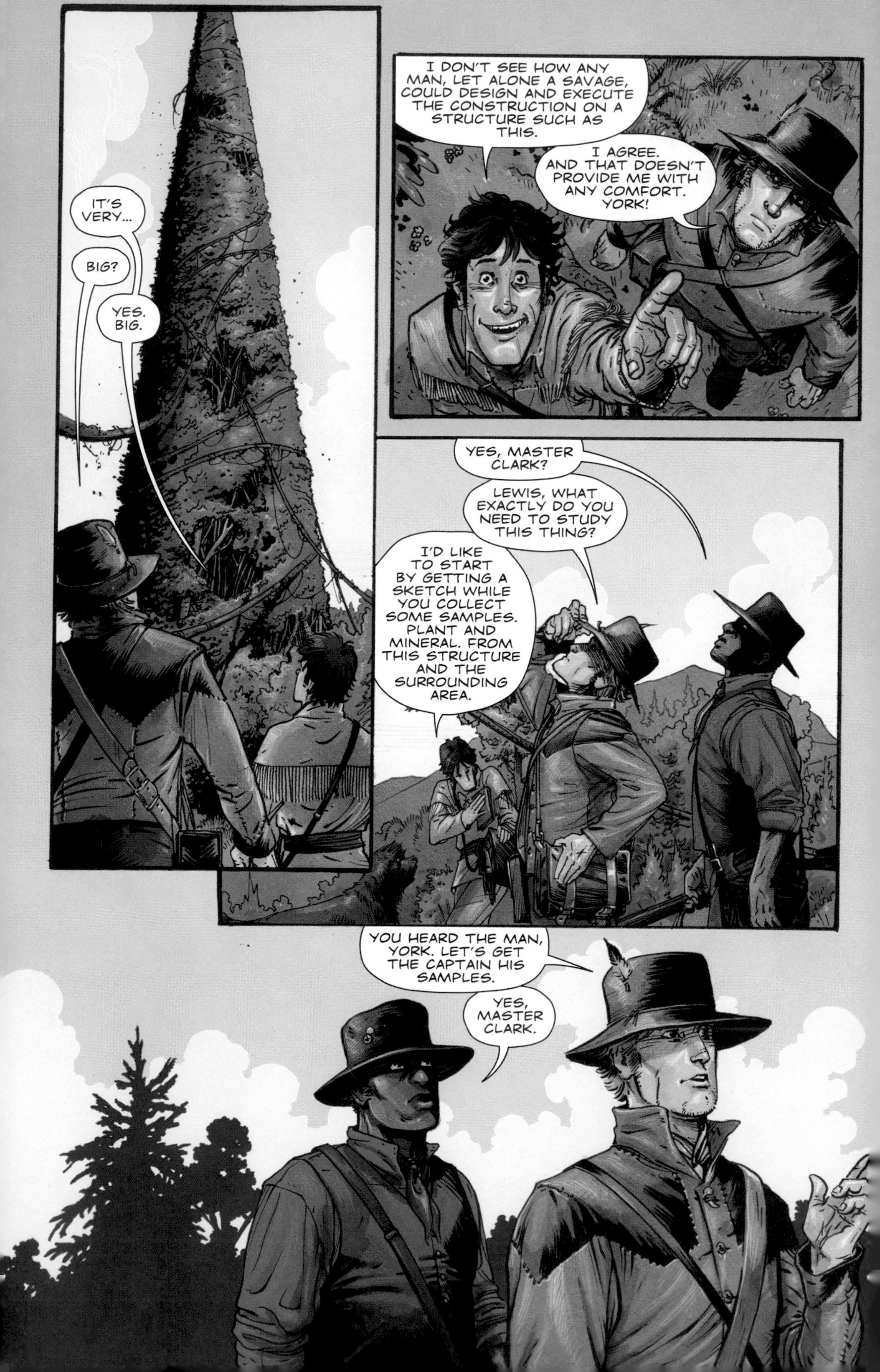
IT'S VERY...
BIG?
YES. BIG.
I DON'T SEE HOW ANY MAN, LET ALONE A SAVAGE, COULD DESIGN AND EXECUTE THE CONSTRUCTION ON A STRUCTURE SUCH AS THIS.
I AGREE. AND THAT DOESN'T PROVIDE ME WITH ANY COMFORT. YORK!
YES, MASTER CLARK?
LEWIS, WHAT EXACTLY DO YOU NEED TO STUDY THIS THING?
I'D LIKE TO START BY GETTING A SKETCH WHILE YOU COLLECT SOME SAMPLES. PLANT AND MINERAL. FROM THIS STRUCTURE AND THE SURROUNDING AREA.
YOU HEARD THE MAN, YORK. LET'S GET THE CAPTAIN HIS SAMPLES.
YES, MASTER CLARK.

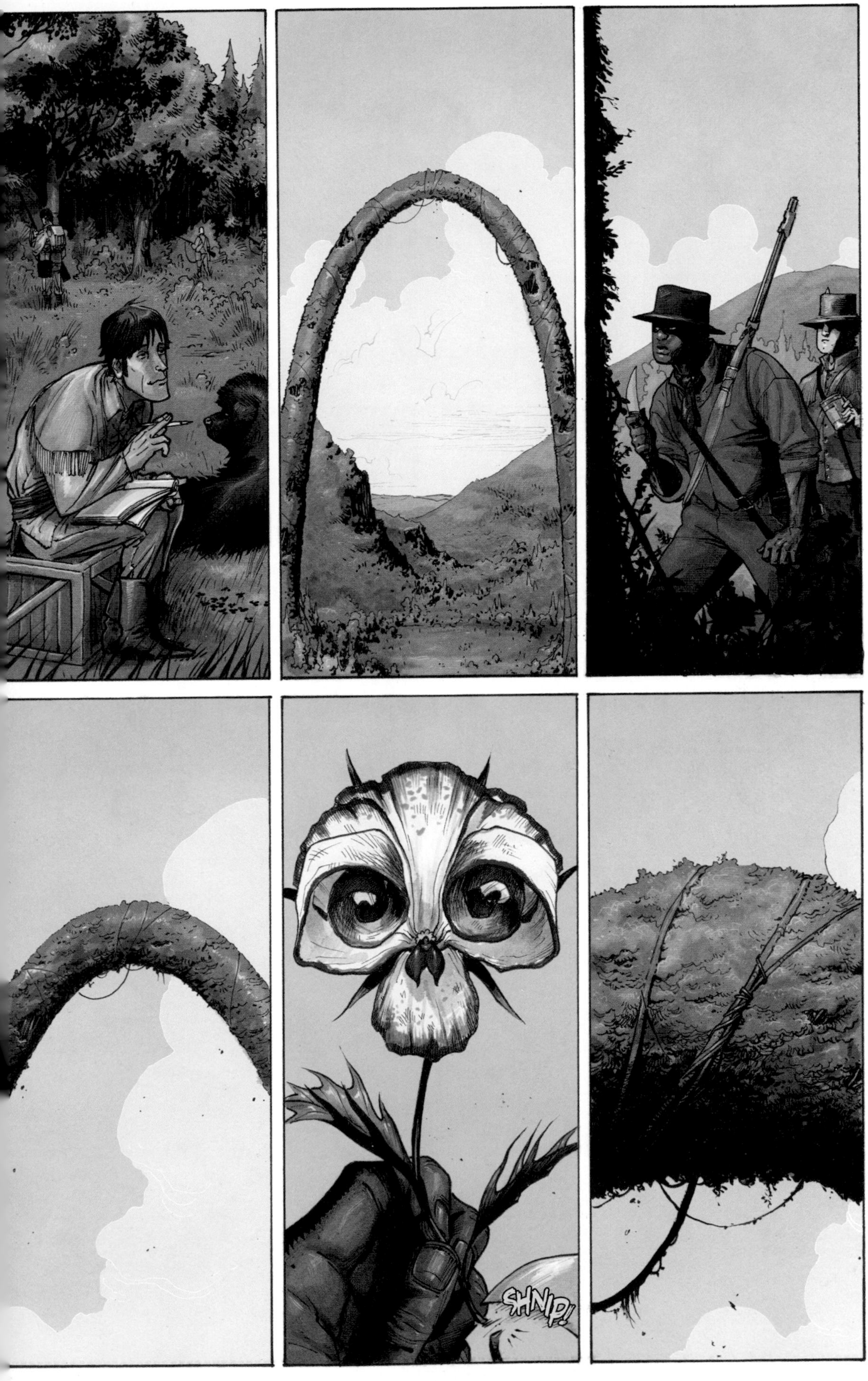
SHNIP!

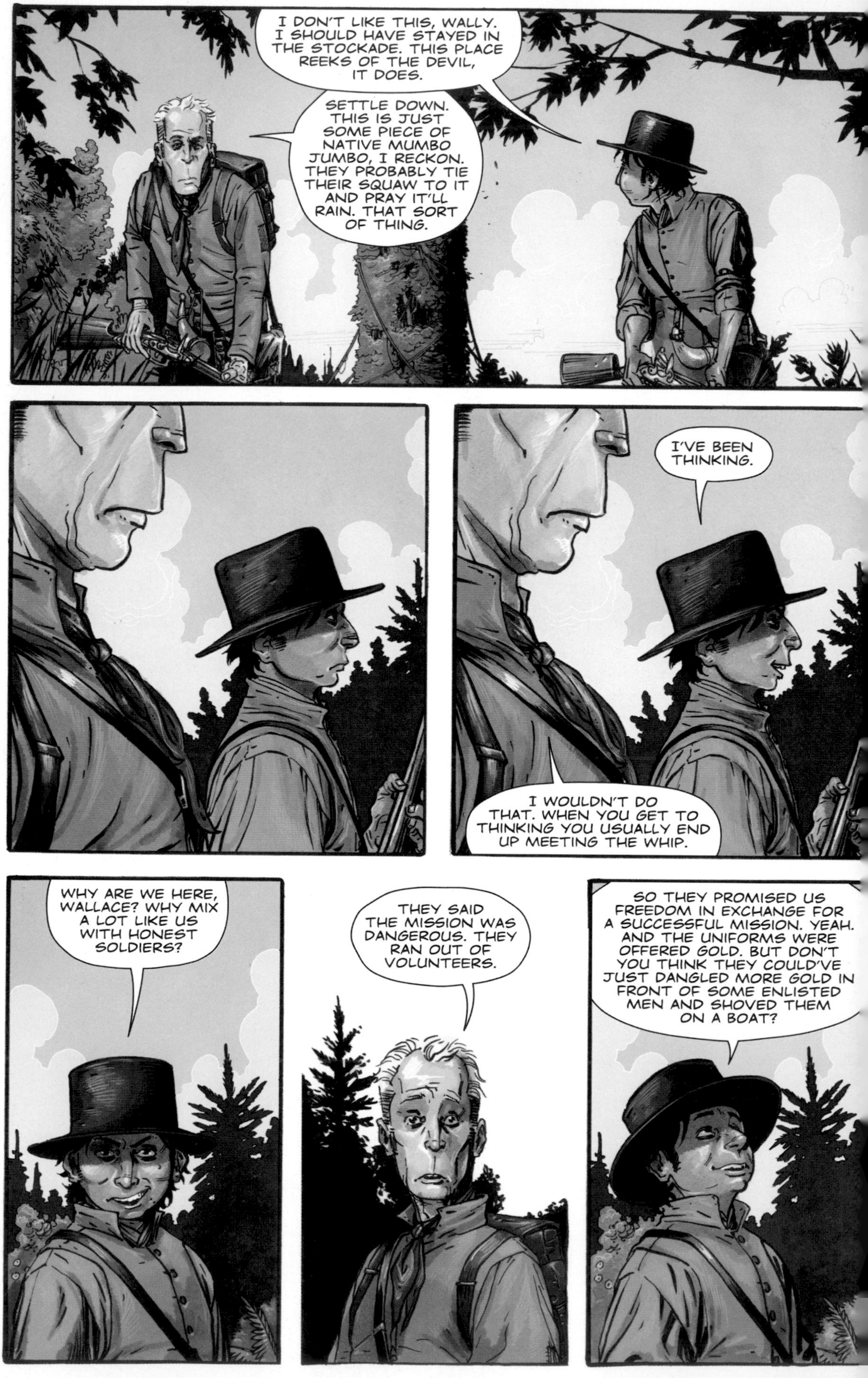
I DON'T LIKE THIS, WALLY. I SHOULD HAVE STAYED IN THE STOCKADE. THIS PLACE REEKS OF THE DEVIL, IT DOES.
SETTLE DOWN. THIS IS JUST SOME PIECE OF NATIVE MUMBO JUMBO, I RECKON. THEY PROBABLY TIE THEIR SQUAW TO IT AND PRAY IT'LL RAIN. THAT SORT OF THING.
I'VE BEEN THINKING.
I WOULDN'T DO THAT. WHEN YOU GET TO THINKING YOU USUALLY END UP MEETING THE WHIP.
WHY ARE WE HERE, WALLACE? WHY MIX A LOT LIKE US WITH HONEST SOLDIERS?
THEY SAID THE MISSION WAS DANGEROUS. THEY RAN OUT OF VOLUNTEERS.
SO THEY PROMISED US FREEDOM IN EXCHANGE FOR A SUCCESSFUL MISSION. YEAH. AND THE UNIFORMS WERE OFFERED GOLD. BUT DON'T YOU THINK THEY COULD'VE JUST DANGLED MORE GOLD IN FRONT OF SOME ENLISTED MEN AND SHOVED THEM ON A BOAT?

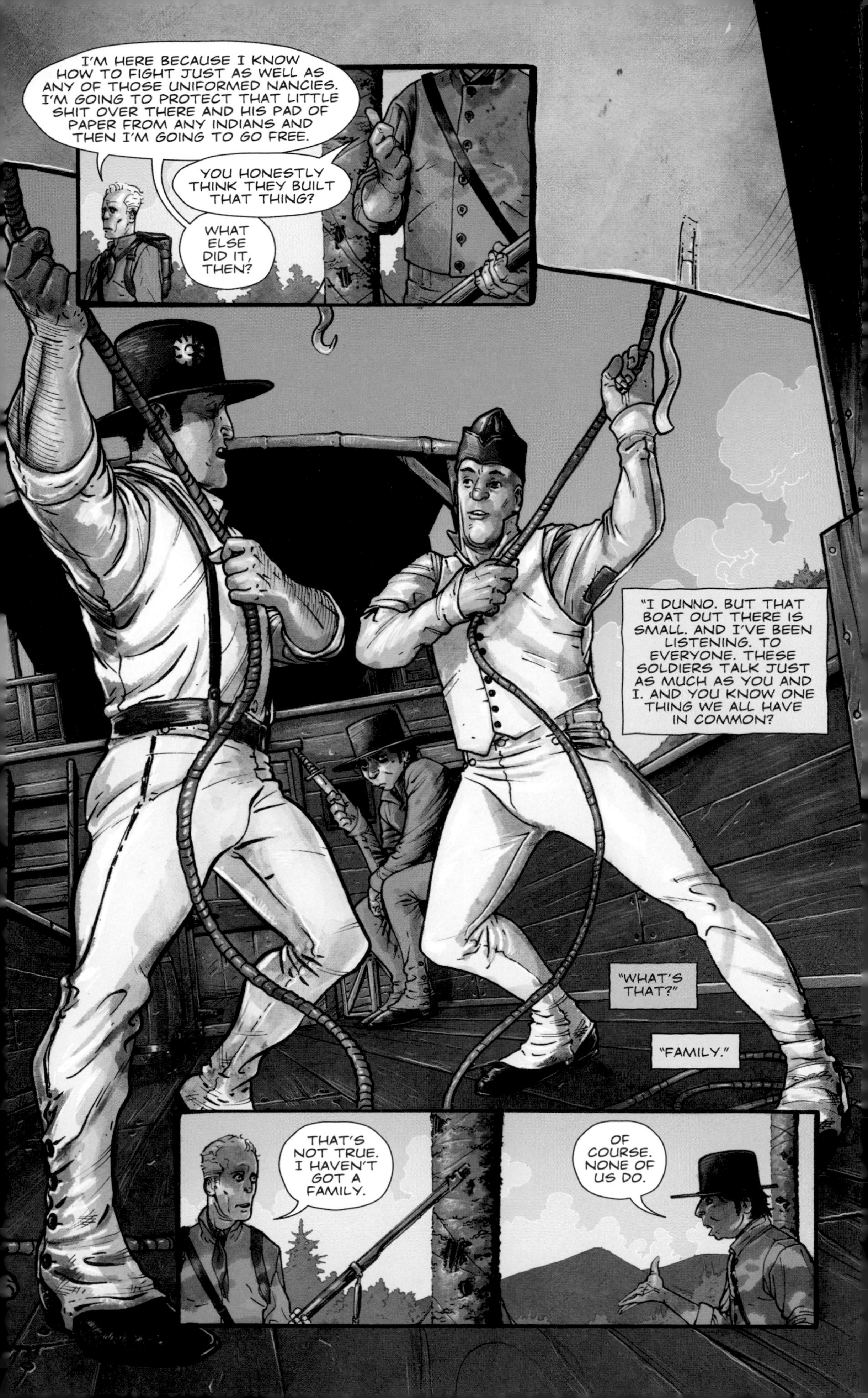
I'M HERE BECAUSE I KNOW HOW TO FIGHT JUST AS WELL AS ANY OF THOSE UNIFORMED NANCIES. I'M GOING TO PROTECT THAT LITTLE SHIT OVER THERE AND HIS PAD OF PAPER FROM ANY INDIANS AND THEN I'M GOING TO GO FREE.
YOU HONESTLY THINK THEY BUILT THAT THING?
WHAT ELSE DID IT, THEN?
"I DUNNO. BUT THAT BOAT OUT THERE IS SMALL. AND I'VE BEEN LISTENING. TO EVERYONE. THESE SOLDIERS TALK JUST AS MUCH AS YOU AND I. AND YOU KNOW ONE THING WE ALL HAVE IN COMMON?
"WHAT'S THAT?"
"FAMILY."
THAT'S NOT TRUE. I HAVEN'T GOT A FAMILY.
OF COURSE. NONE OF US DO.

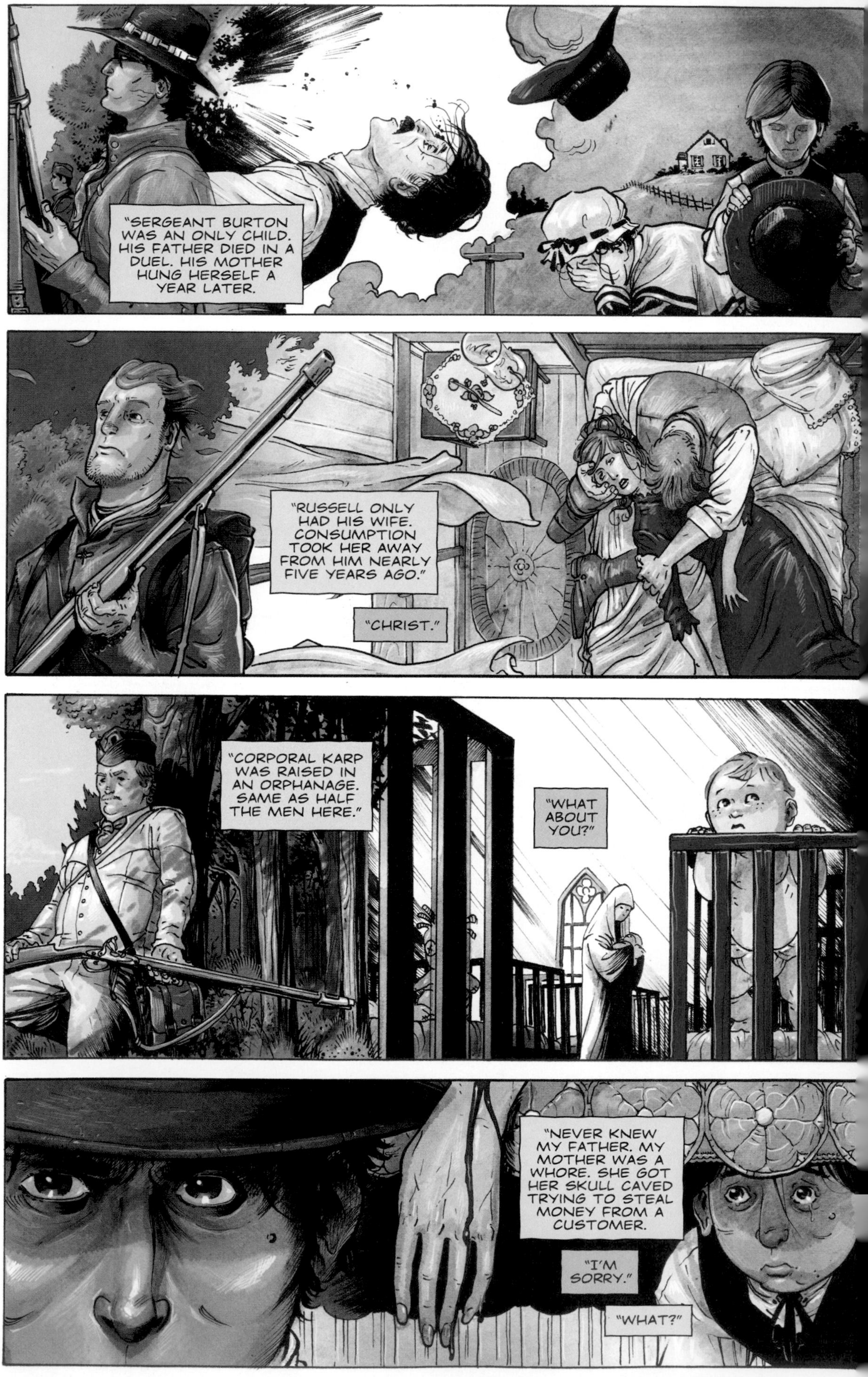

"SERGEANT BURTON WAS AN ONLY CHILD. HIS FATHER DIED IN A DUEL. HIS MOTHER HUNG HERSELF A YEAR LATER.
"RUSSELL ONLY HAD HIS WIFE. CONSUMPTION TOOK HER AWAY FROM HIM NEARLY FIVE YEARS AGO."
"CHRIST."
"CORPORAL KARP WAS RAISED IN AN ORPHANAGE. SAME AS HALF THE MEN HERE."
"WHAT ABOUT YOU?"
"NEVER KNEW MY FATHER. MY MOTHER WAS A WHORE. SHE GOT HER SKULL CAVED TRYING TO STEAL MONEY FROM A CUSTOMER.
"I'M SORRY."
"WHAT?"

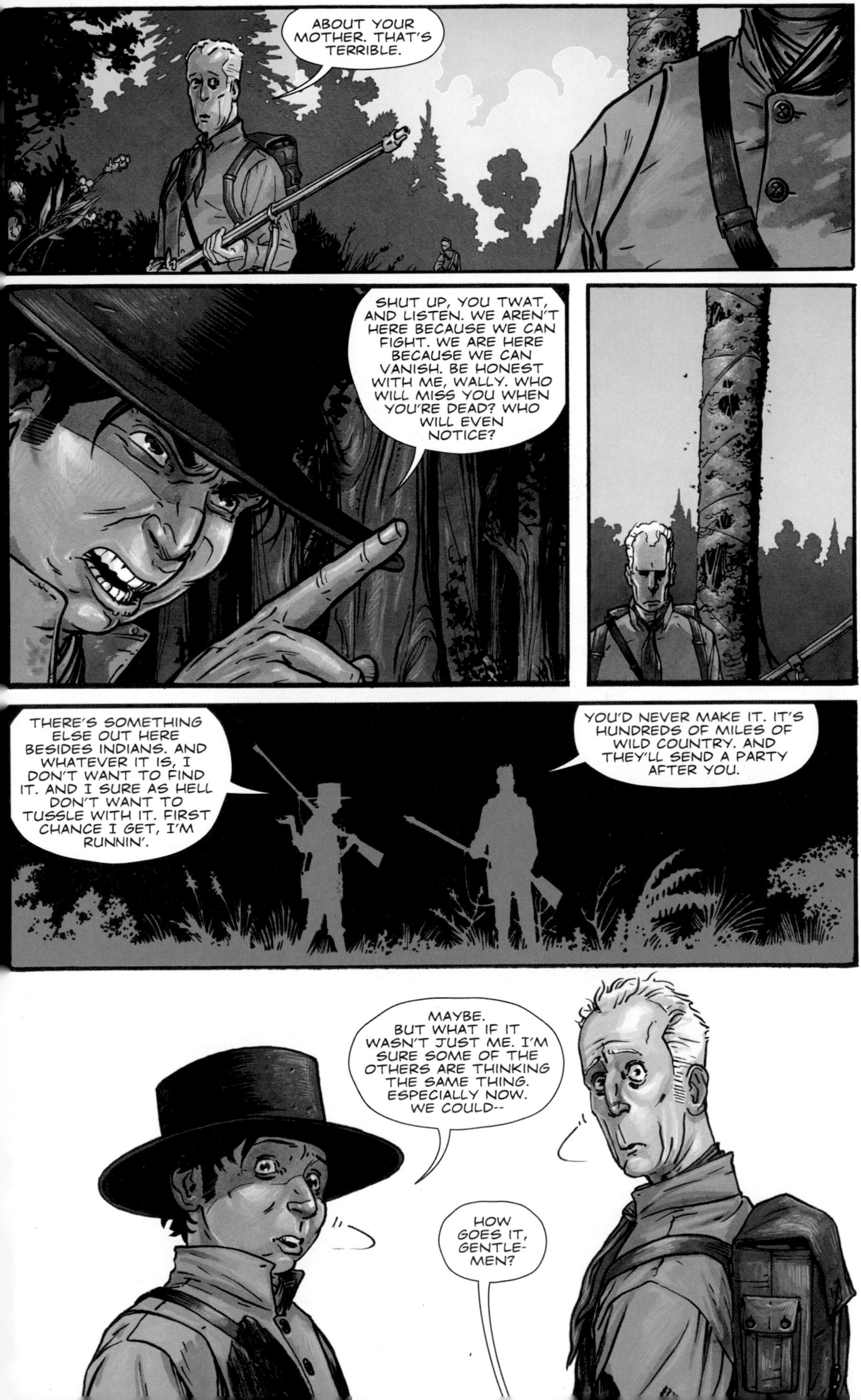
ABOUT YOUR MOTHER. THAT'S TERRIBLE.
SHUT UP, YOU TWAT, AND LISTEN. WE AREN'T HERE BECAUSE WE CAN FIGHT. WE ARE HERE BECAUSE WE CAN VANISH. BE HONEST WITH ME, WALLY. WHO WILL MISS YOU WHEN YOU'RE DEAD? WHO WILL EVEN NOTICE?
THERE'S SOMETHING ELSE OUT HERE BESIDES INDIANS. AND WHATEVER IT IS, I DON'T WANT TO FIND IT. AND I SURE AS HELL DON'T WANT TO TUSSLE WITH IT. FIRST CHANCE I GET, I'M RUNNIN'.
YOU'D NEVER MAKE IT. IT'S HUNDREDS OF MILES OF WILD COUNTRY. AND THEY'LL SEND A PARTY AFTER YOU.
MAYBE. BUT WHAT IF IT WASN'T JUST ME. I'M SURE SOME OF THE OTHERS ARE THINKING THE SAME THING. ESPECIALLY NOW. WE COULD--
HOW GOES IT, GENTLE-MEN?

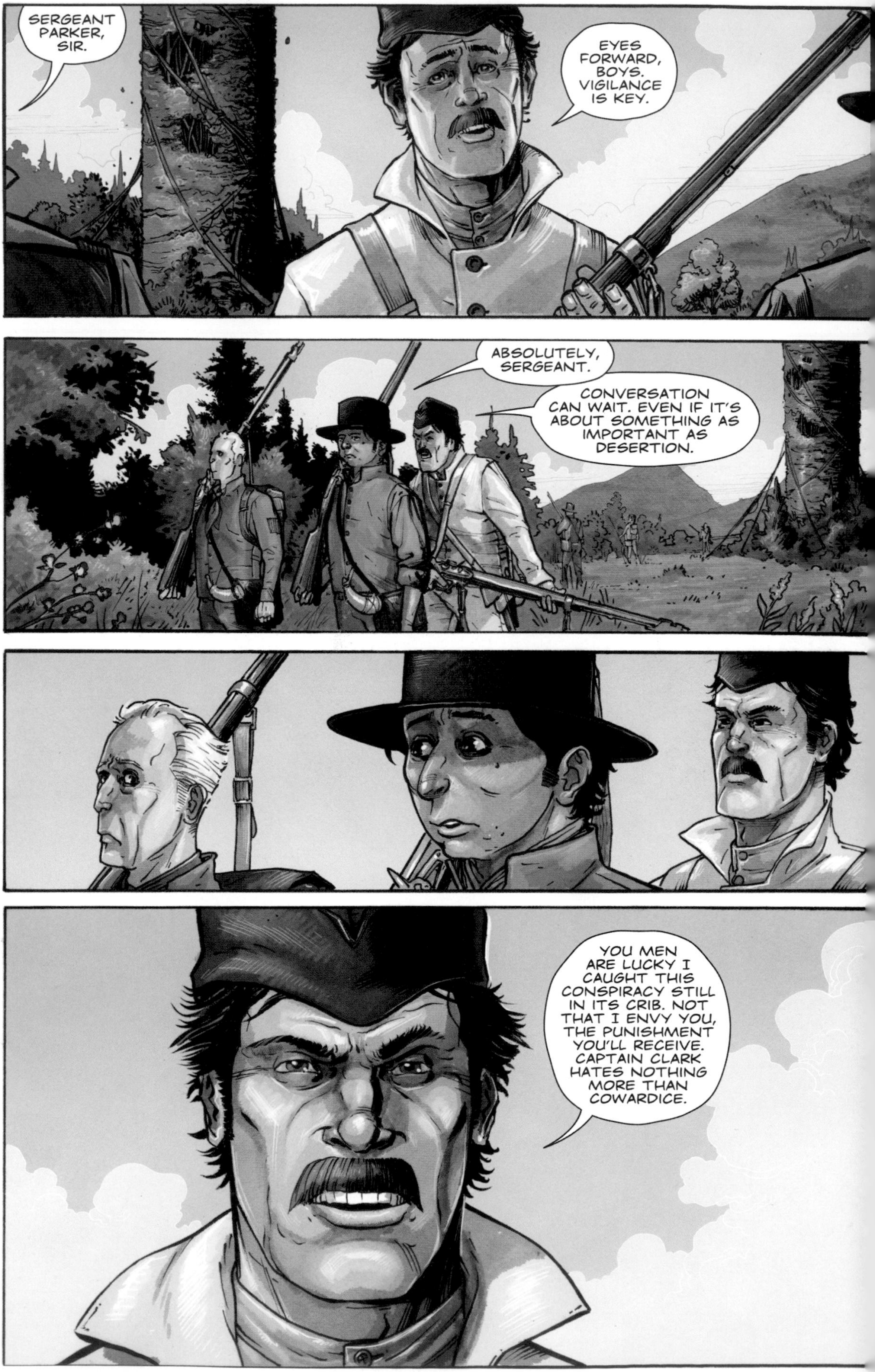
SERGEANT PARKER, SIR.
EYES FORWARD, BOYS. VIGILANCE IS KEY.
ABSOLUTELY, SERGEANT.
CONVERSATION CAN WAIT. EVEN IF IT'S ABOUT SOMETHING AS IMPORTANT AS DESERTION.
YOU MEN ARE LUCKY I CAUGHT THIS CONSPIRACY STILL IN ITS CRIB. NOT THAT I ENVY YOU, THE PUNISHMENT YOU'LL RECEIVE. CAPTAIN CLARK HATES NOTHING MORE THAN COWARDICE.

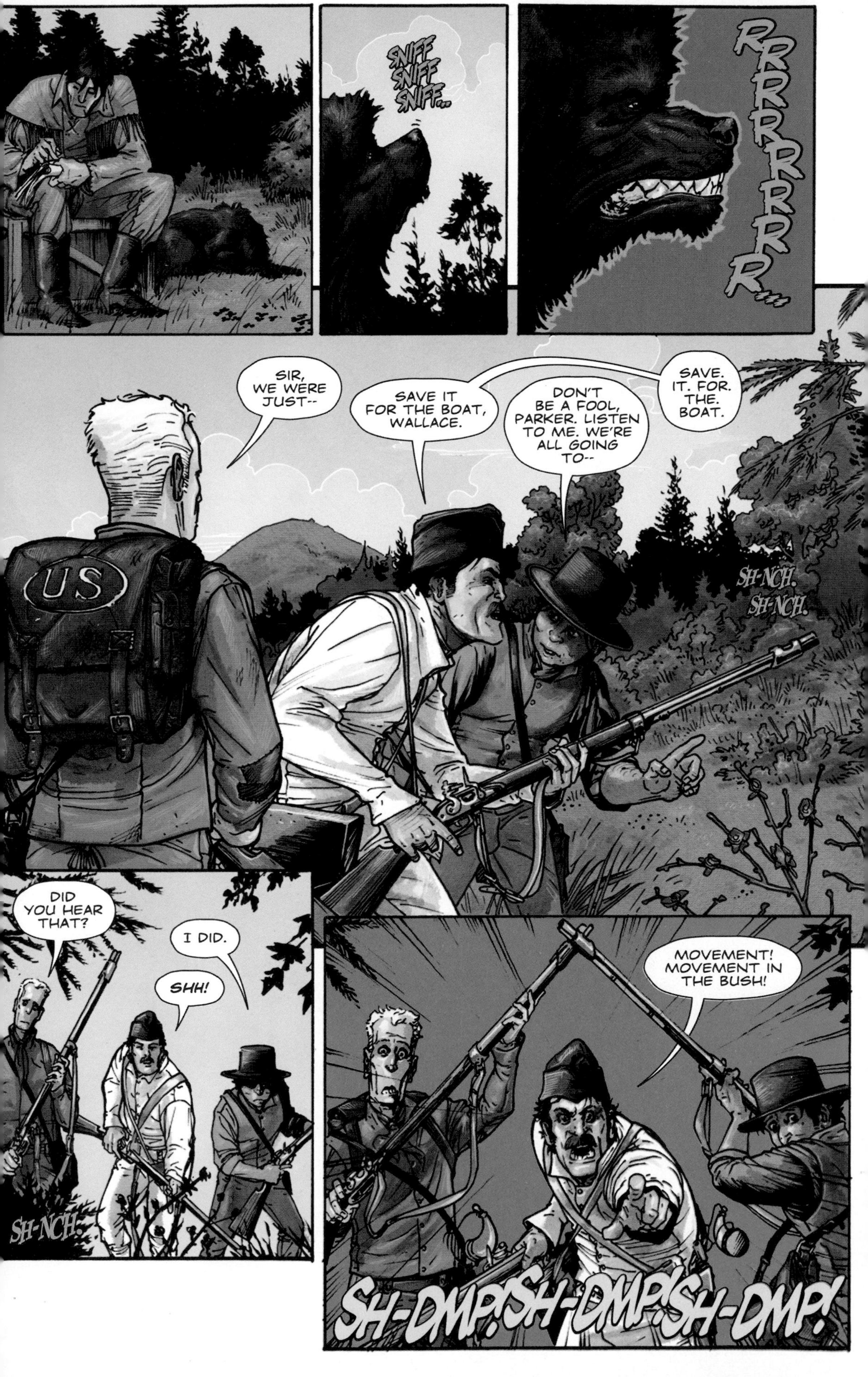
SNIFF SNIFF SNIFF...
RRRRRRRRRR...
SIR, WE WERE JUST--
SAVE IT FOR THE BOAT, WALLACE.
DON'T BE A FOOL, PARKER. LISTEN TO ME. WE'RE ALL GOING TO--
SAVE. IT. FOR. THE. BOAT.
US
SH-NCH. SH-NCH.
DID YOU HEAR THAT?
I DID.
SHH!
SH-NCH.
MOVEMENT! MOVEMENT IN THE BUSH!
SH-DMP! SH-DMP! SH-DMP!

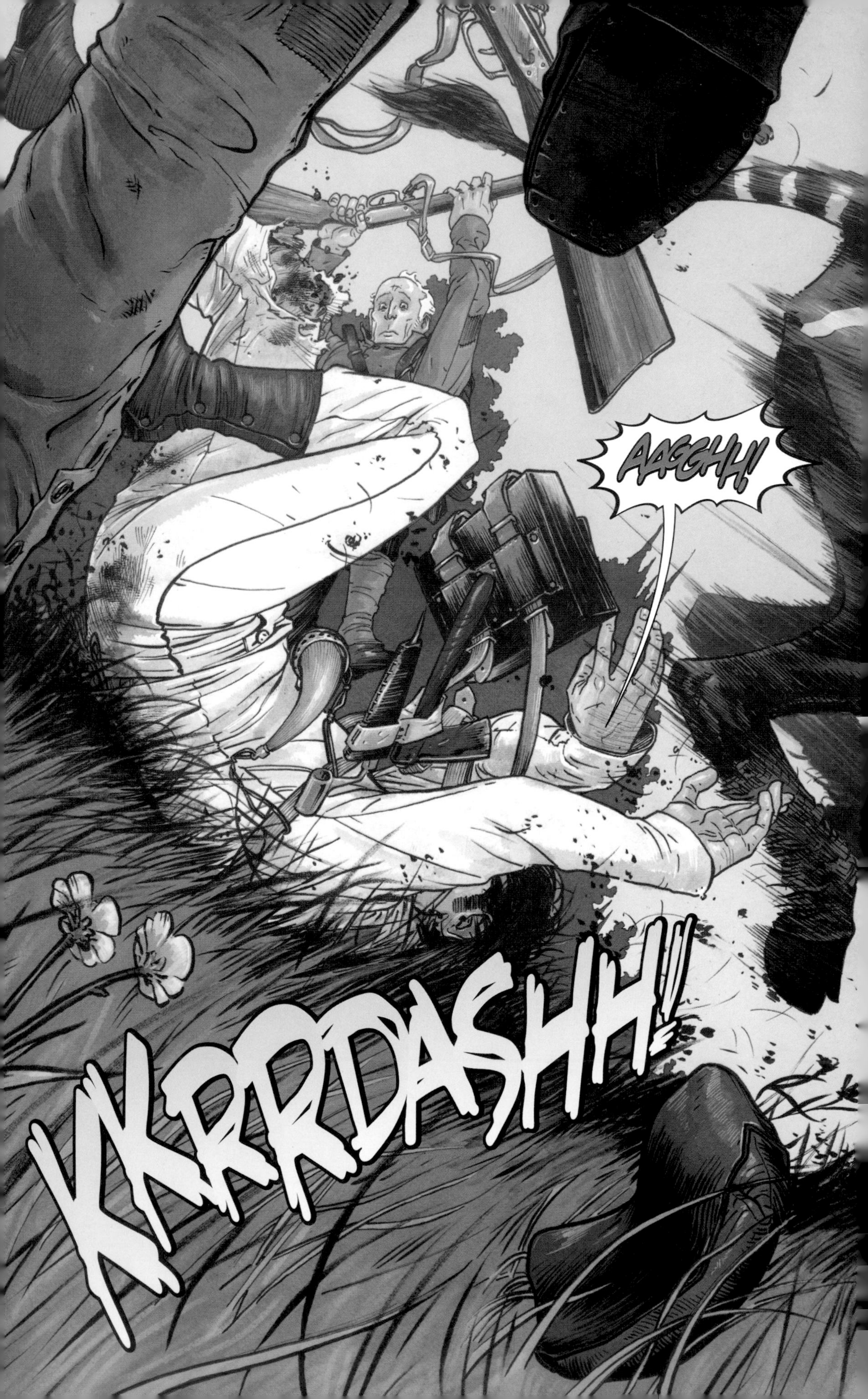
AAGGHH!
KKRRDASHH!

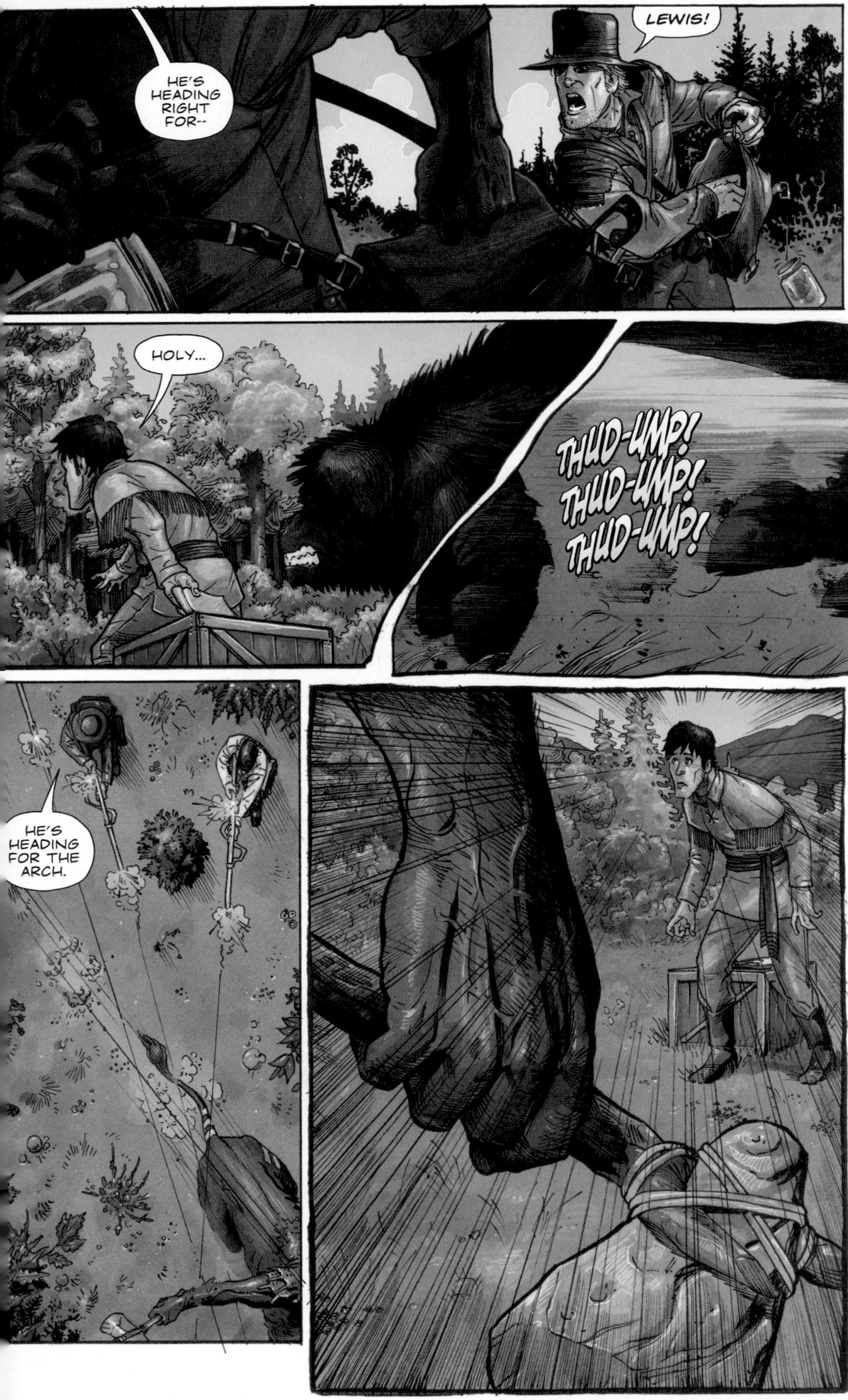
HE'S HEADING RIGHT FOR--
LEWIS!
HOLY...
THUD-UMP! THUD-UMP! THUD-UMP!
HE'S HEADING FOR THE ARCH.

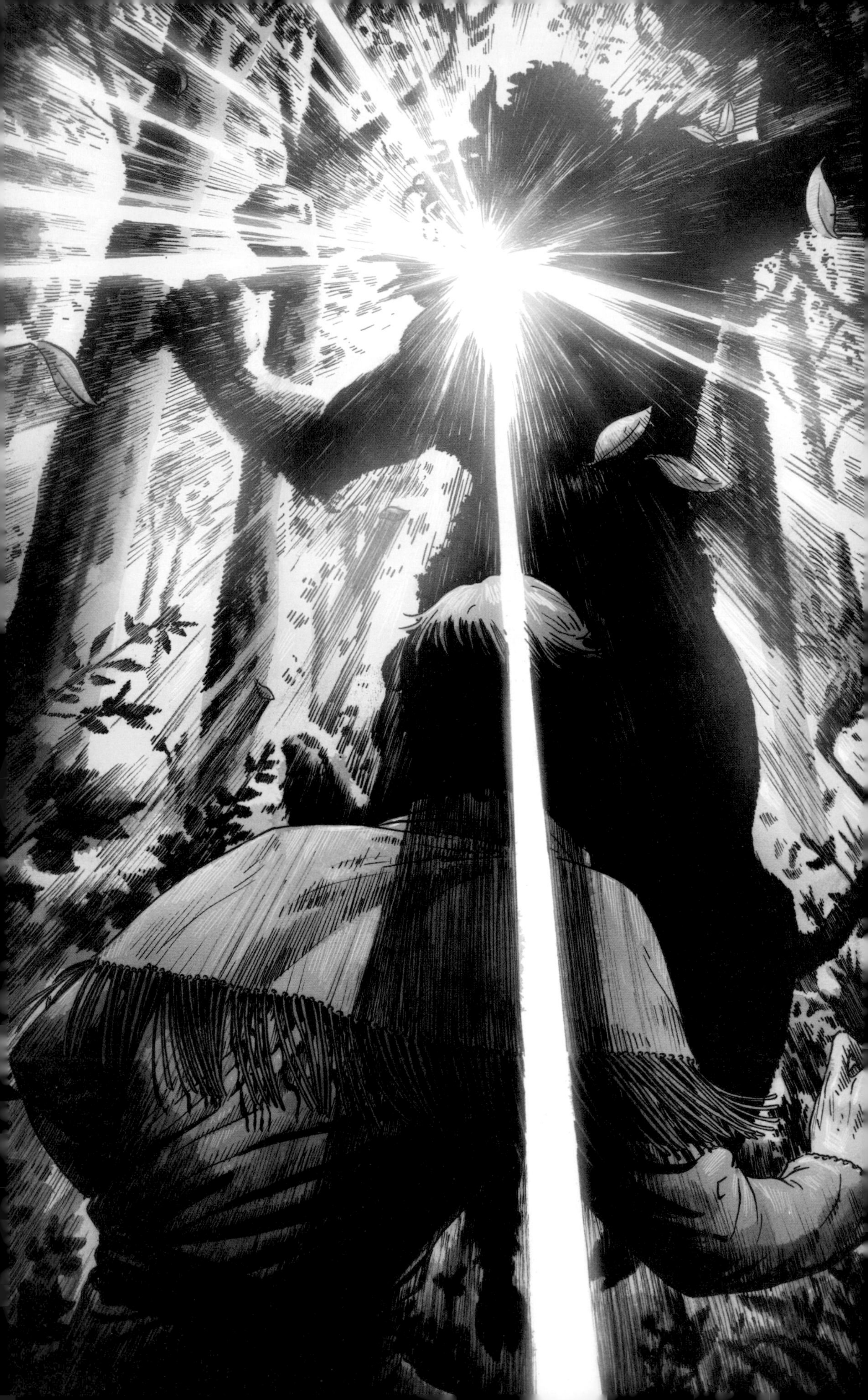

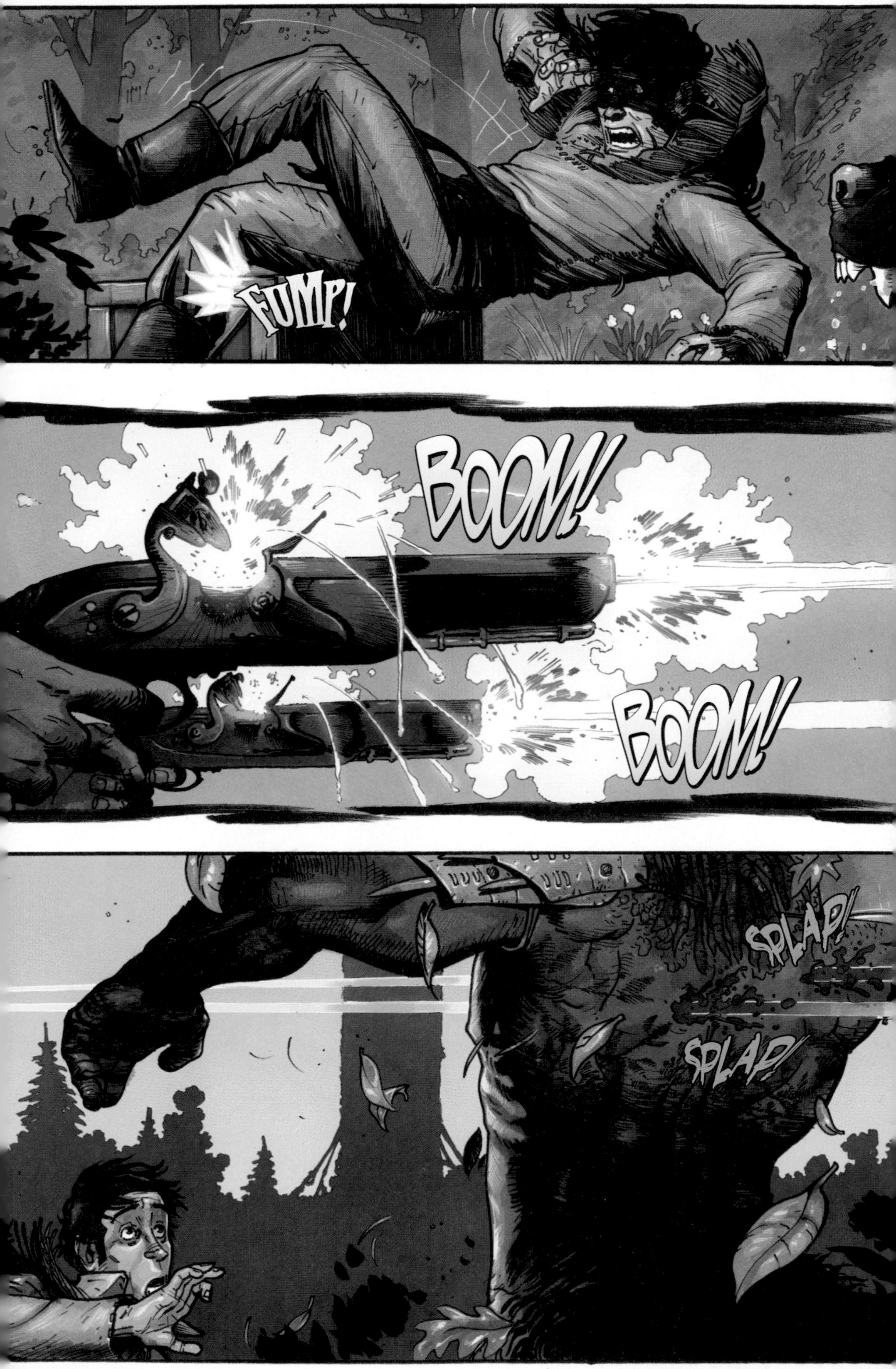
FUMP!
BOOM!
BOOM!
SPLAP!
SPLAP!

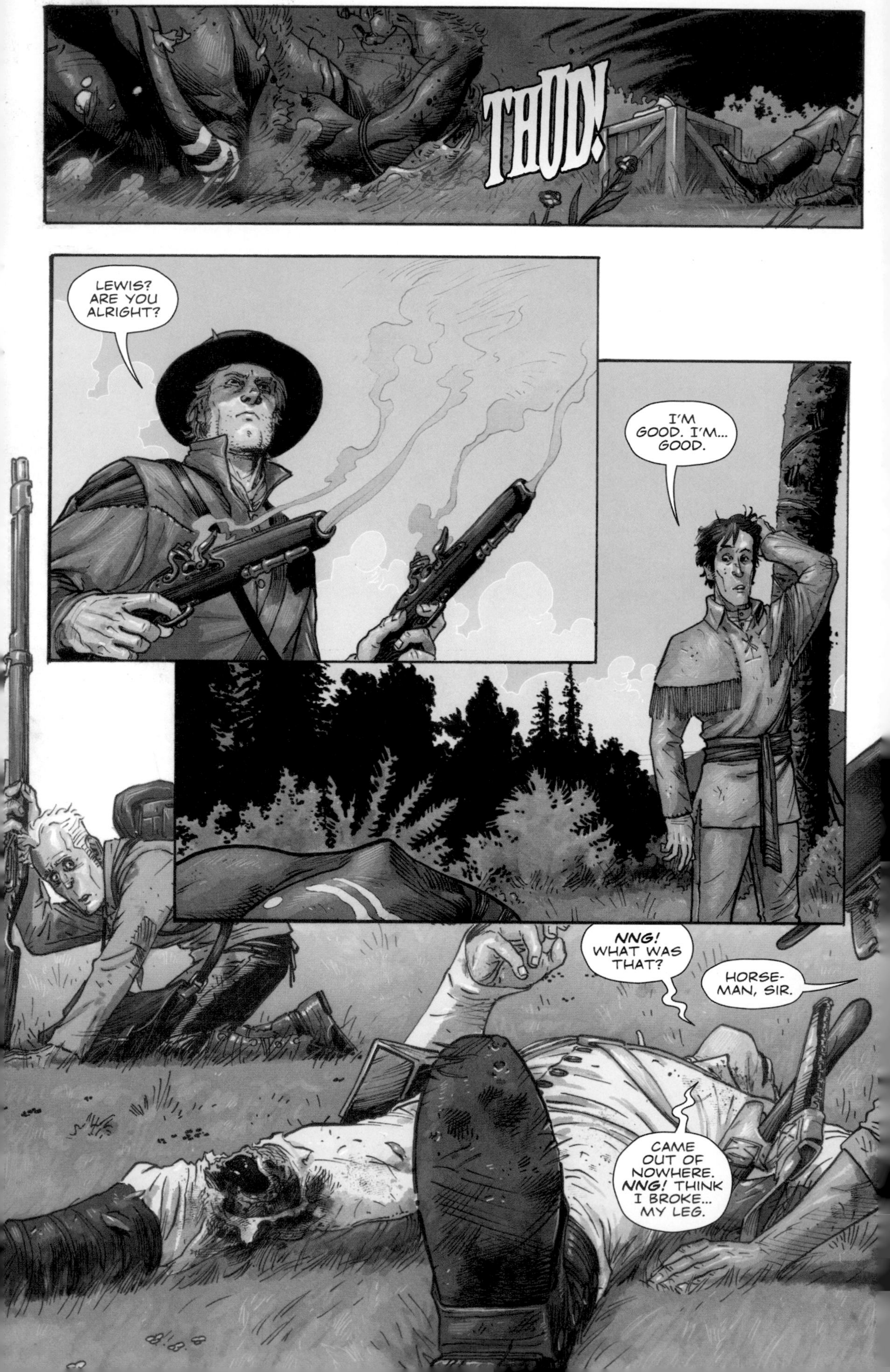
THUD!
LEWIS? ARE YOU ALRIGHT?
I'M GOOD. I'M... GOOD.
NNG! WHAT WAS THAT?
HORSE-MAN, SIR.
CAME OUT OF NOWHERE. NNG! THINK I BROKE... MY LEG.

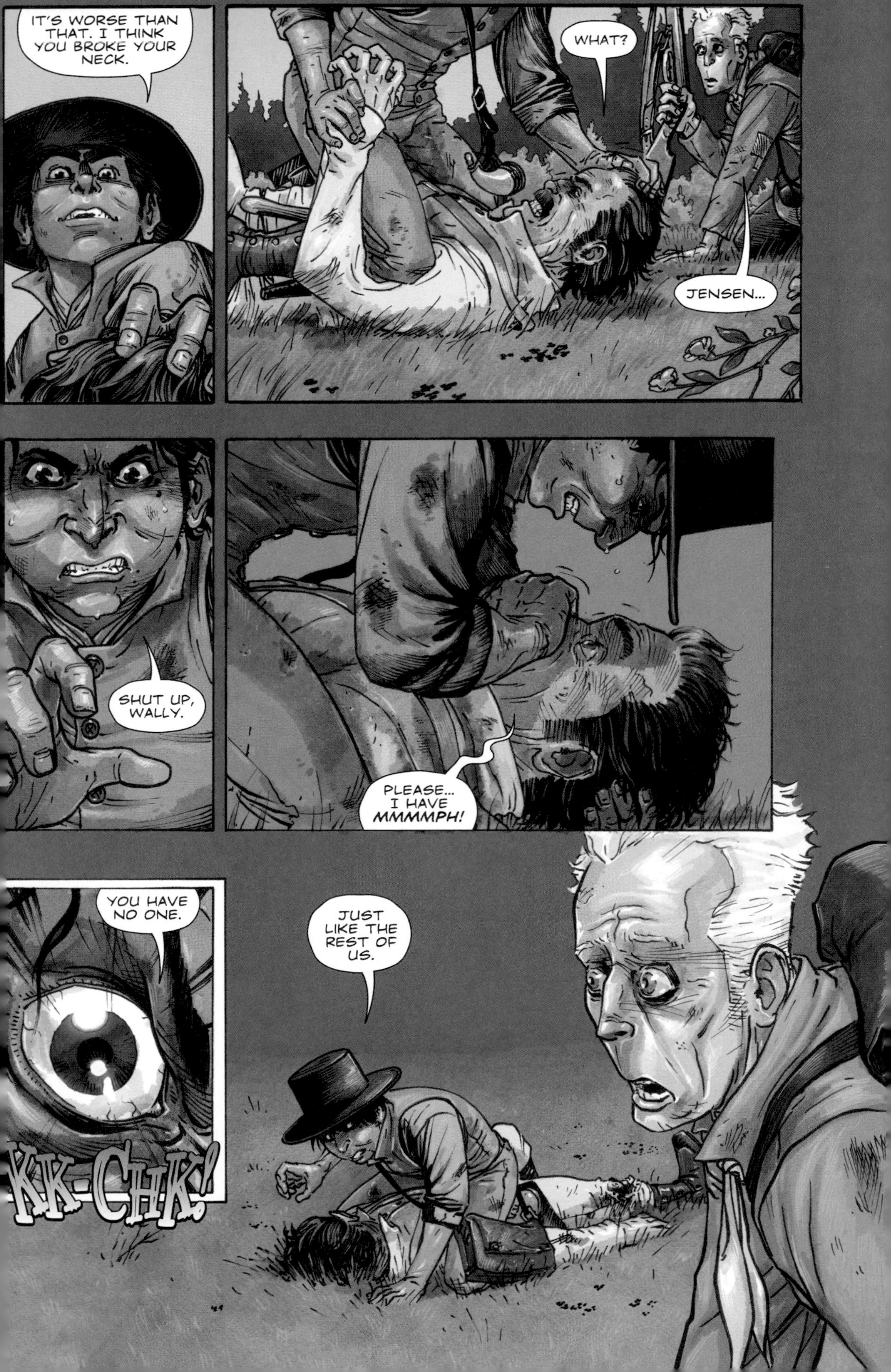
IT'S WORSE THAN THAT. I THINK YOU BROKE YOUR NECK.
WHAT?
JENSEN...
SHUT UP, WALLY.
PLEASE... I HAVE MMMMPH!
YOU HAVE NO ONE.
KK-CHK!
JUST LIKE THE REST OF US.

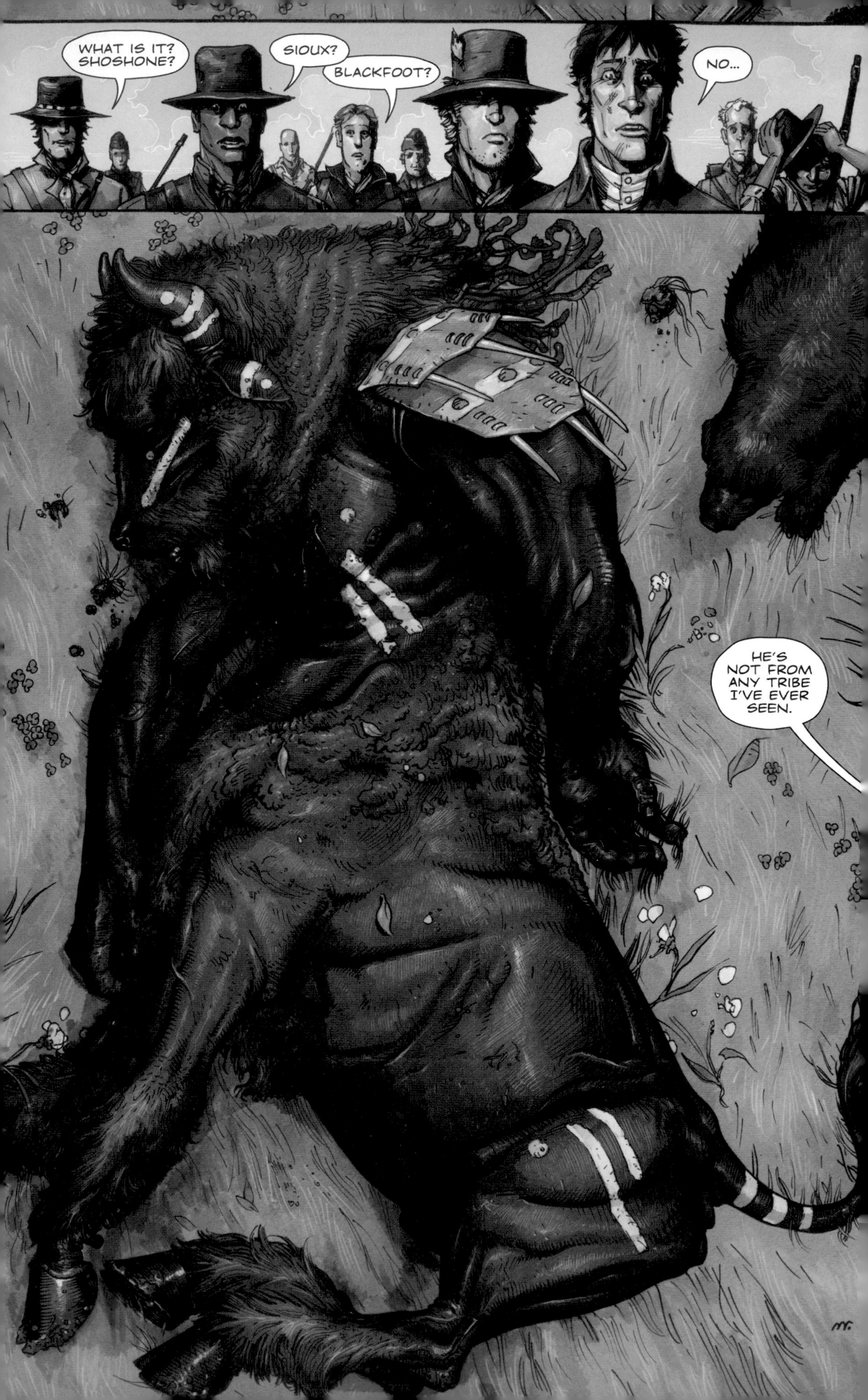
WHAT IS IT? SHOSHONE?
SIOUX?
BLACKFOOT?
NO...
HE'S NOT FROM ANY TRIBE I'VE EVER SEEN.

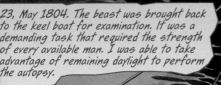

23, May 1804. The beast was brought back to the keel boat for examination. It was a demanding task that required the strength of every available man. I was able to take advantage of remaining daylight to perform the autopsy.

Began by dissecting three major components. Bison carriage separated from human torso. Torso separated from head, which appears to be a hybrid.

First cuts were difficult. Though some of the flesh appears human, it is actually tougher. Thicker. Like animal hide. Scalpel was useless.

Progress demanded a skinning knife. From there, it was a routine autopsy, with the exception of my subject.

For the most part, only most basic information has been obtained:
Cause of Death: Shooting (head and lung)
Species: ? (Human, Buffalo)
Height: 7 feet 8 inches
Weight: ? (est. 700 pounds)
Sex: Male
Organs appear to coincide with region/species they are located in.

Heart appears human, though is larger than usual and weighed approx. 13 ounces.

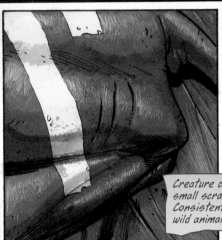

Creature covered in small scratches. Consistent with wild animals.

One note of worth. During examination of the creature's head, a tooth was abstracted. Upon examination it was determined that this was a deciduous tooth, or "baby tooth." This beast, whatever it is, is only a child and at close to 8 feet, I must wonder: how large is an adult?

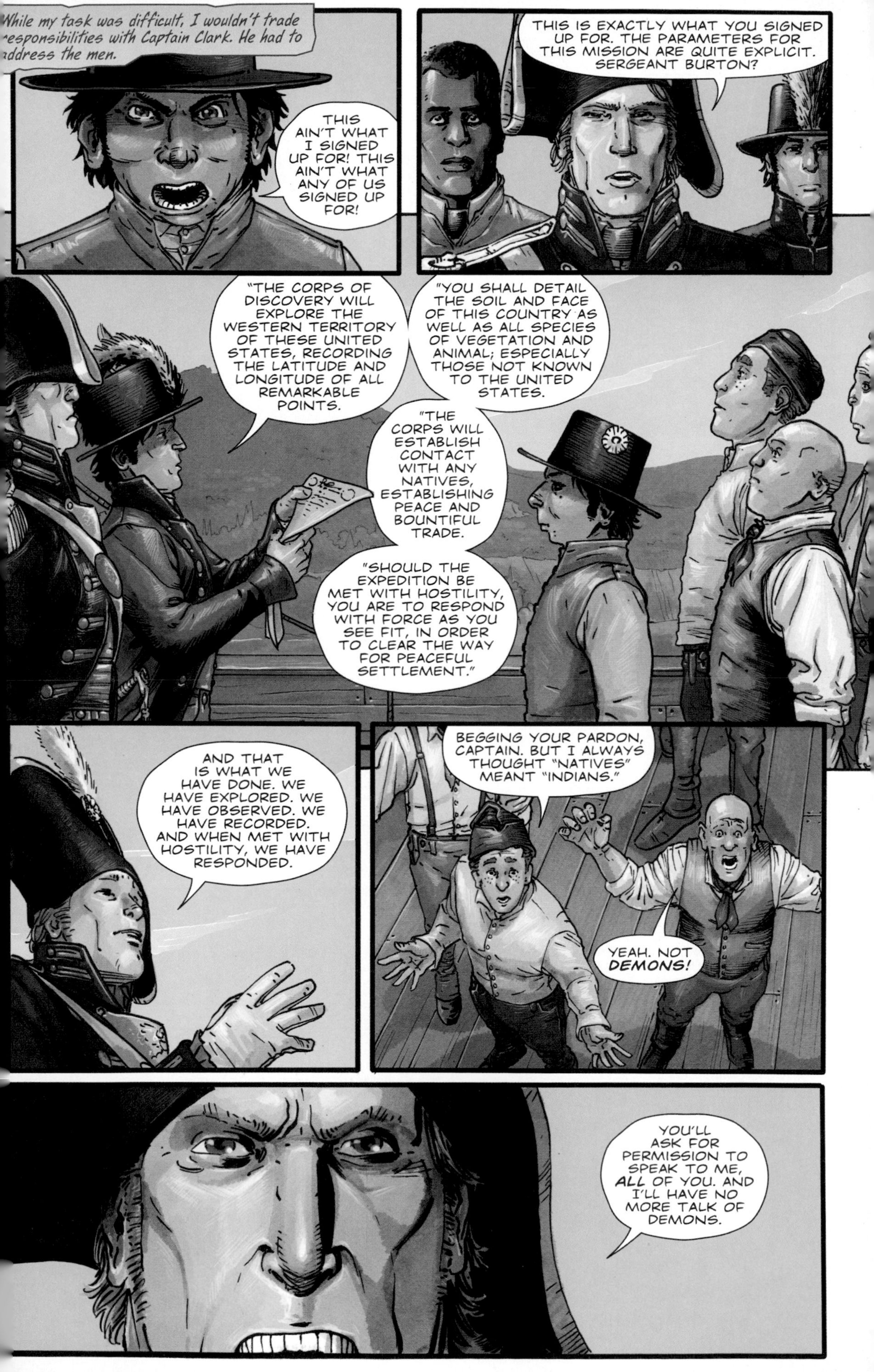

While my task was difficult, I wouldn't trade responsibilities with Captain Clark. He had to address the men.
THIS AIN'T WHAT I SIGNED UP FOR! THIS AIN'T WHAT ANY OF US SIGNED UP FOR!
THIS IS EXACTLY WHAT YOU SIGNED UP FOR. THE PARAMETERS FOR THIS MISSION ARE QUITE EXPLICIT. SERGEANT BURTON?
"THE CORPS OF DISCOVERY WILL EXPLORE THE WESTERN TERRITORY OF THESE UNITED STATES, RECORDING THE LATITUDE AND LONGITUDE OF ALL REMARKABLE POINTS.
"YOU SHALL DETAIL THE SOIL AND FACE OF THIS COUNTRY AS WELL AS ALL SPECIES OF VEGETATION AND ANIMAL; ESPECIALLY THOSE NOT KNOWN TO THE UNITED STATES.
"THE CORPS WILL ESTABLISH CONTACT WITH ANY NATIVES, ESTABLISHING PEACE AND BOUNTIFUL TRADE.
"SHOULD THE EXPEDITION BE MET WITH HOSTILITY, YOU ARE TO RESPOND WITH FORCE AS YOU SEE FIT, IN ORDER TO CLEAR THE WAY FOR PEACEFUL SETTLEMENT."
AND THAT IS WHAT WE HAVE DONE. WE HAVE EXPLORED. WE HAVE OBSERVED. WE HAVE RECORDED. AND WHEN MET WITH HOSTILITY, WE HAVE RESPONDED.
BEGGING YOUR PARDON, CAPTAIN. BUT I ALWAYS THOUGHT "NATIVES" MEANT "INDIANS."
YEAH. NOT DEMONS!
YOU'LL ASK FOR PERMISSION TO SPEAK TO ME, ALL OF YOU. AND I'LL HAVE NO MORE TALK OF DEMONS.

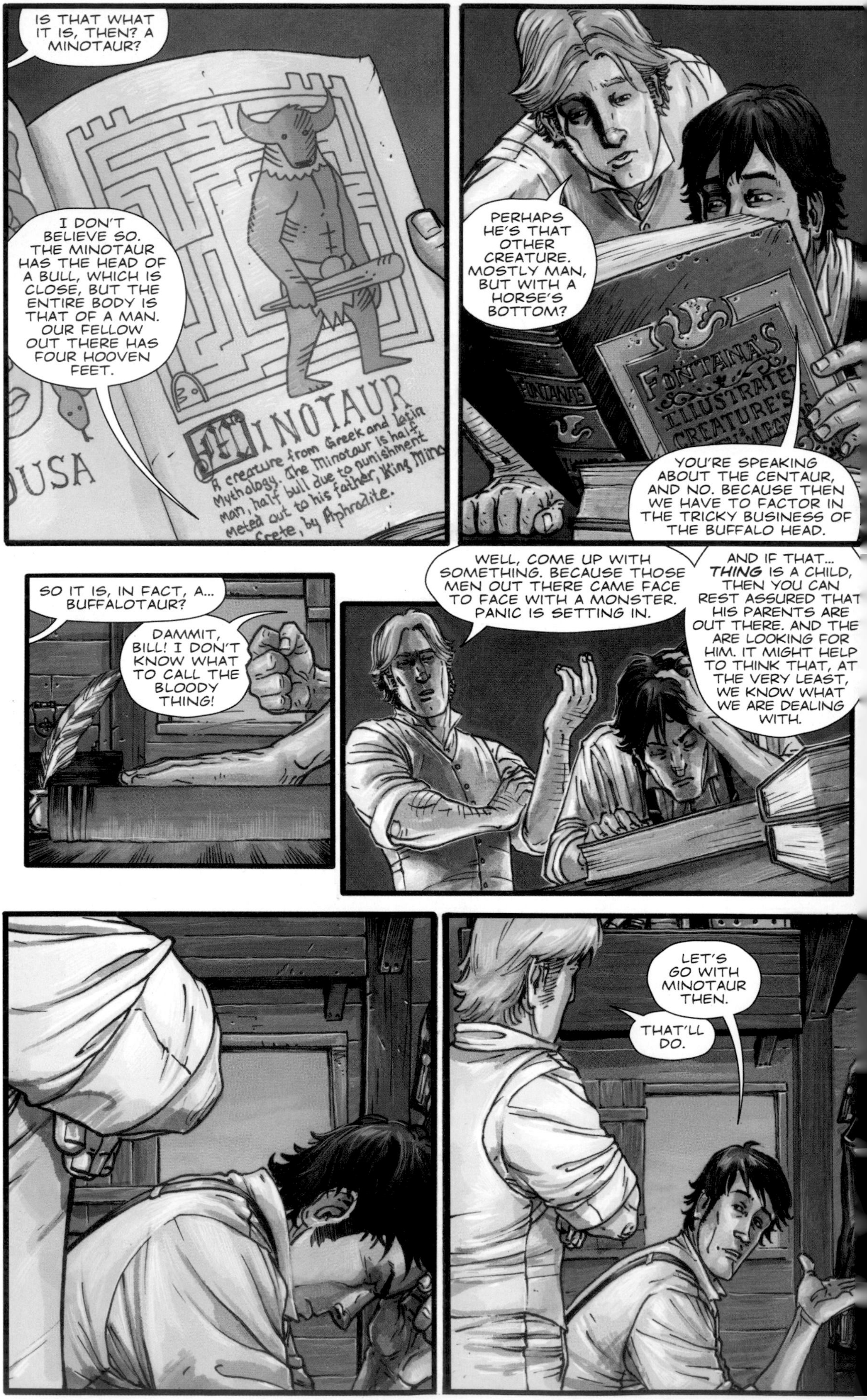
IS THAT WHAT IT IS, THEN? A MINOTAUR?
I DON'T BELIEVE SO. THE MINOTAUR HAS THE HEAD OF A BULL, WHICH IS CLOSE, BUT THE ENTIRE BODY IS THAT OF A MAN. OUR FELLOW OUT THERE HAS FOUR HOOVEN FEET.
MINOTAUR
A creature from Greek and Latin Mythology. The Minotaur is half man, half bull due to punishment meted out to his father,
by Aphrodite.
PERHAPS HE'S THAT OTHER CREATURE. MOSTLY MAN, BUT WITH A HORSE'S BOTTOM?
FONTANA'S ILLUSTRATED
YOU'RE SPEAKING ABOUT THE CENTAUR, AND NO. BECAUSE THEN WE HAVE TO FACTOR IN THE TRICKY BUSINESS OF THE BUFFALO HEAD.
SO IT IS, IN FACT, A... BUFFALOTAUR?
DAMMIT, BILL! I DON'T KNOW WHAT TO CALL THE BLOODY THING!
WELL, COME UP WITH SOMETHING. BECAUSE THOSE MEN OUT THERE CAME FACE TO FACE WITH A MONSTER. PANIC IS SETTING IN.
AND IF THAT... *THING* IS A CHILD, THEN YOU CAN REST ASSURED THAT HIS PARENTS ARE OUT THERE. AND THE ARE LOOKING FOR HIM. IT MIGHT HELP TO THINK THAT, AT THE VERY LEAST, WE KNOW WHAT WE ARE DEALING WITH.
LET'S GO WITH MINOTAUR THEN.
THAT'LL DO.

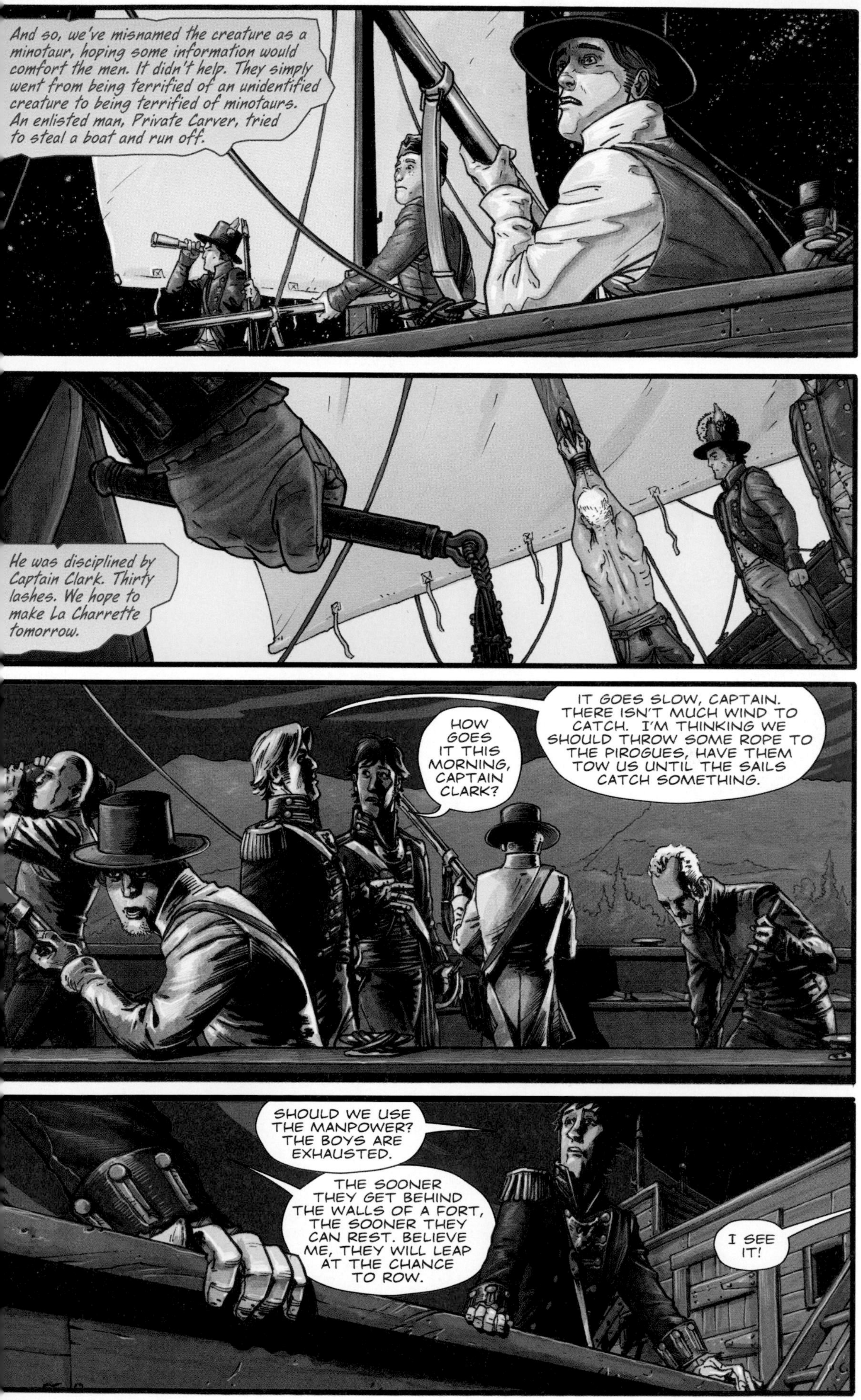
And so, we've misnamed the creature as a minotaur, hoping some information would comfort the men. It didn't help. They simply went from being terrified of an unidentified creature to being terrified of minotaurs. An enlisted man, Private Carver, tried to steal a boat and run off.
He was disciplined by Captain Clark. Thirty lashes. We hope to make La Charrette tomorrow.
HOW GOES IT THIS MORNING, CAPTAIN CLARK?
IT GOES SLOW, CAPTAIN. THERE ISN'T MUCH WIND TO CATCH. I'M THINKING WE SHOULD THROW SOME ROPE TO THE PIROGUES, HAVE THEM TOW US UNTIL THE SAILS CATCH SOMETHING.
SHOULD WE USE THE MANPOWER? THE BOYS ARE EXHAUSTED.
THE SOONER THEY GET BEHIND THE WALLS OF A FORT, THE SOONER THEY CAN REST. BELIEVE ME, THEY WILL LEAP AT THE CHANCE TO ROW.
I SEE IT!

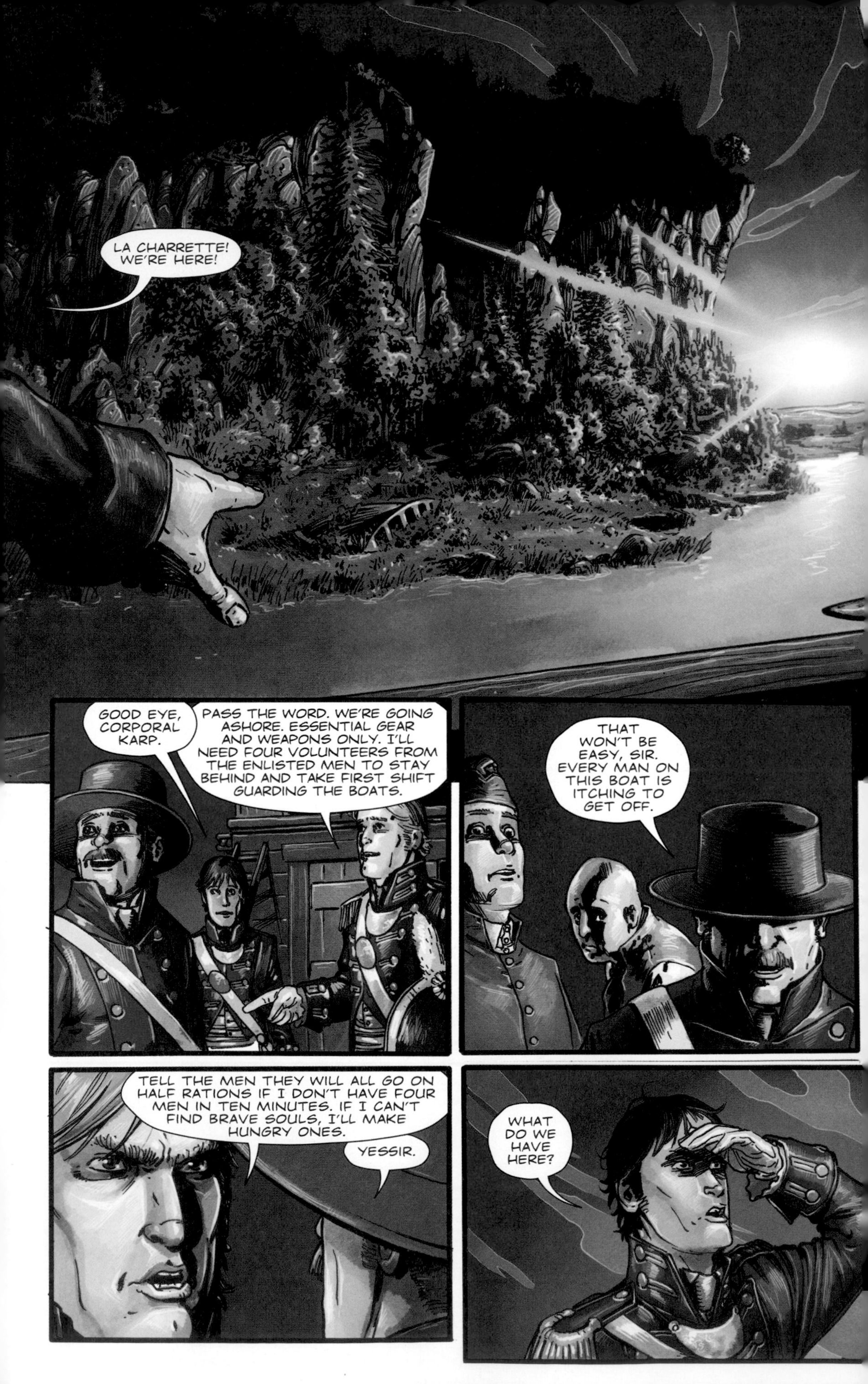
LA CHARRETTE! WE'RE HERE!
GOOD EYE, CORPORAL KARP.
PASS THE WORD. WE'RE GOING ASHORE. ESSENTIAL GEAR AND WEAPONS ONLY. I'LL NEED FOUR VOLUNTEERS FROM THE ENLISTED MEN TO STAY BEHIND AND TAKE FIRST SHIFT GUARDING THE BOATS.
THAT WON'T BE EASY, SIR. EVERY MAN ON THIS BOAT IS ITCHING TO GET OFF.
TELL THE MEN THEY WILL ALL GO ON HALF RATIONS IF I DON'T HAVE FOUR MEN IN TEN MINUTES. IF I CAN'T FIND BRAVE SOULS, I'LL MAKE HUNGRY ONES.
YESSIR.
WHAT DO WE HAVE HERE?

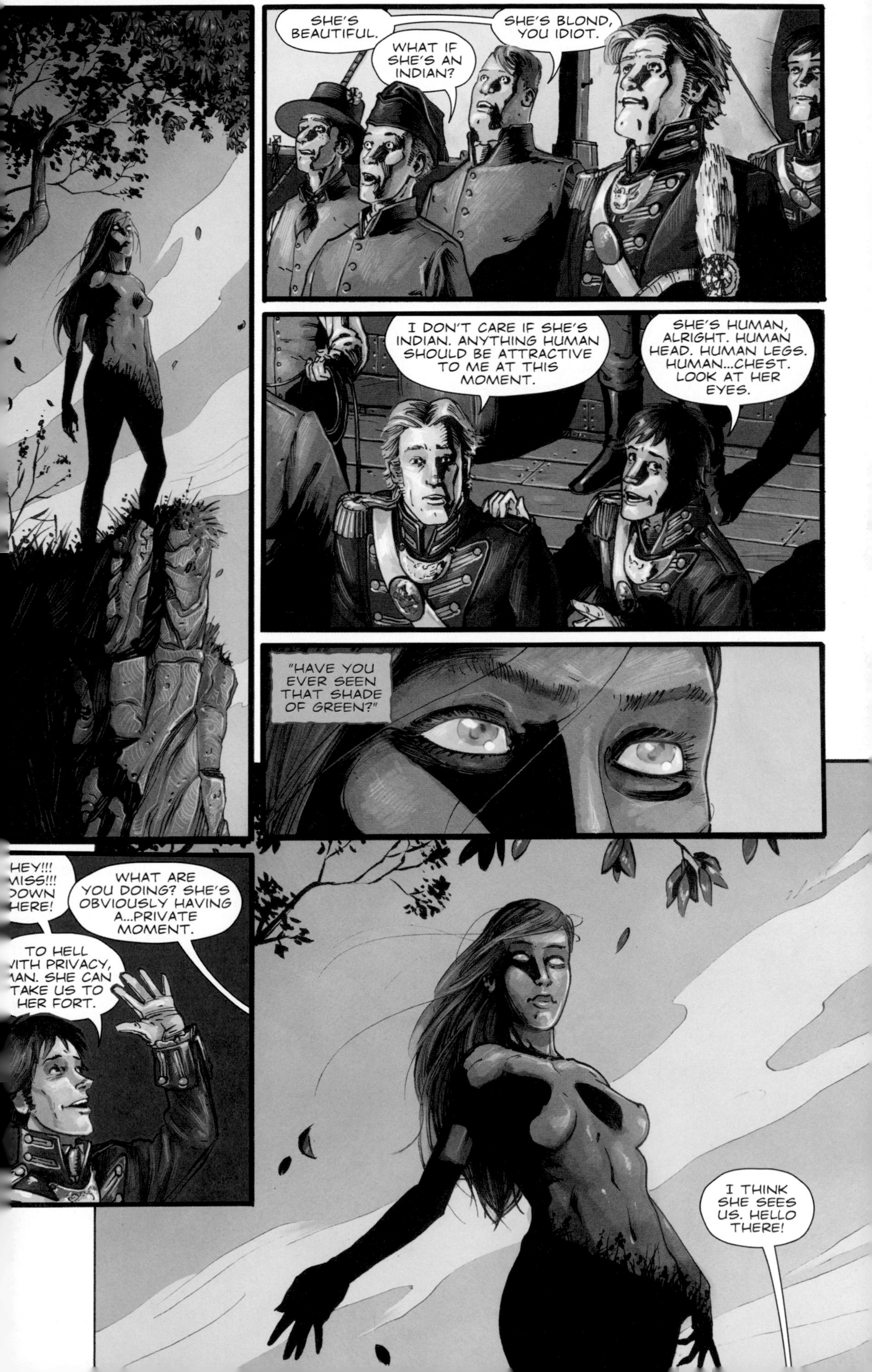
SHE'S BEAUTIFUL.
WHAT IF SHE'S AN INDIAN?
SHE'S BLOND, YOU IDIOT.
I DON'T CARE IF SHE'S INDIAN. ANYTHING HUMAN SHOULD BE ATTRACTIVE TO ME AT THIS MOMENT.
SHE'S HUMAN, ALRIGHT. HUMAN HEAD. HUMAN LEGS. HUMAN...CHEST. LOOK AT HER EYES.
"HAVE YOU EVER SEEN THAT SHADE OF GREEN?"
HEY!!! MISS!!! DOWN HERE!
WHAT ARE YOU DOING? SHE'S OBVIOUSLY HAVING A...PRIVATE MOMENT.
TO HELL WITH PRIVACY, MAN. SHE CAN TAKE US TO HER FORT.
I THINK SHE SEES US. HELLO THERE!

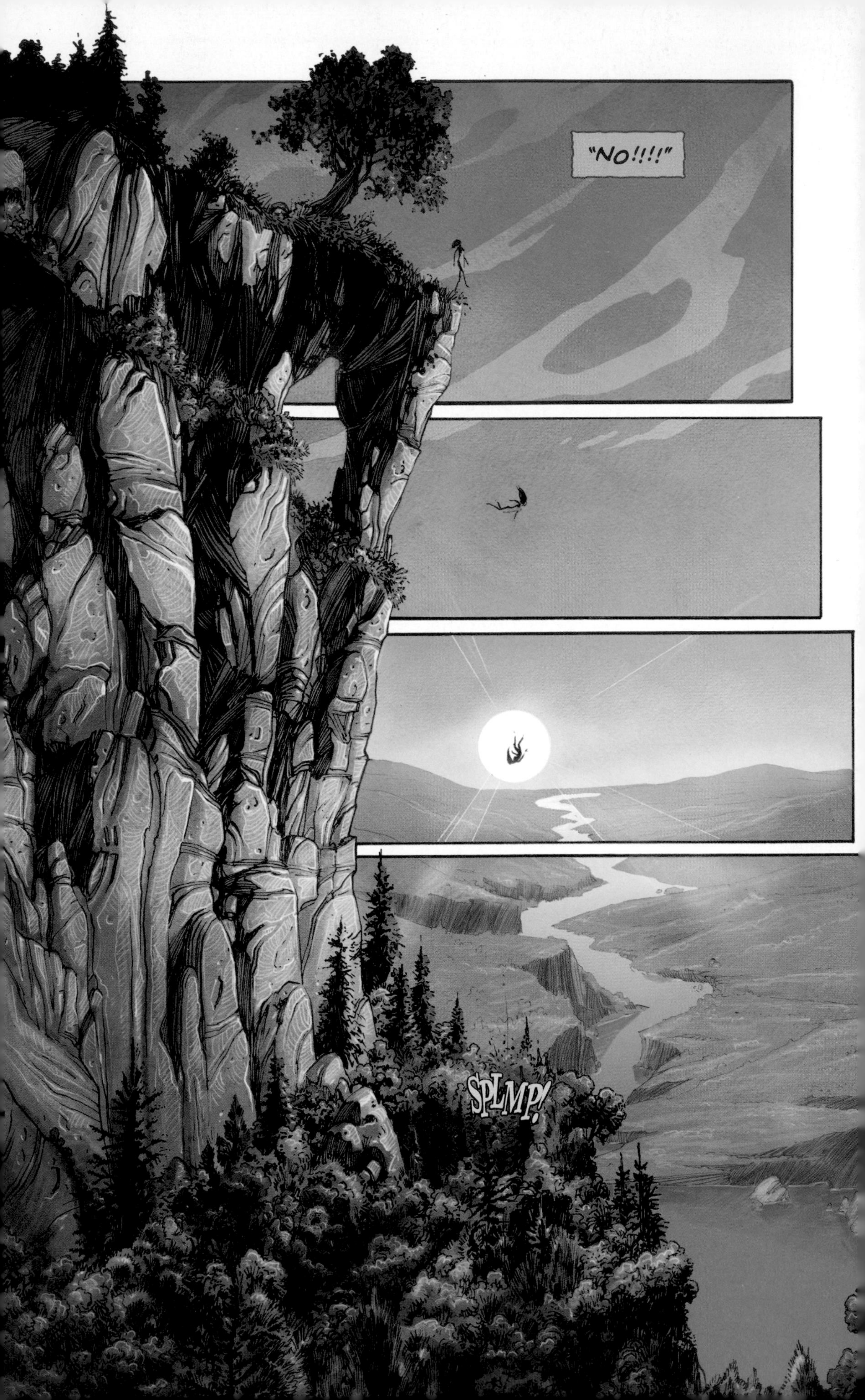
"NO!!!!"
SPLMP!

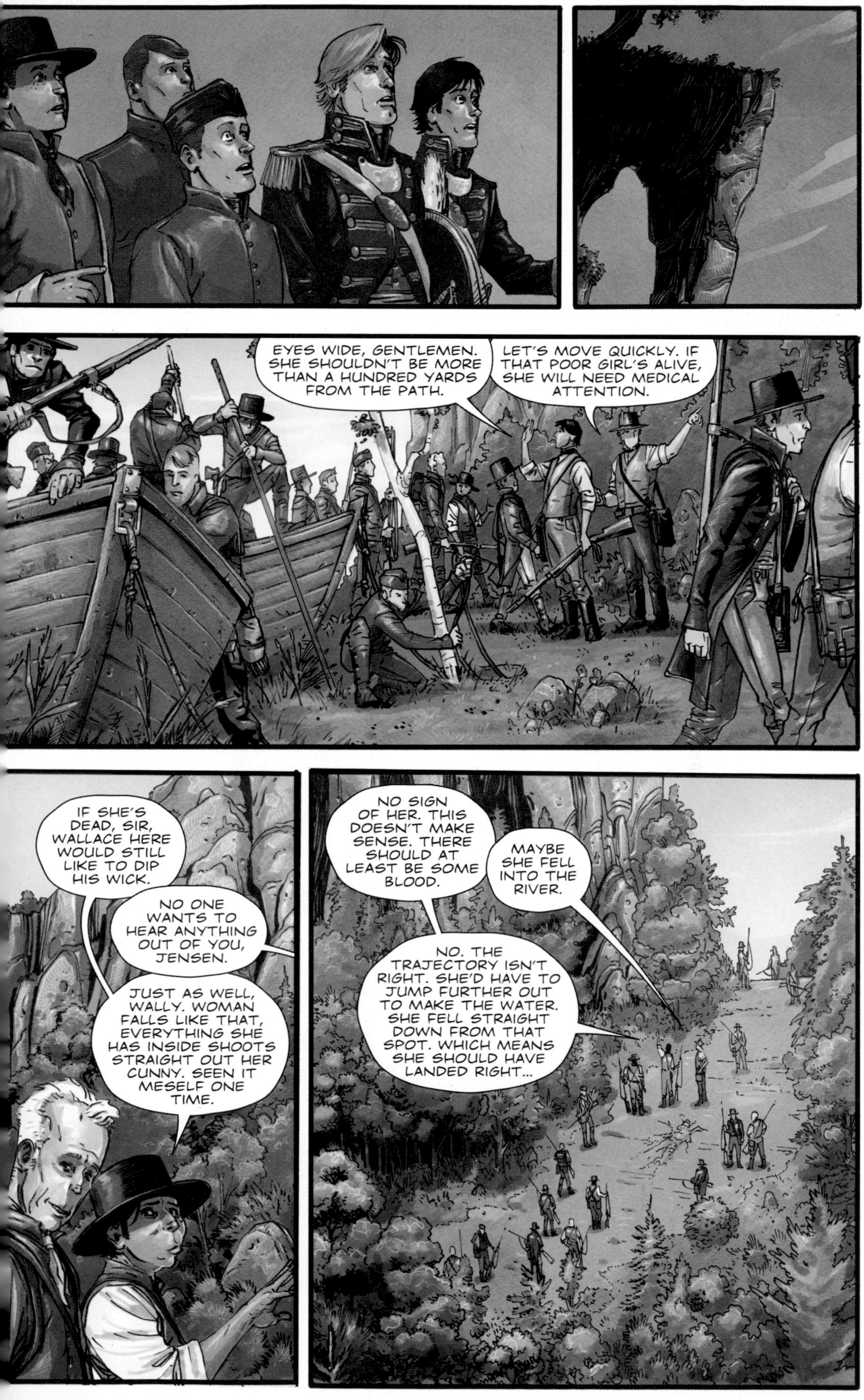
EYES WIDE, GENTLEMEN. SHE SHOULDN'T BE MORE THAN A HUNDRED YARDS FROM THE PATH.
LET'S MOVE QUICKLY. IF THAT POOR GIRL'S ALIVE, SHE WILL NEED MEDICAL ATTENTION.
IF SHE'S DEAD, SIR, WALLACE HERE WOULD STILL LIKE TO DIP HIS WICK.
NO ONE WANTS TO HEAR ANYTHING OUT OF YOU, JENSEN.
JUST AS WELL, WALLY. WOMAN FALLS LIKE THAT, EVERYTHING SHE HAS INSIDE SHOOTS STRAIGHT OUT HER CUNNY. SEEN IT MESELF ONE TIME.
NO SIGN OF HER. THIS DOESN'T MAKE SENSE. THERE SHOULD AT LEAST BE SOME BLOOD.
MAYBE SHE FELL INTO THE RIVER.
NO. THE TRAJECTORY ISN'T RIGHT. SHE'D HAVE TO JUMP FURTHER OUT TO MAKE THE WATER. SHE FELL STRAIGHT DOWN FROM THAT SPOT. WHICH MEANS SHE SHOULD HAVE LANDED RIGHT...

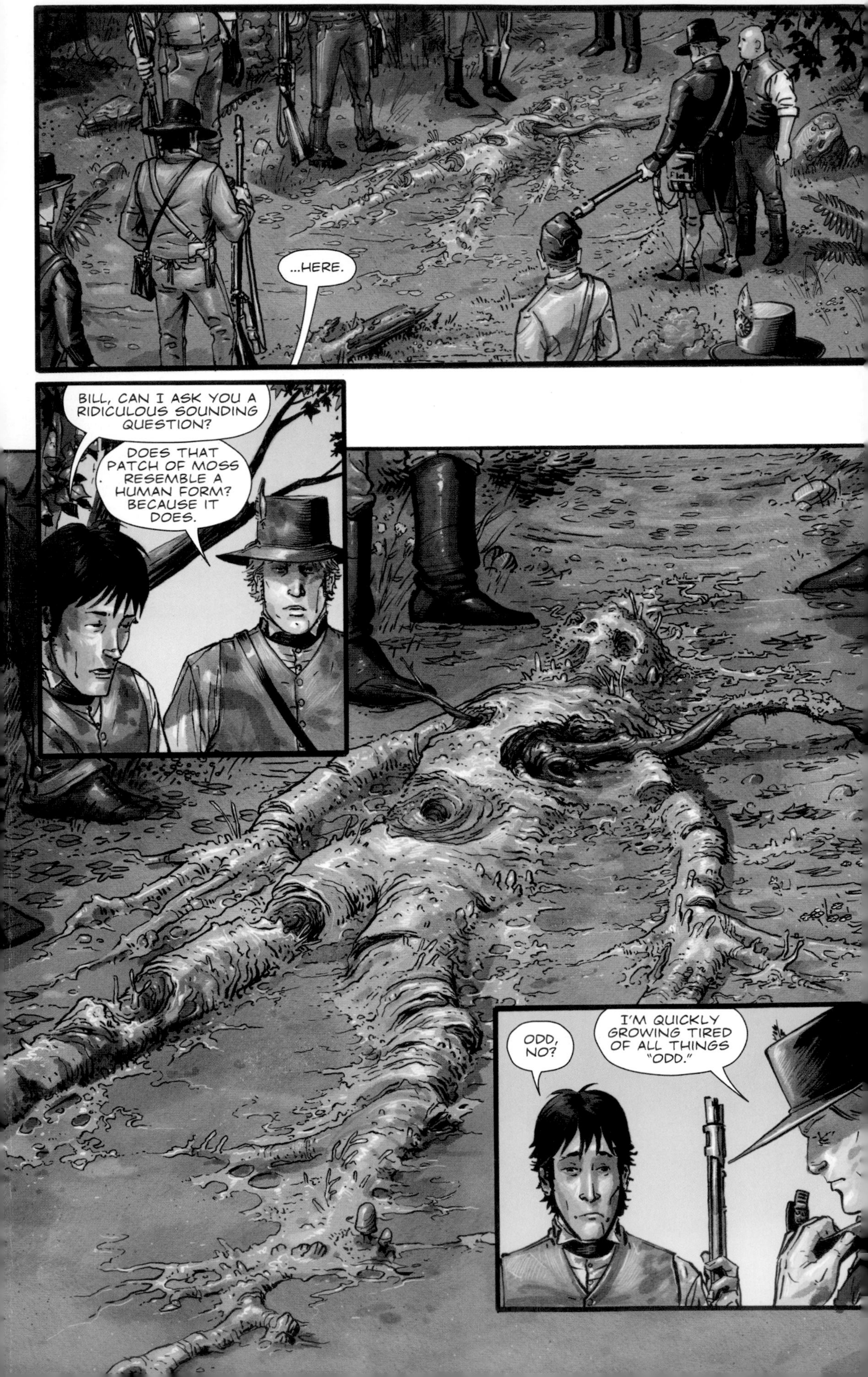
...HERE.
BILL, CAN I ASK YOU A RIDICULOUS SOUNDING QUESTION?
DOES THAT PATCH OF MOSS RESEMBLE A HUMAN FORM? BECAUSE IT DOES.
ODD, NO?
I'M QUICKLY GROWING TIRED OF ALL THINGS "ODD."

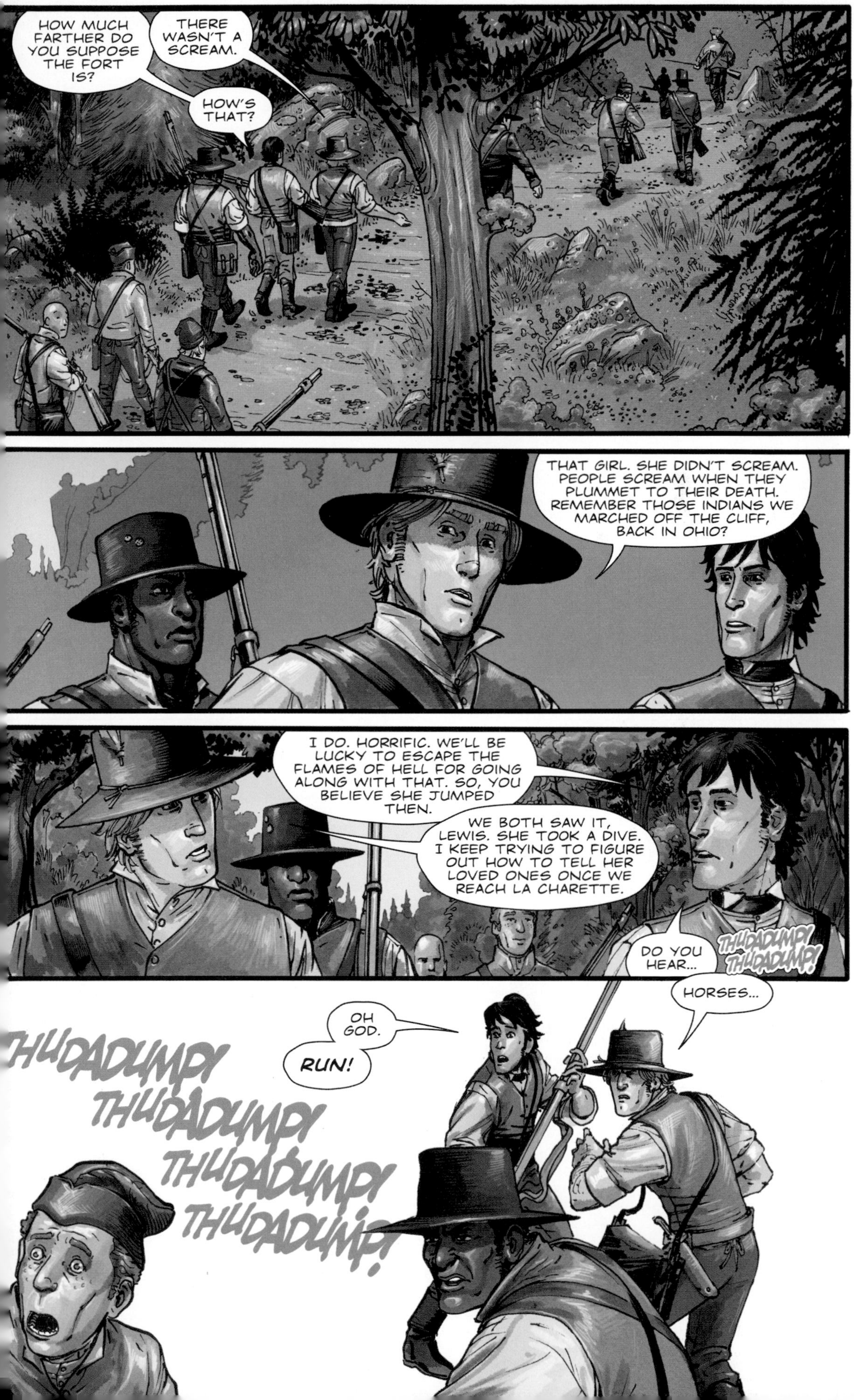
HOW MUCH FARTHER DO YOU SUPPOSE THE FORT IS?
THERE WASN'T A SCREAM.
HOW'S THAT?
THAT GIRL. SHE DIDN'T SCREAM. PEOPLE SCREAM WHEN THEY PLUMMET TO THEIR DEATH. REMEMBER THOSE INDIANS WE MARCHED OFF THE CLIFF, BACK IN OHIO?
I DO. HORRIFIC. WE'LL BE LUCKY TO ESCAPE THE FLAMES OF HELL FOR GOING ALONG WITH THAT. SO, YOU BELIEVE SHE JUMPED THEN.
WE BOTH SAW IT, LEWIS. SHE TOOK A DIVE. I KEEP TRYING TO FIGURE OUT HOW TO TELL HER LOVED ONES ONCE WE REACH LA CHARETTE.
DO YOU HEAR...
THUDADUMP! THUDADUMP!
HORSES...
OH GOD.
RUN!
THUDADUMP! THUDADUMP! THUDADUMP! THUDADUMP!

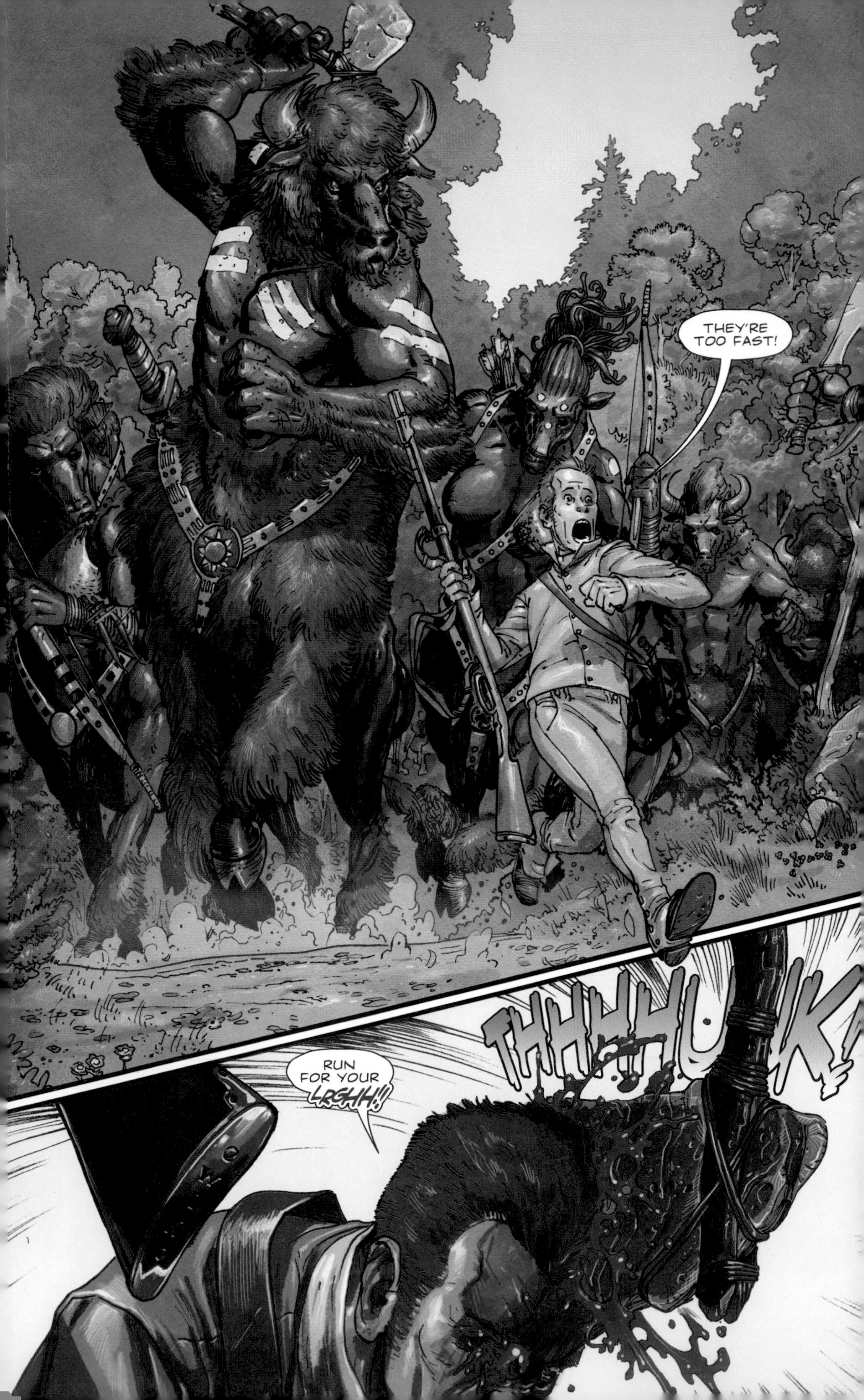
THEY'RE TOO FAST!
THHHHUK
RUN FOR YOUR LRGHH!!

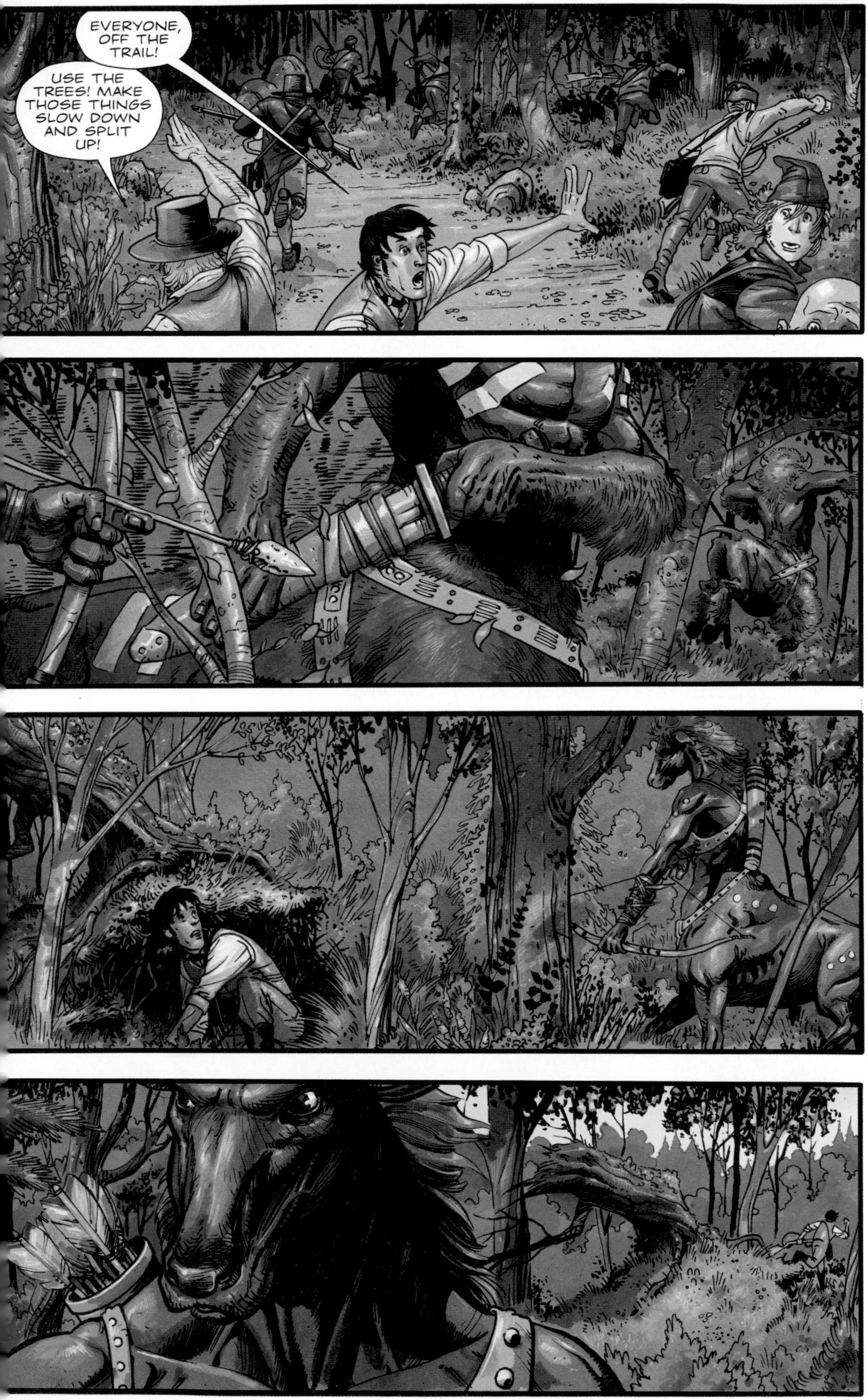
EVERYONE, OFF THE TRAIL!
USE THE TREES! MAKE THOSE THINGS SLOW DOWN AND SPLIT UP!

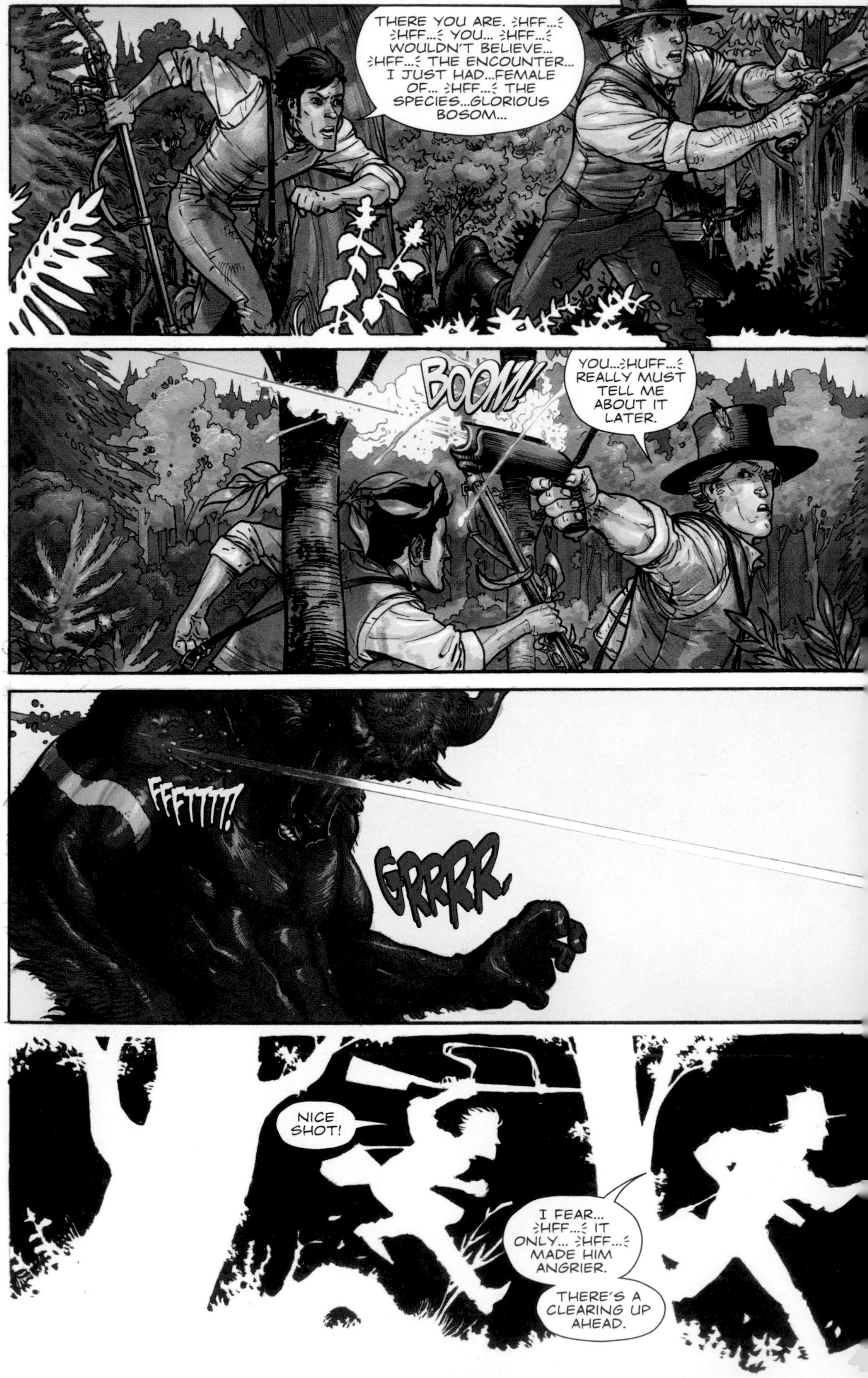
THERE YOU ARE. HFF... HFF... YOU... HFF... WOULDN'T BELIEVE... HFF... THE ENCOUNTER... I JUST HAD...FEMALE OF... HFF... THE SPECIES...GLORIOUS BOSOM...
BOOM!
YOU...HUFF... REALLY MUST TELL ME ABOUT IT LATER.
FFFTTTT!
GRRRR.
NICE SHOT!
I FEAR... HFF... IT ONLY... HFF... MADE HIM ANGRIER.
THERE'S A CLEARING UP AHEAD.

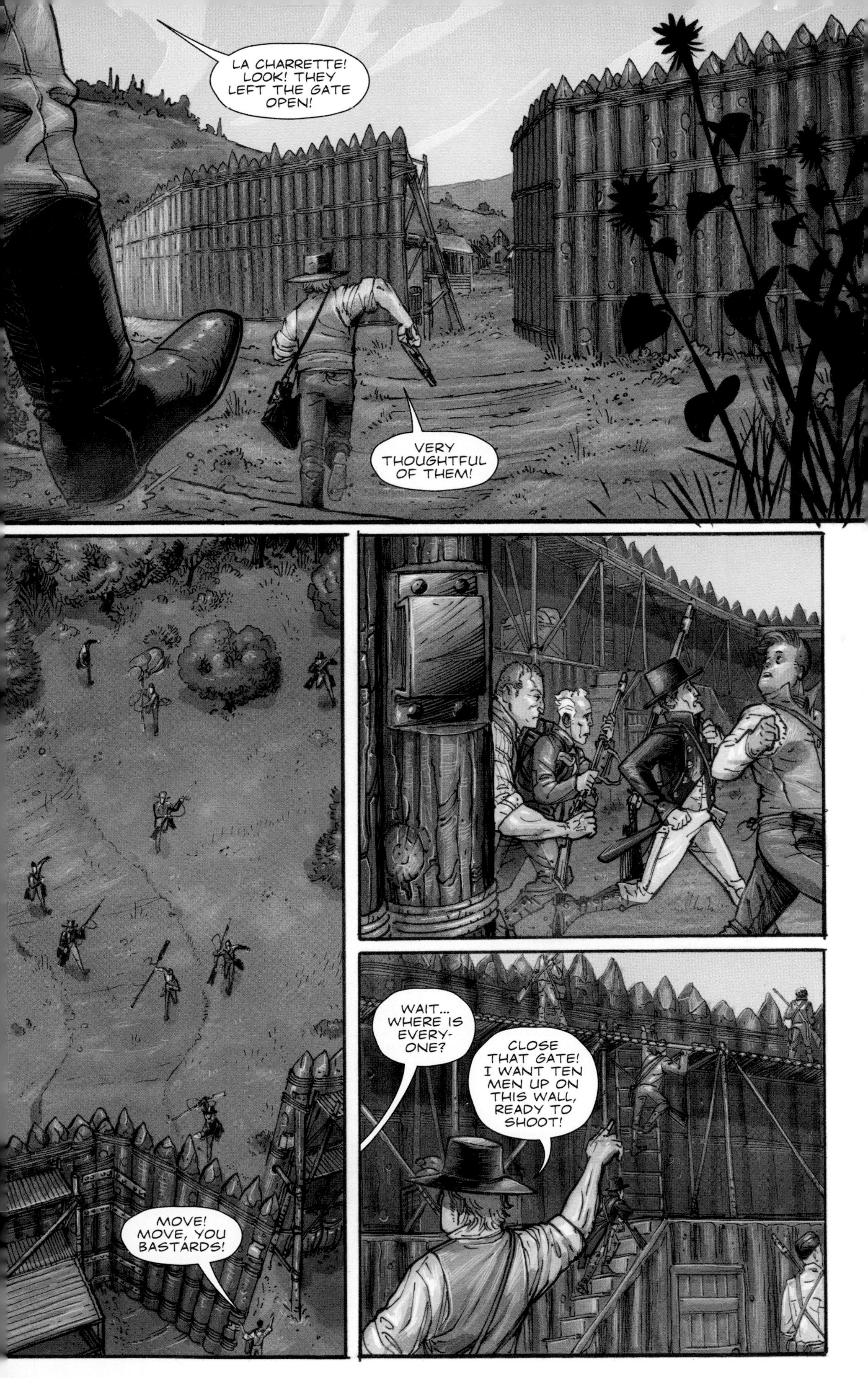
LA CHARRETTE! LOOK! THEY LEFT THE GATE OPEN!
VERY THOUGHTFUL OF THEM!
MOVE! MOVE, YOU BASTARDS!
WAIT... WHERE IS EVERY-ONE?
CLOSE THAT GATE! I WANT TEN MEN UP ON THIS WALL, READY TO SHOOT!

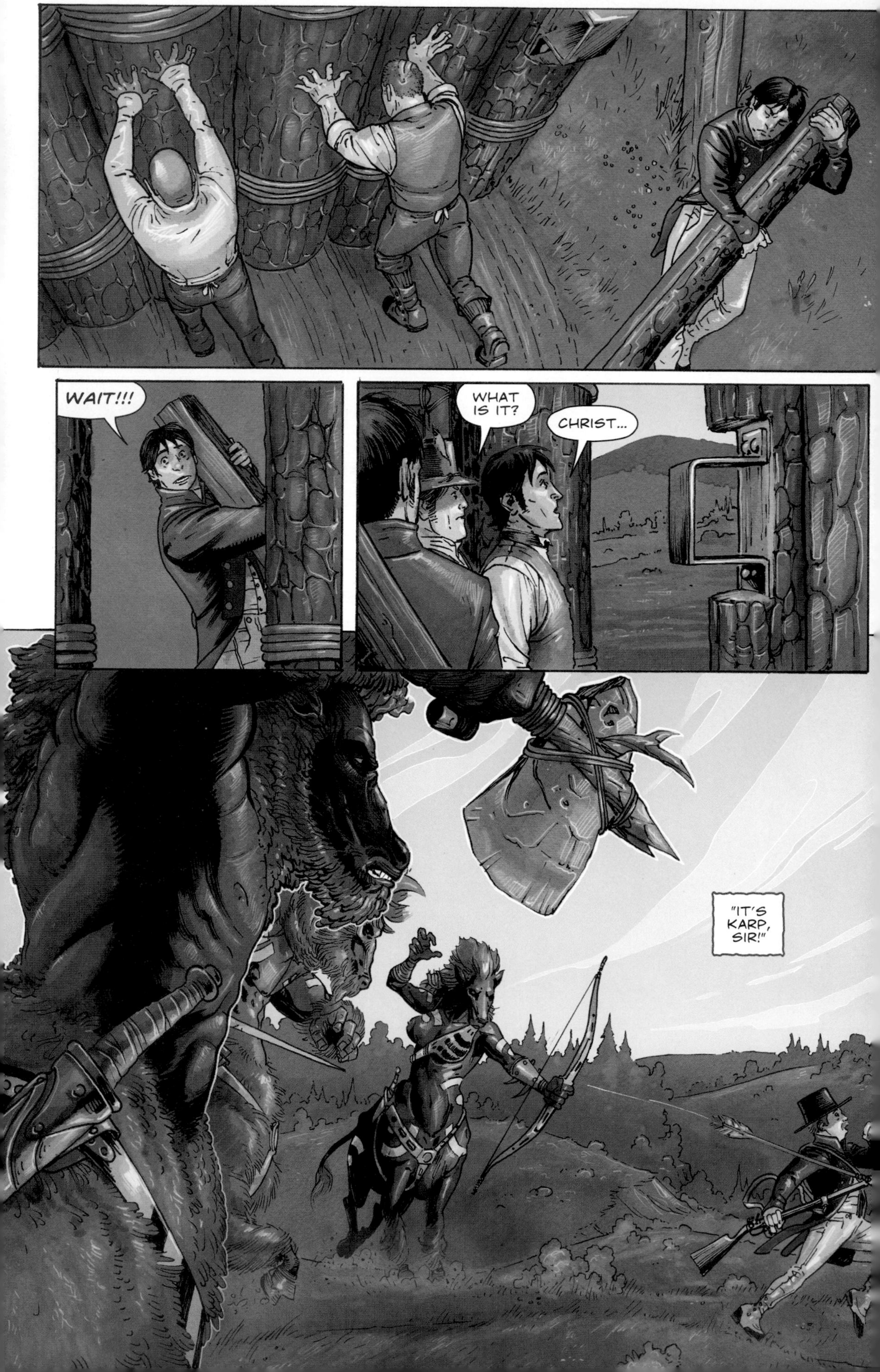
WAIT!!!
WHAT IS IT?
CHRIST...
"IT'S KARP, SIR!"

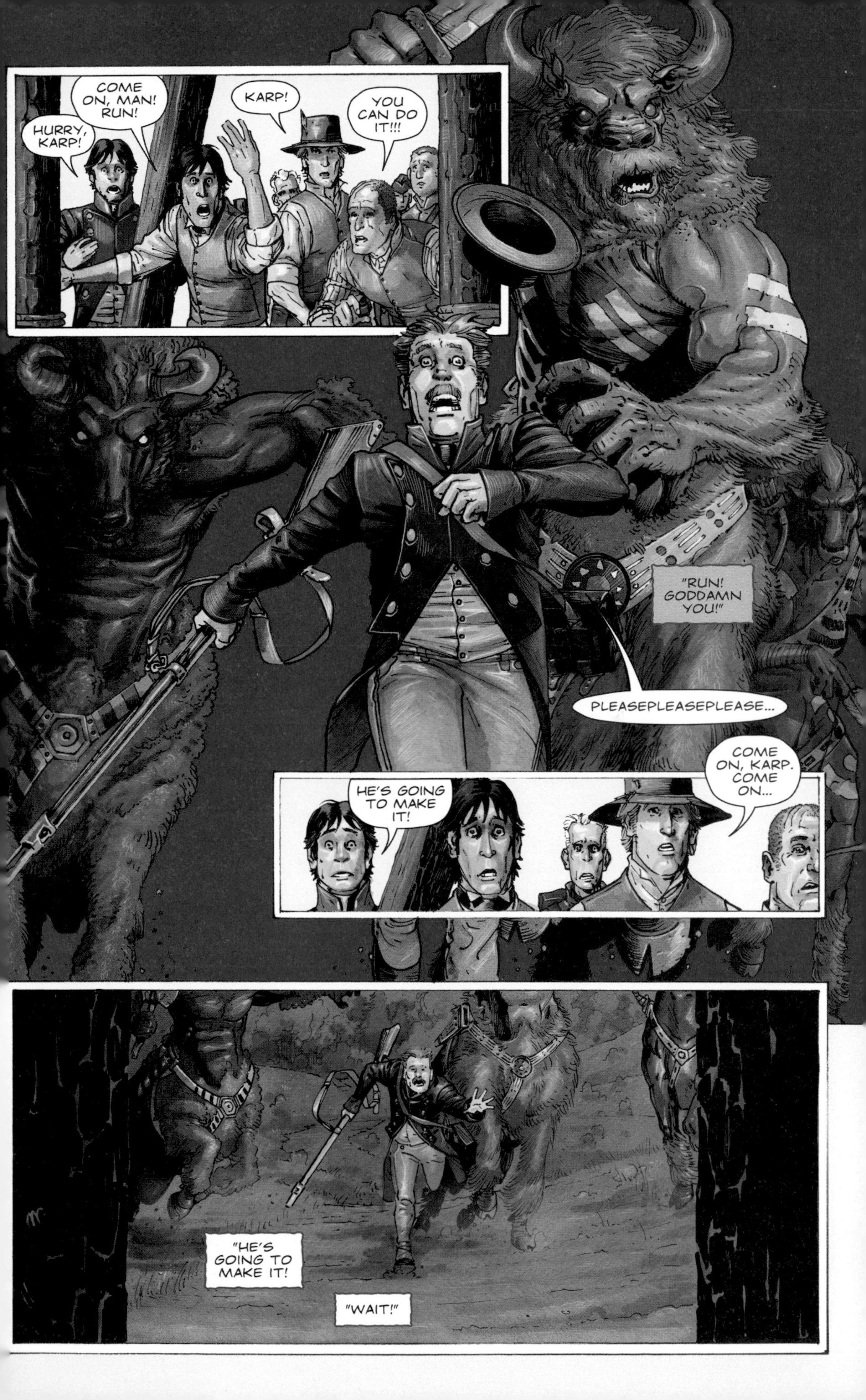
HURRY, KARP!
COME ON, MAN! RUN!
KARP!
YOU CAN DO IT!!!
"RUN! GODDAMN YOU!"
PLEASEPLEASEPLEASE...
HE'S GOING TO MAKE IT!
COME ON, KARP. COME ON...
"HE'S GOING TO MAKE IT!
"WAIT!"

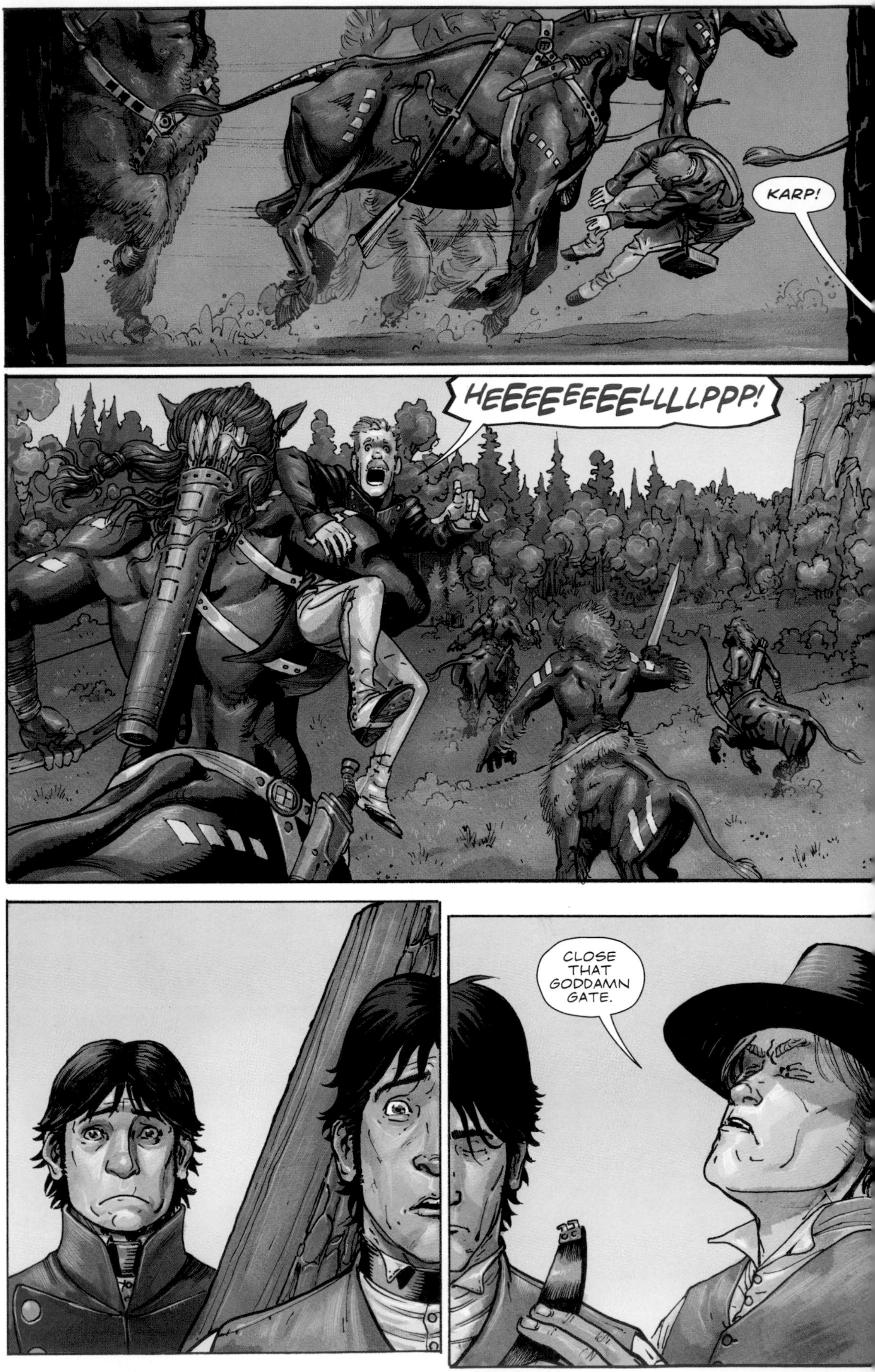
KARP!
HEEEEEEEELLLLPPP!
CLOSE THAT GODDAMN GATE.

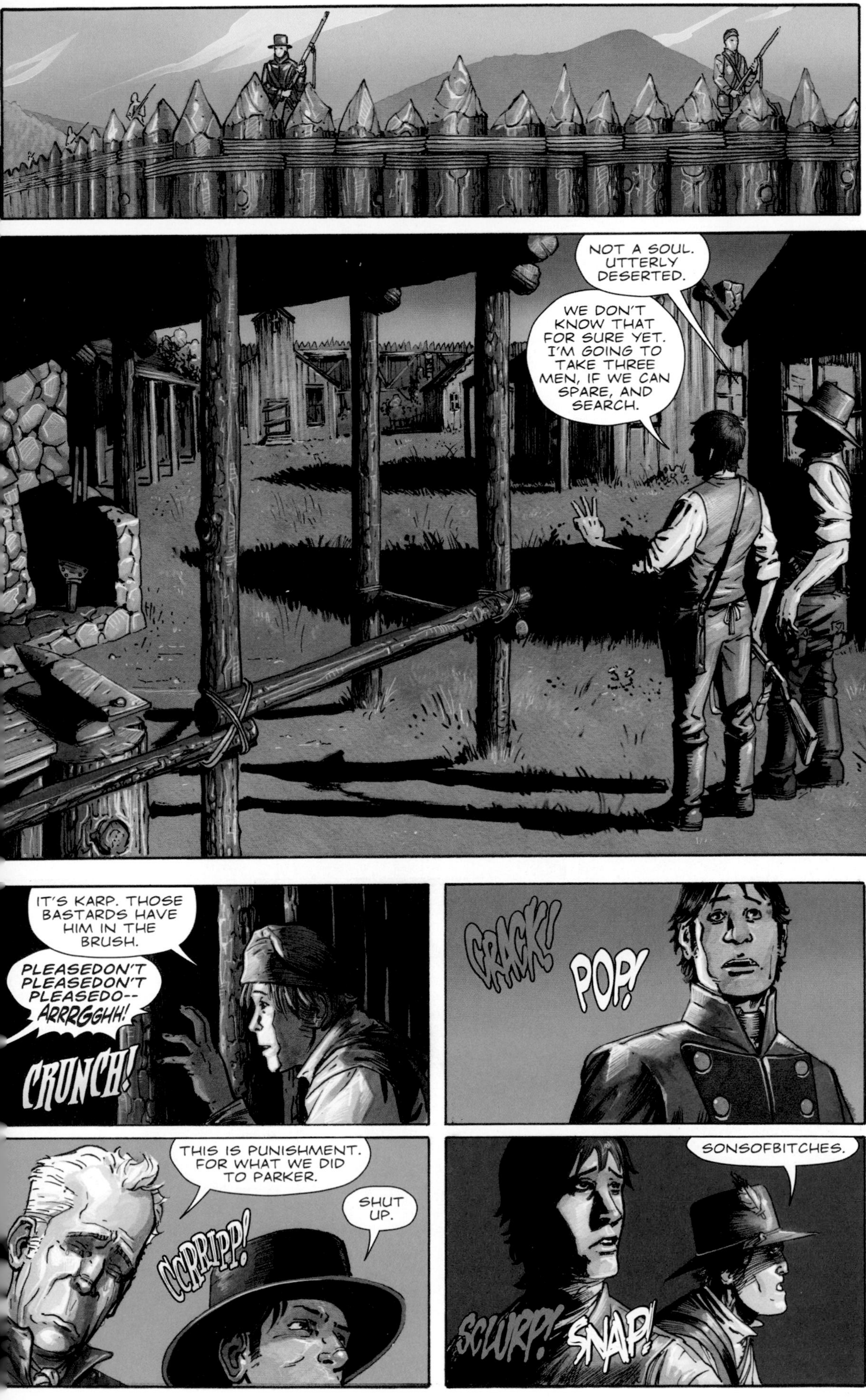
NOT A SOUL. UTTERLY DESERTED.
WE DON'T KNOW THAT FOR SURE YET. I'M GOING TO TAKE THREE MEN, IF WE CAN SPARE, AND SEARCH.
IT'S KARP. THOSE BASTARDS HAVE HIM IN THE BRUSH.
PLEASEDON'T PLEASEDON'T PLEASEDO-- ARRRGGHH!
CRUNCH!
CRACK!
POP!
THIS IS PUNISHMENT. FOR WHAT WE DID TO PARKER.
SHUT UP.
CCRRIPP!
SONSOFBITCHES.
SCLURP!
SNAP!

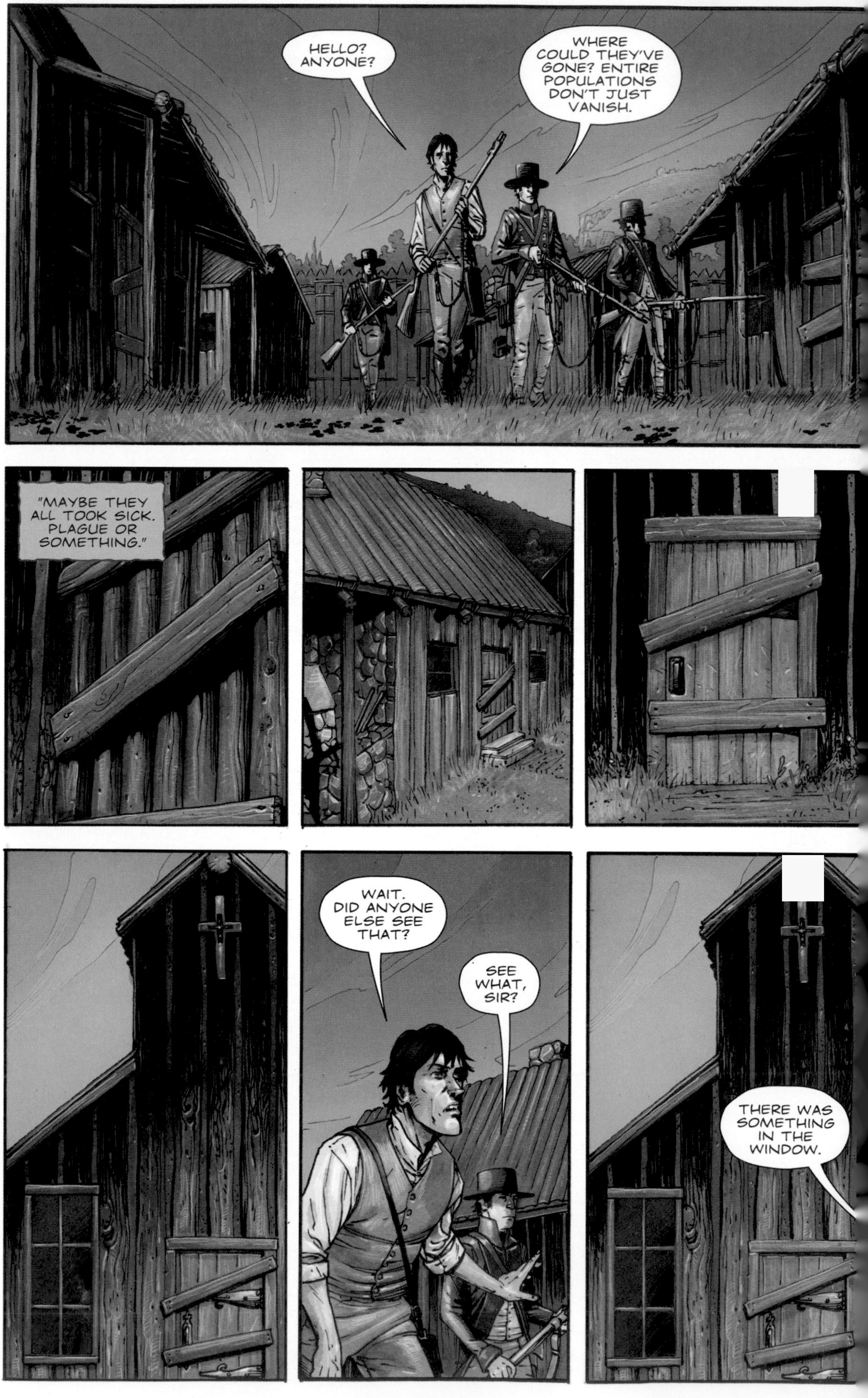
HELLO? ANYONE?
WHERE COULD THEY'VE GONE? ENTIRE POPULATIONS DON'T JUST VANISH.
"MAYBE THEY ALL TOOK SICK. PLAGUE OR SOMETHING."
WAIT. DID ANYONE ELSE SEE THAT?
SEE WHAT, SIR?
THERE WAS SOMETHING IN THE WINDOW.

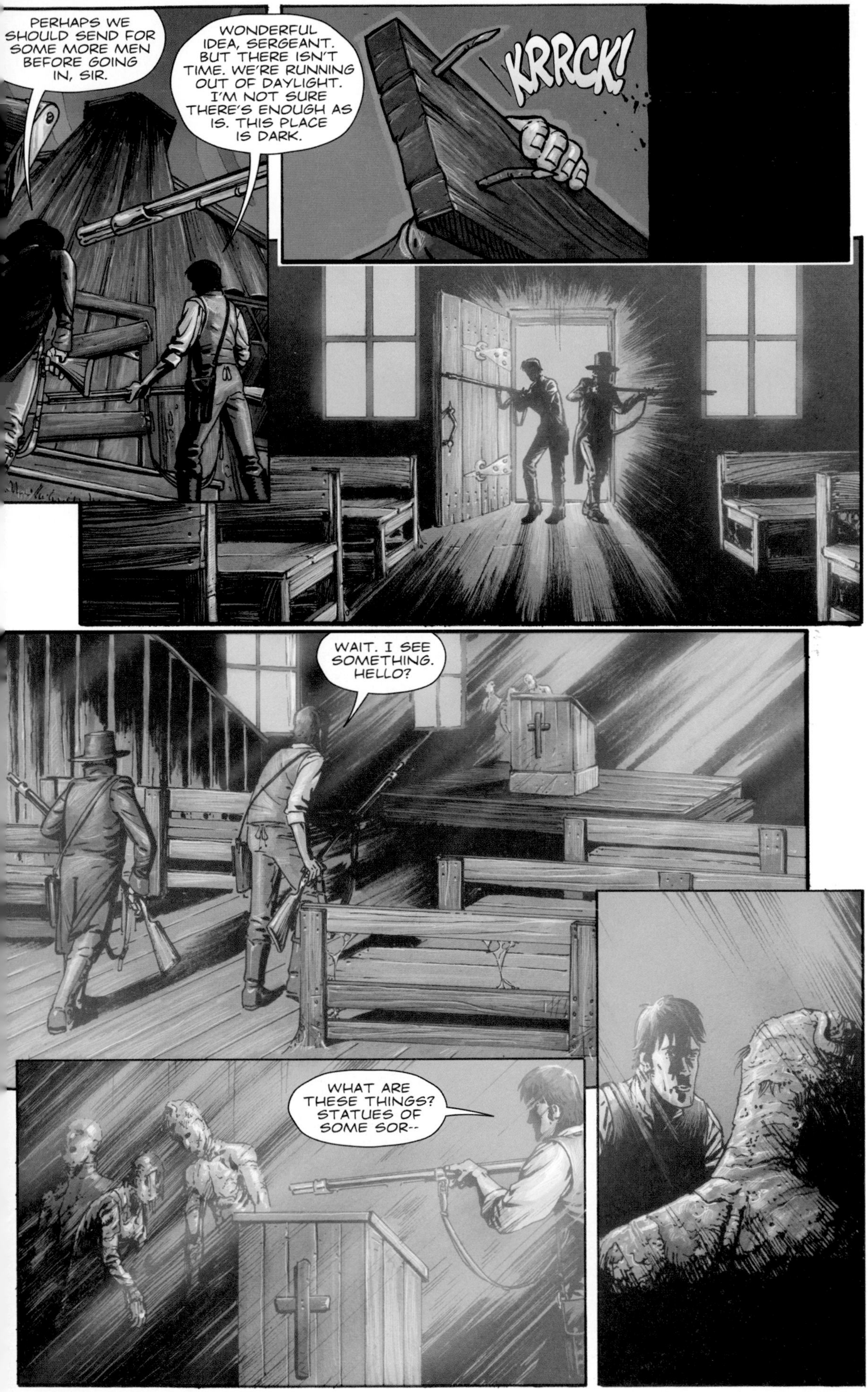

PERHAPS WE SHOULD SEND FOR SOME MORE MEN BEFORE GOING IN, SIR.
WONDERFUL IDEA, SERGEANT. BUT THERE ISN'T TIME. WE'RE RUNNING OUT OF DAYLIGHT. I'M NOT SURE THERE'S ENOUGH AS IS. THIS PLACE IS DARK.
KRRCK!
WAIT. I SEE SOMETHING. HELLO?
WHAT ARE THESE THINGS? STATUES OF SOME SOR--

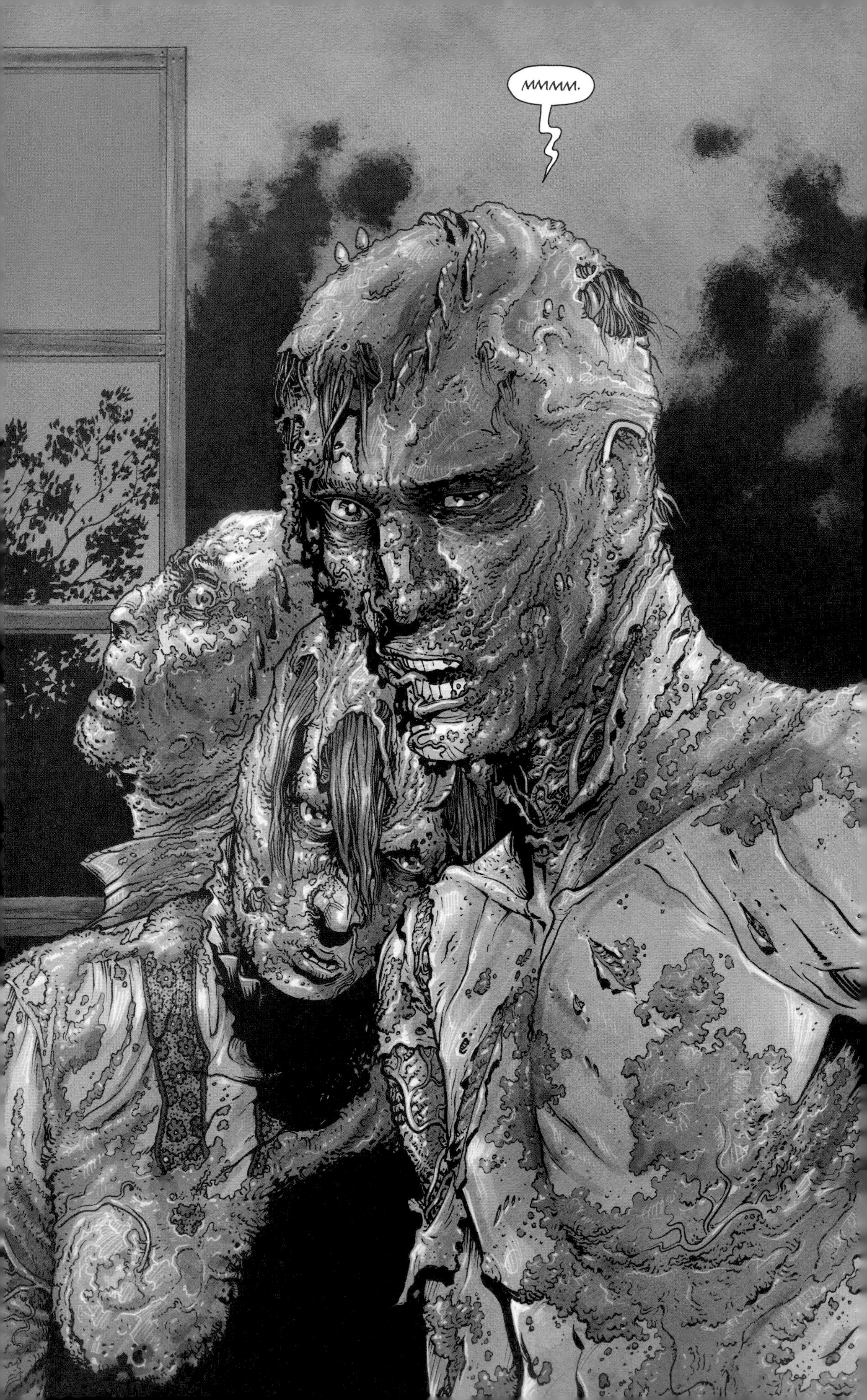
MMMM.

26. May 1804. With beasts watching from the woods, we made camp at the seemingly abandoned La Charrette. As the last white settlement due west, La Charrette had been our objective. A safe rendezvous point to encounter the additional members of our party.

THOSE THINGS HAVE BUILT A FIRE, CAPTAIN CLARK.

AT LEAST WE KNOW WHERE THEY ARE.

Now this deserted, ominous place had become our haven. Its walls providing a respite from what appeared to be certain death waiting outside. Many of us were certain this respite would be temporary.

THEY'RE GOING TO WAIT US OUT, AREN'T THEY? HOW LONG DO YOU SUPPOSE WE CAN LAST IN HERE?

WE'LL HAVE TO SEE WHAT CAPTAIN LEWIS FINDS IN HIS SEARCH, MISTER COLLINS. AND PRAY THEY AREN'T PATIENT CREATURES.

CLARK!

BACK ALREADY. HOW DID THE SEARCH GO?

I was tasked with searching La Charrette for inhabitants and supplies. What I found was horror.

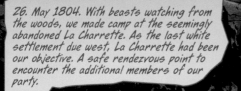

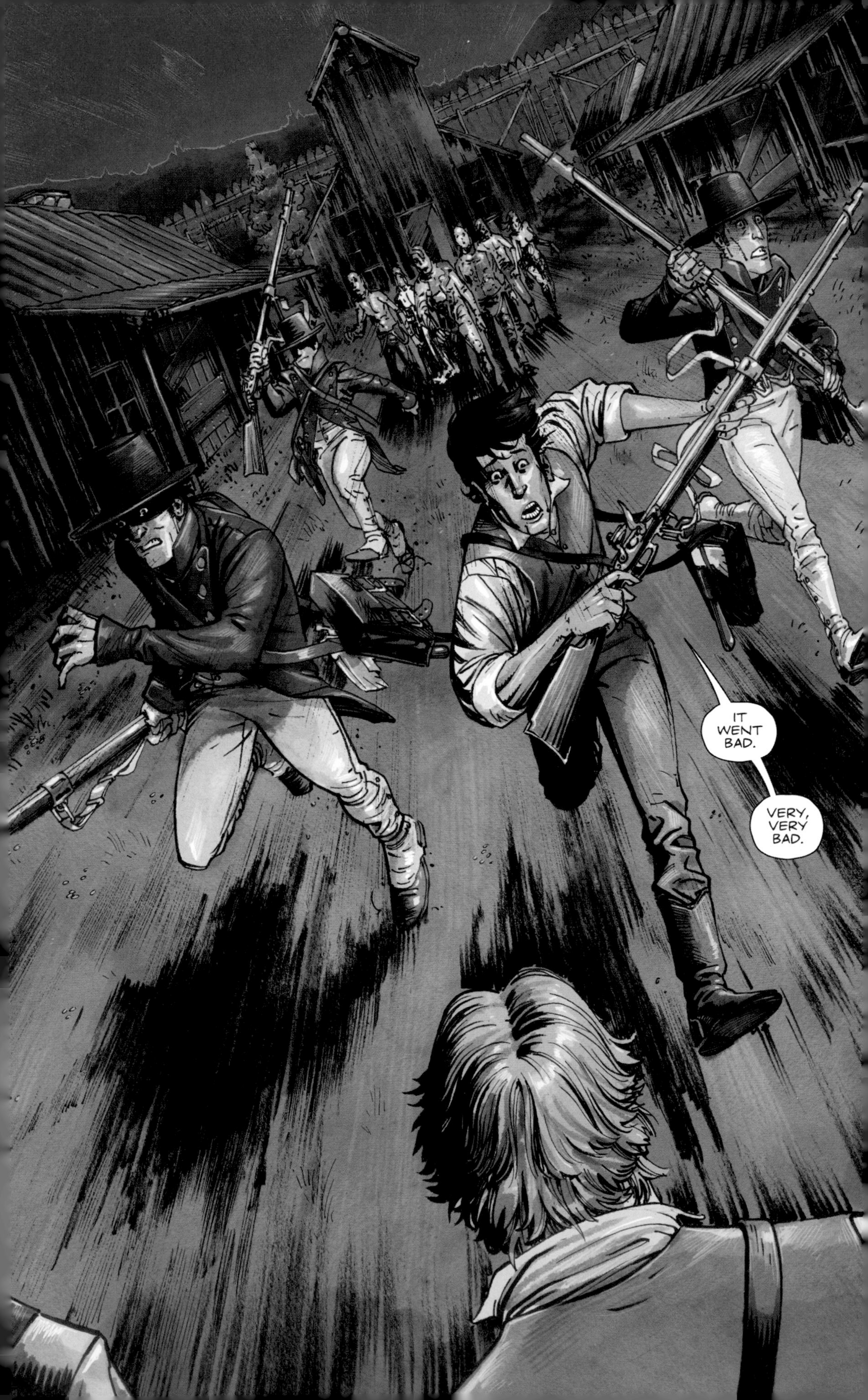
IT WENT BAD.
VERY, VERY BAD.

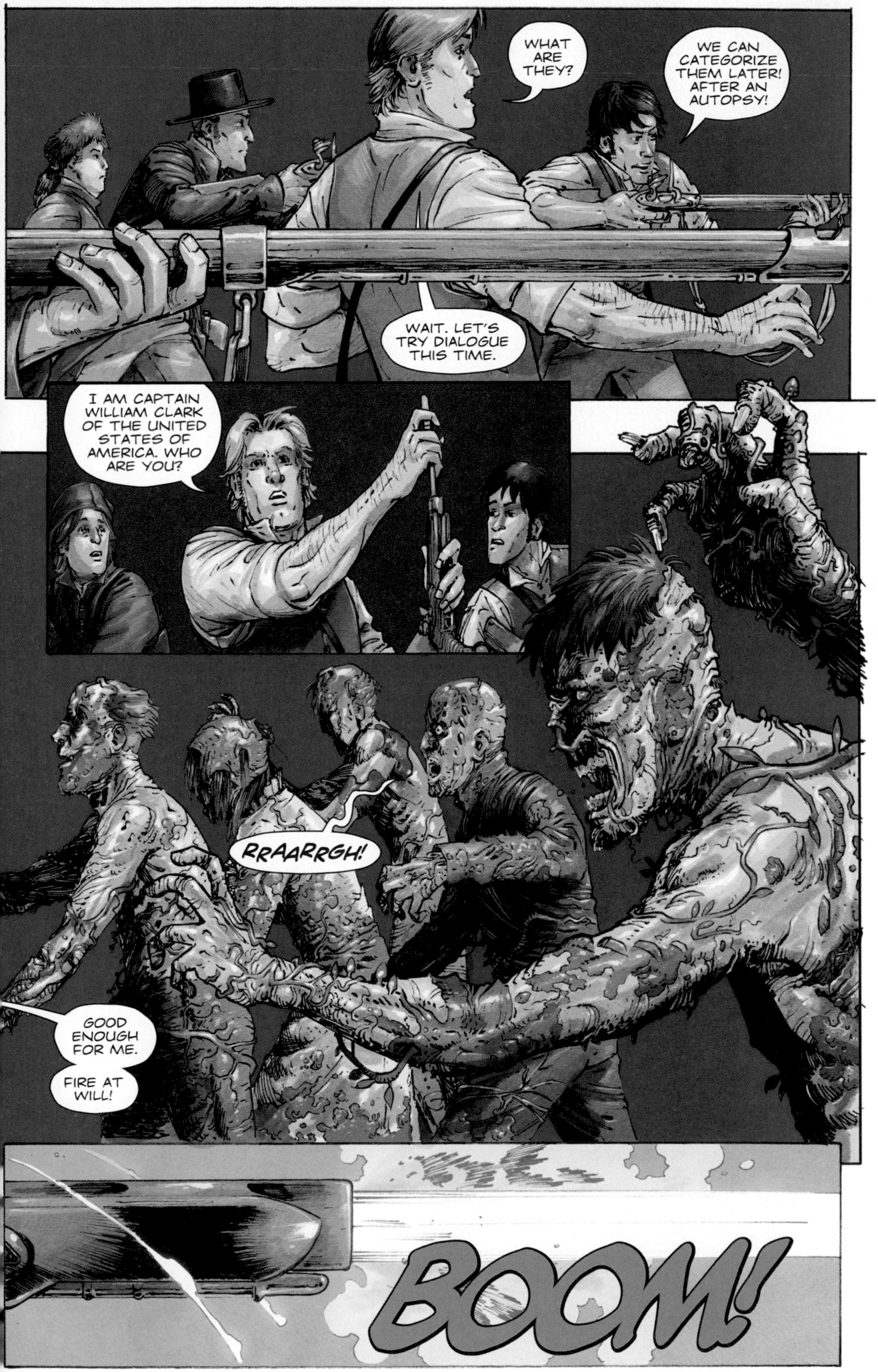
WHAT ARE THEY?
WE CAN CATEGORIZE THEM LATER! AFTER AN AUTOPSY!
WAIT. LET'S TRY DIALOGUE THIS TIME.
I AM CAPTAIN WILLIAM CLARK OF THE UNITED STATES OF AMERICA. WHO ARE YOU?
RRAARRGH!
GOOD ENOUGH FOR ME.
FIRE AT WILL!
BOOM!

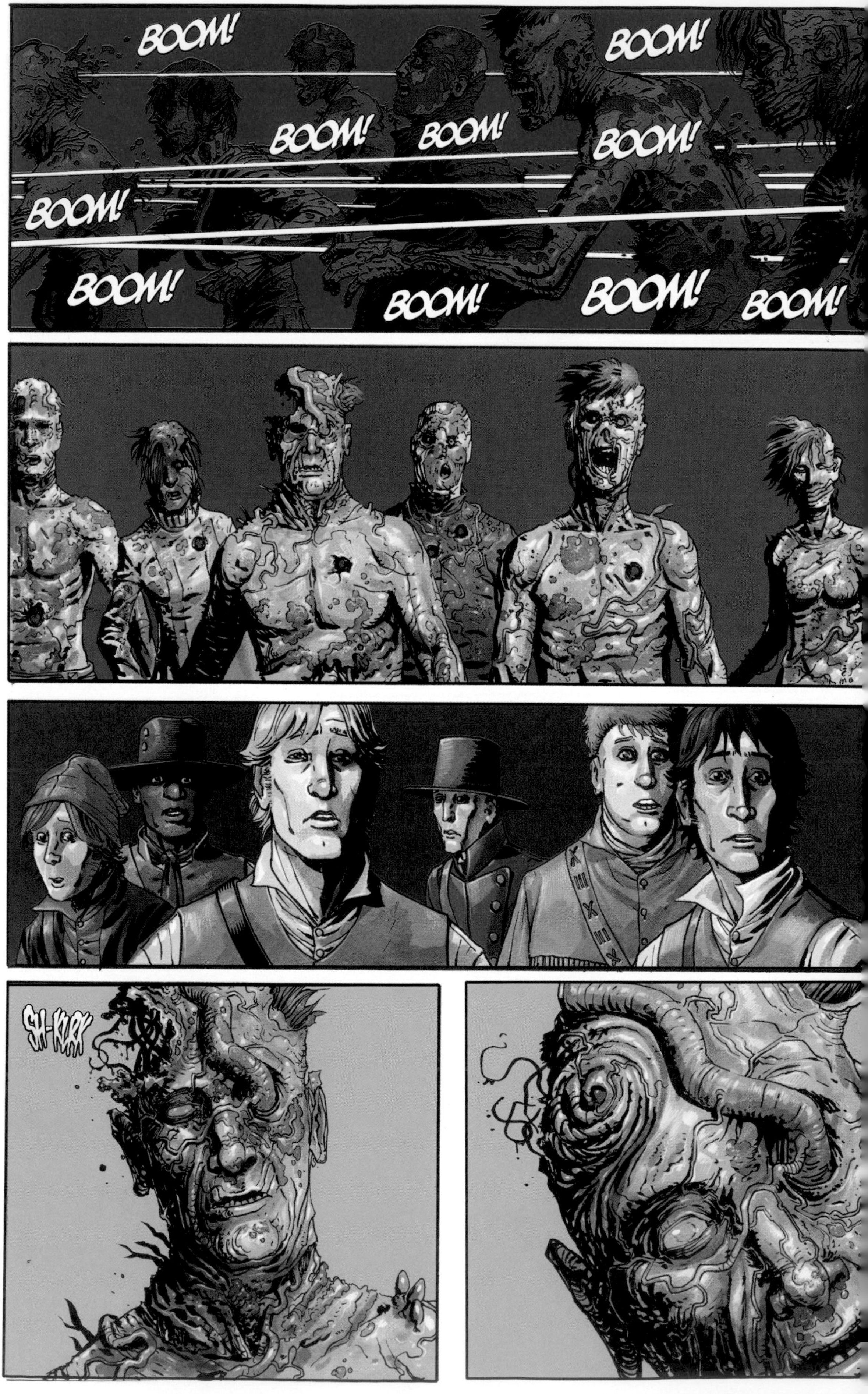
BOOM!
BOOM!
BOOM!
BOOM!
BOOM!
BOOM!
BOOM!
BOOM!
BOOM!
BOOM!
SH-KLRK

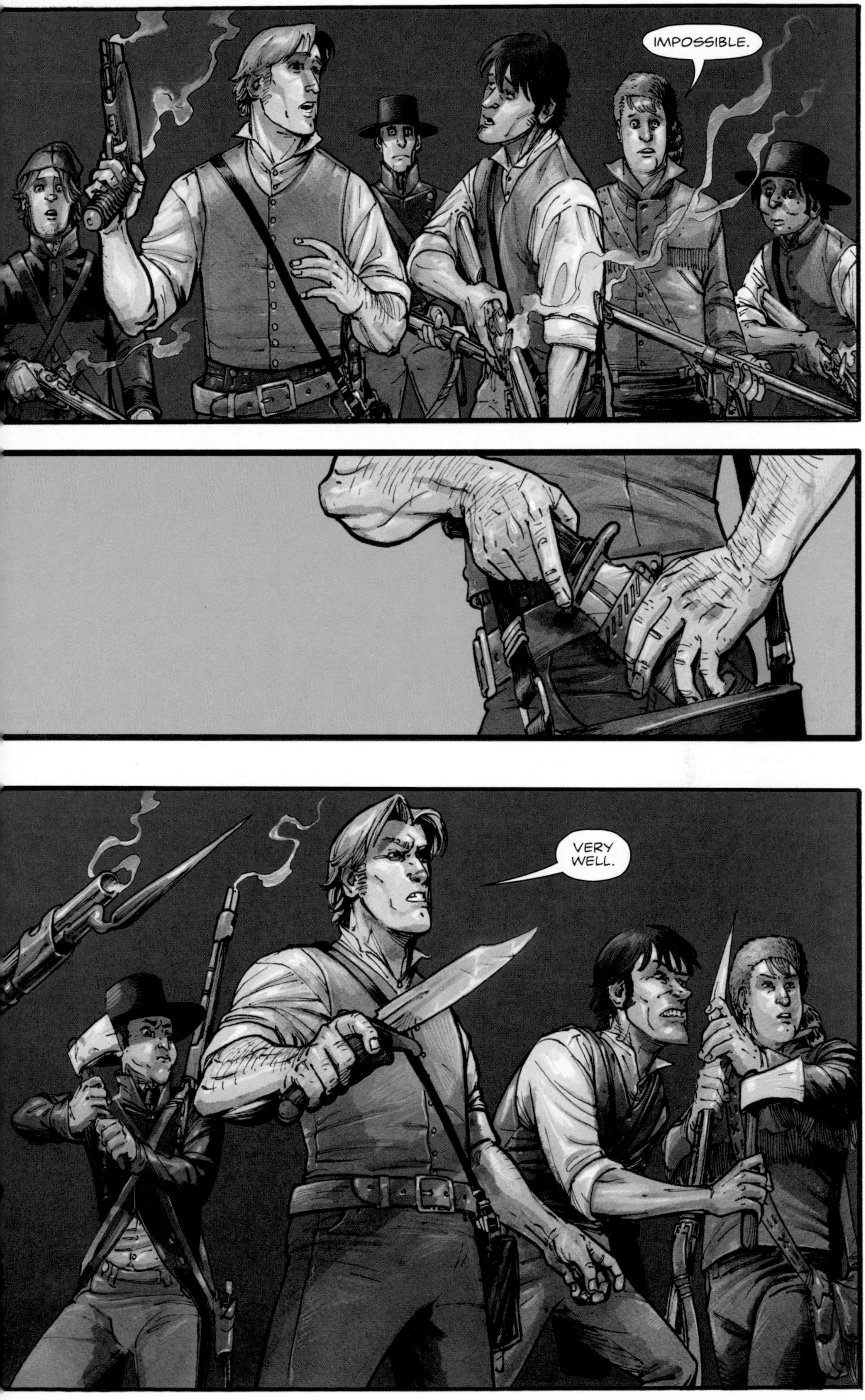
IMPOSSIBLE.
VERY WELL.

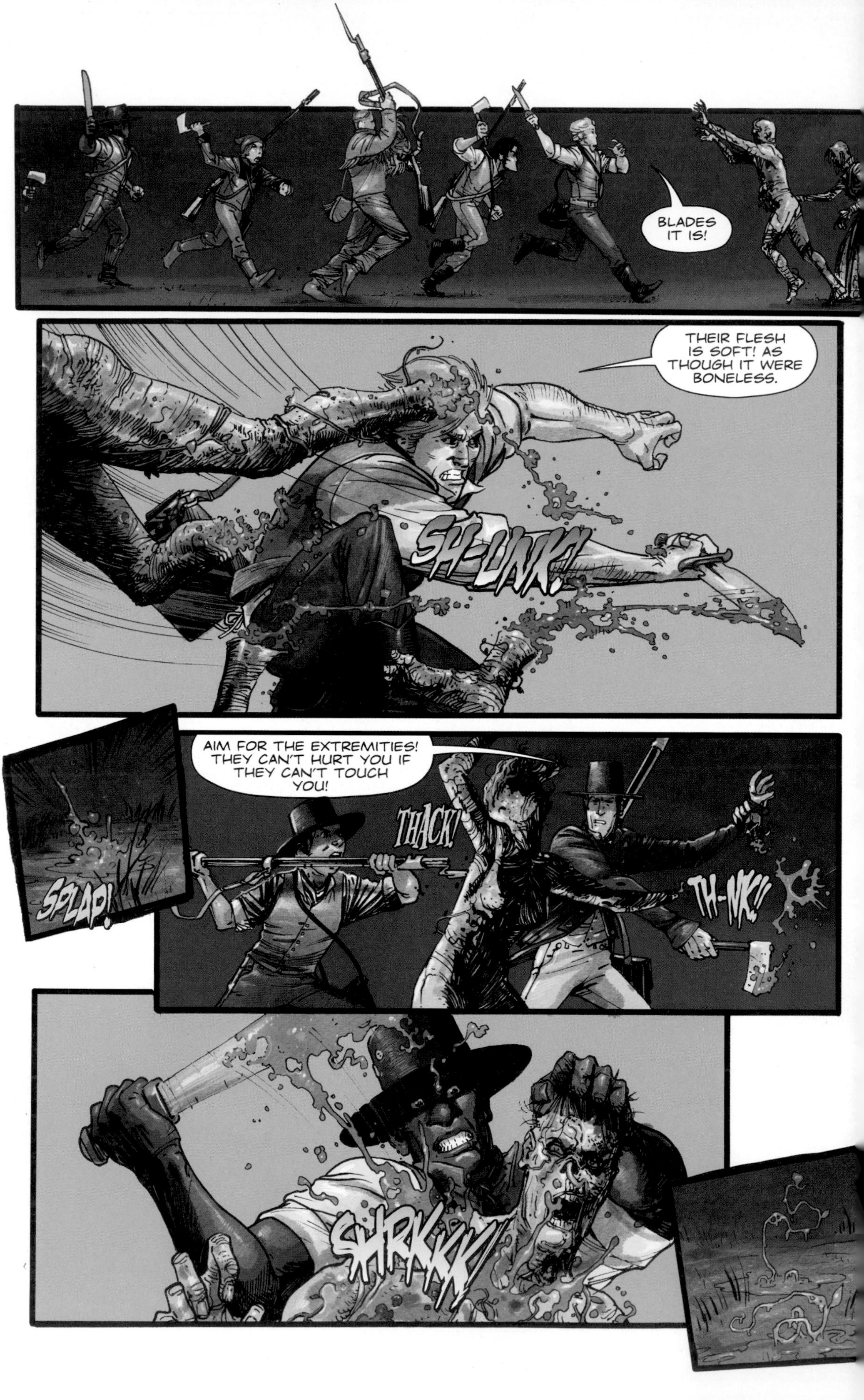
BLADES IT IS!
THEIR FLESH IS SOFT! AS THOUGH IT WERE BONELESS.
SH-UNK!
SPLAP!
AIM FOR THE EXTREMITIES! THEY CAN'T HURT YOU IF THEY CAN'T TOUCH YOU!
THACK!
TH-NK!!
SHRKKK!

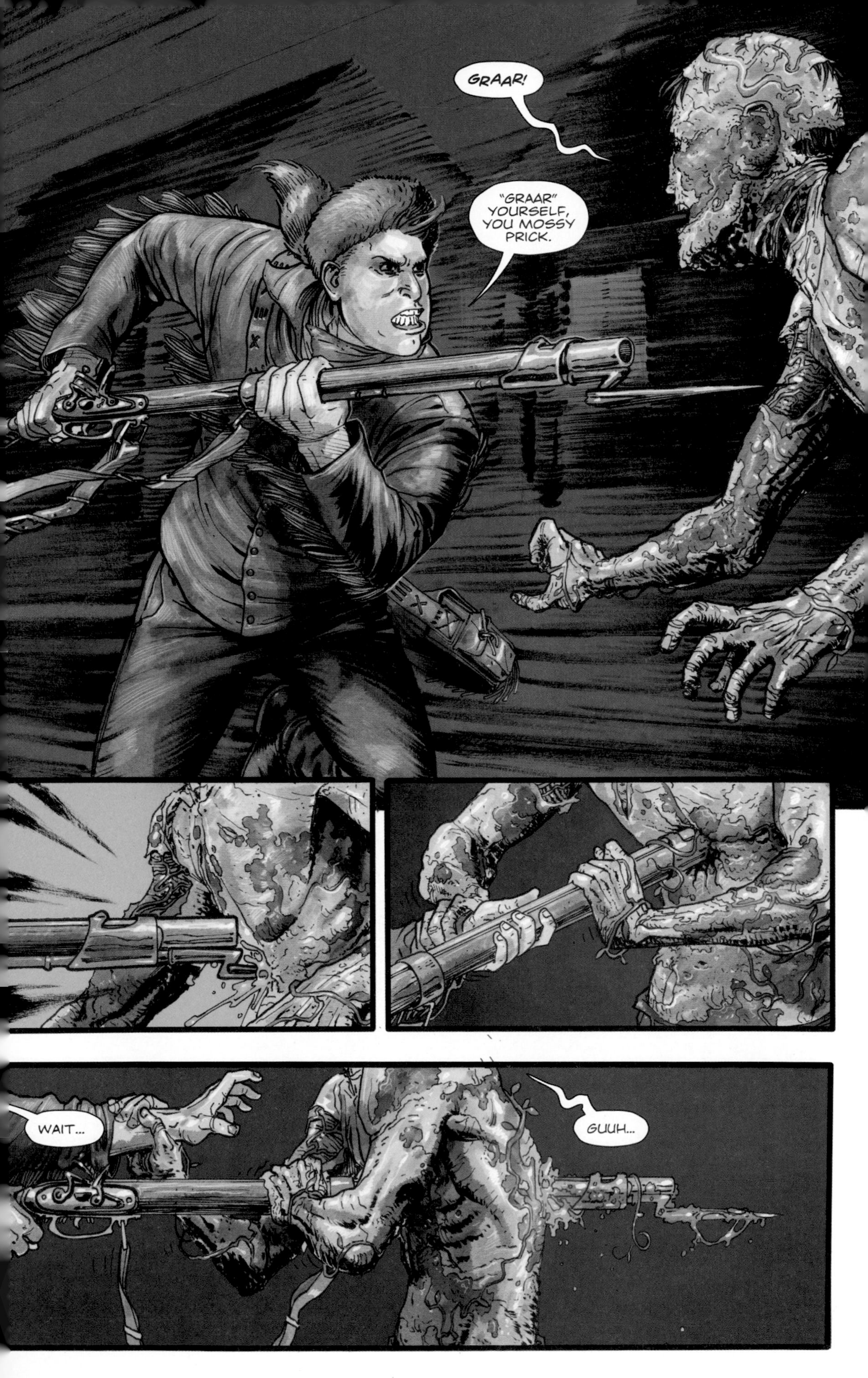
GRAAR!
"GRAAR" YOURSELF, YOU MOSSY PRICK.
WAIT...
GUUH...

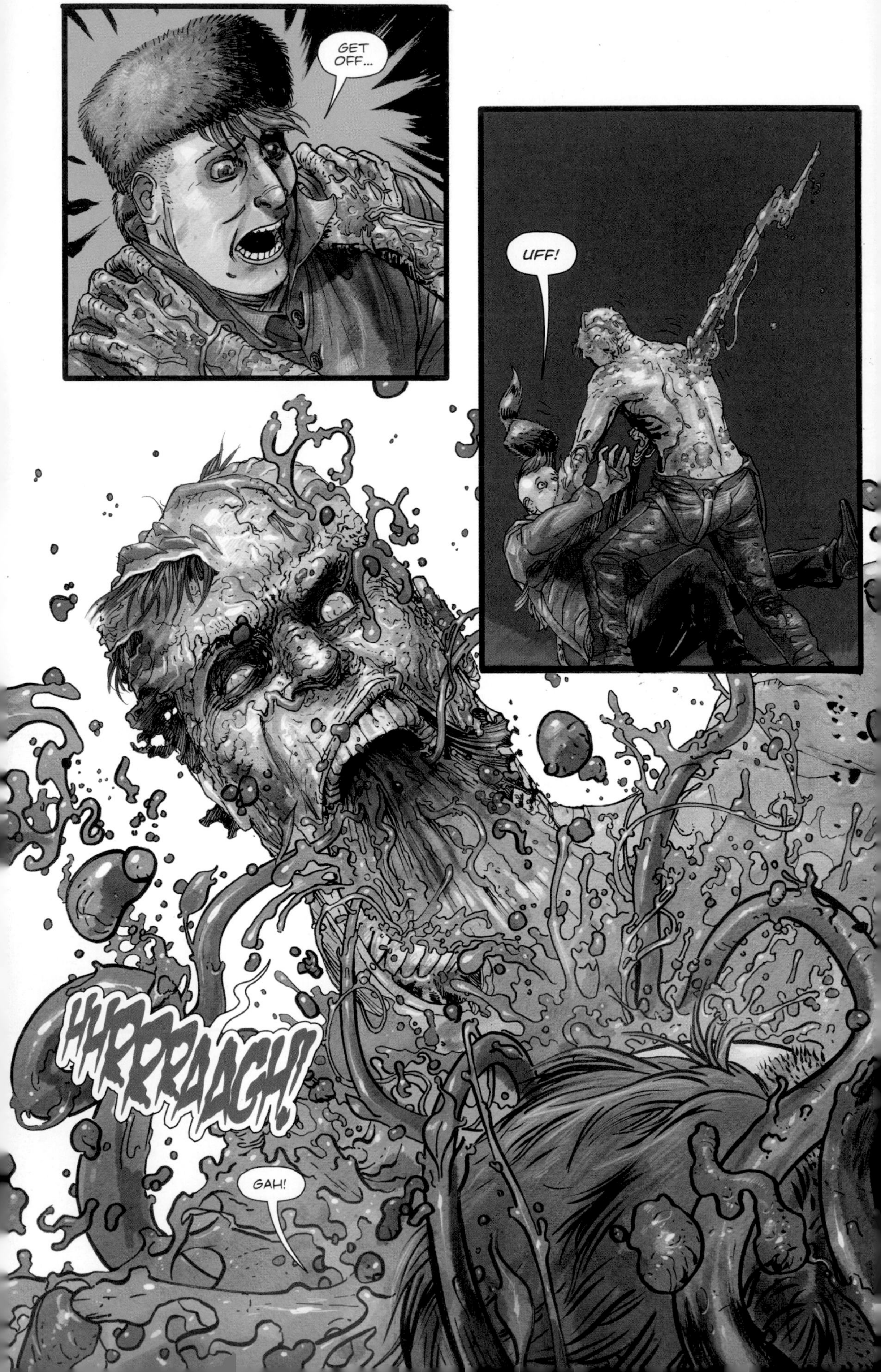
GET OFF...
UFF!
HHRRRAAGH!
GAH!

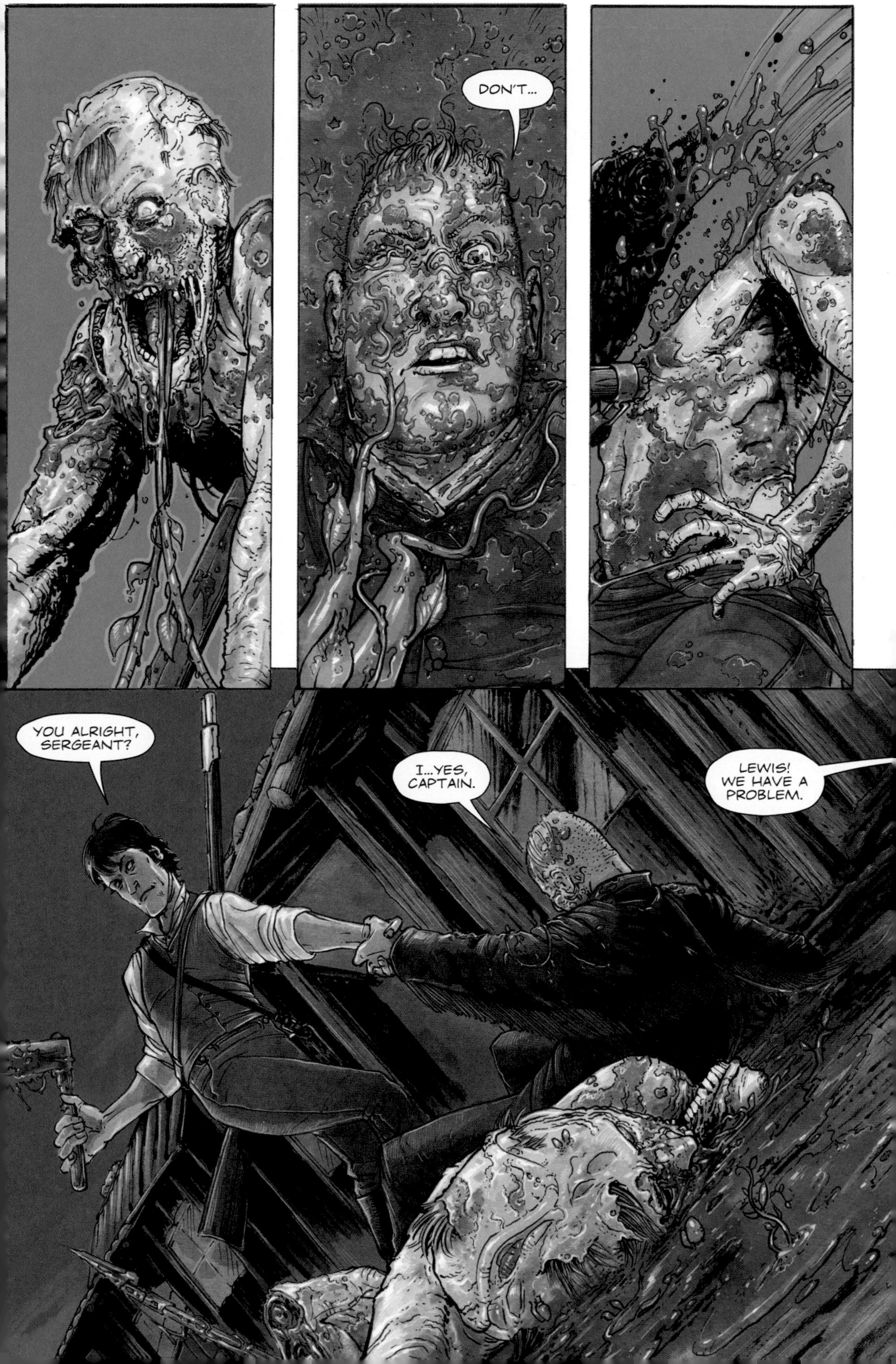
DON'T...
YOU ALRIGHT, SERGEANT?
I...YES, CAPTAIN.
LEWIS! WE HAVE A PROBLEM.

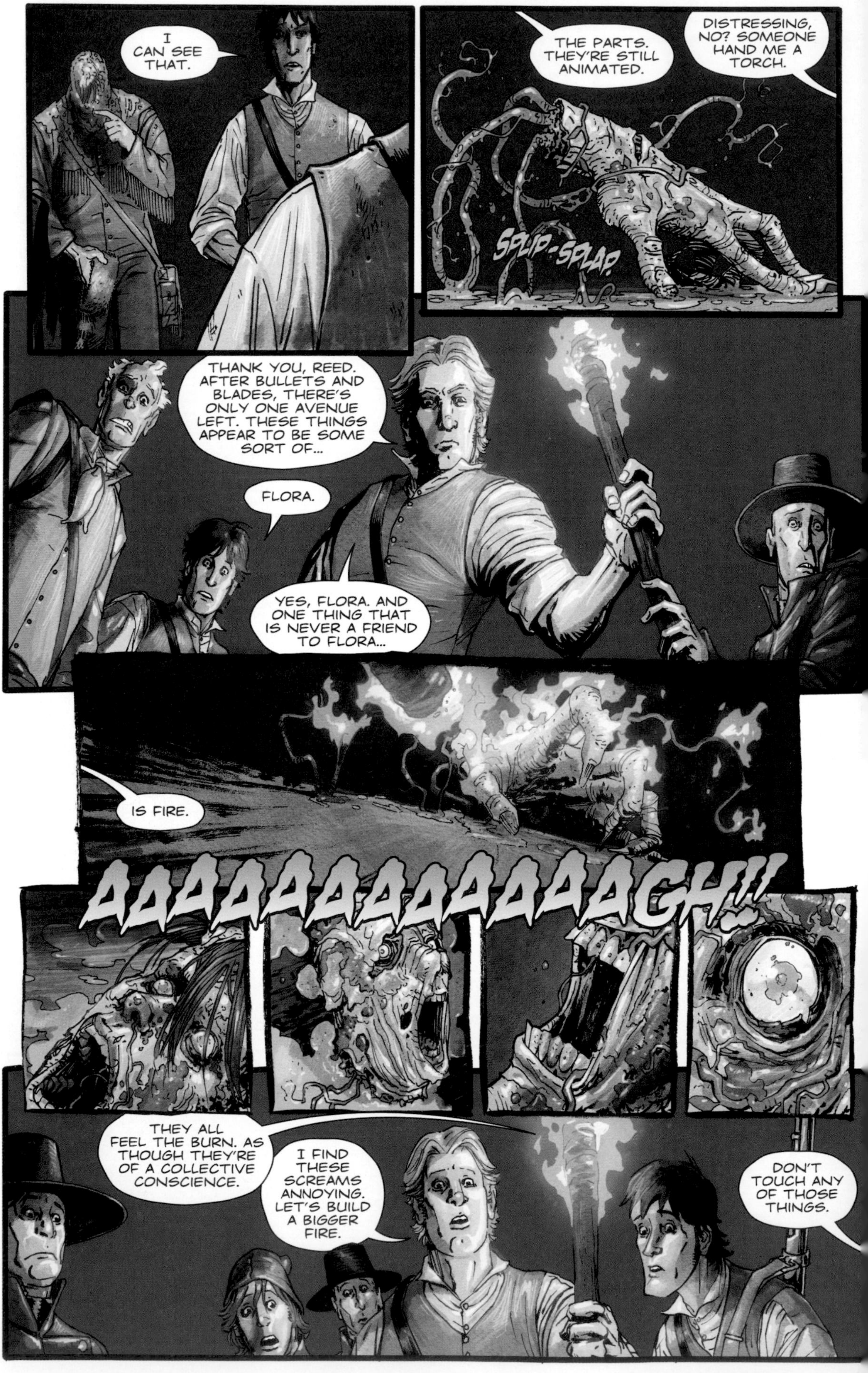
I CAN SEE THAT.
THE PARTS. THEY'RE STILL ANIMATED.
DISTRESSING, NO? SOMEONE HAND ME A TORCH.
SPLIP-SPLAP.
THANK YOU, REED. AFTER BULLETS AND BLADES, THERE'S ONLY ONE AVENUE LEFT. THESE THINGS APPEAR TO BE SOME SORT OF...
FLORA.
YES, FLORA. AND ONE THING THAT IS NEVER A FRIEND TO FLORA...
IS FIRE.
AAAAAAAAAAAAAGH!!
THEY ALL FEEL THE BURN. AS THOUGH THEY'RE OF A COLLECTIVE CONSCIENCE.
I FIND THESE SCREAMS ANNOYING. LET'S BUILD A BIGGER FIRE.
DON'T TOUCH ANY OF THOSE THINGS.

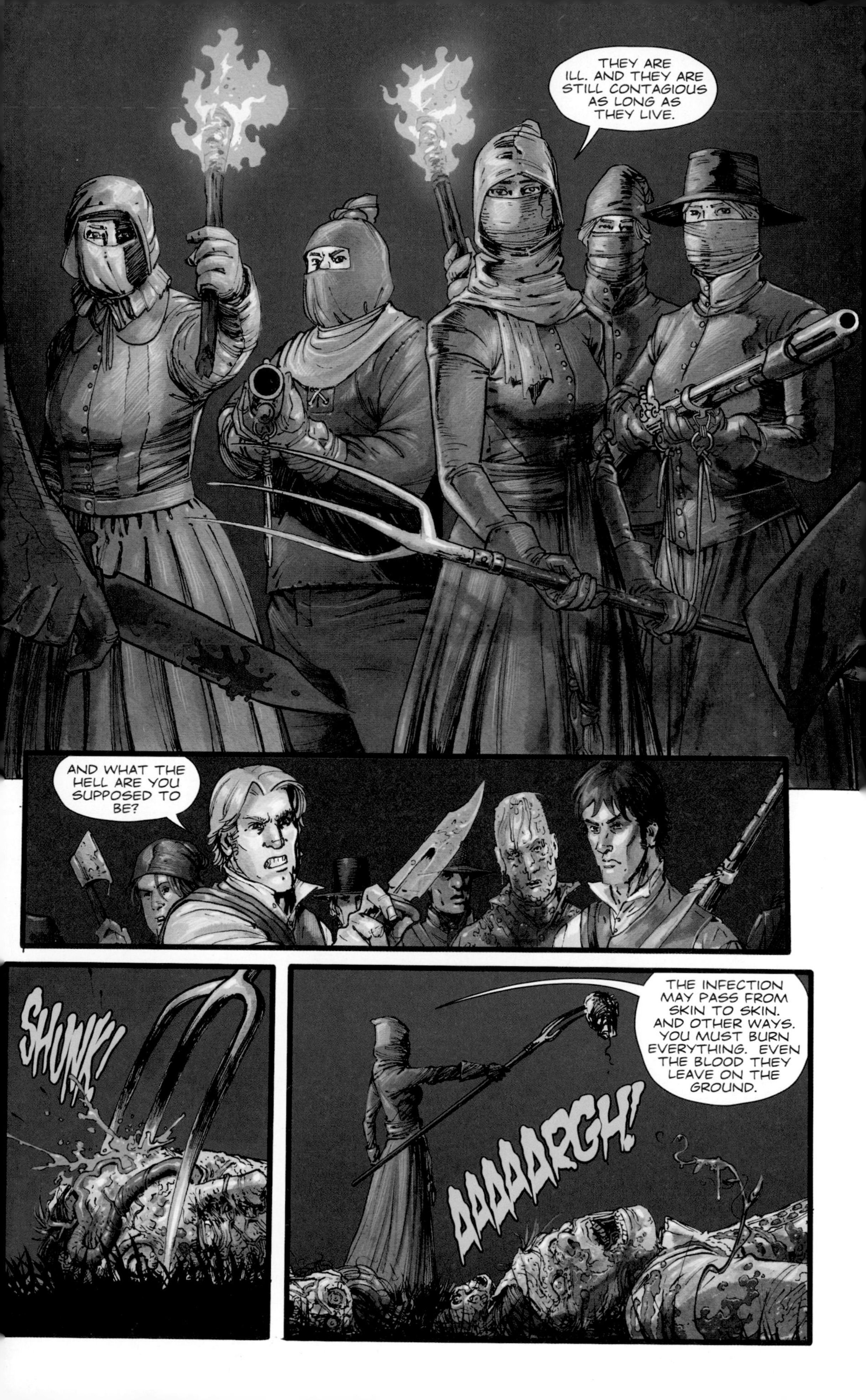
THEY ARE ILL. AND THEY ARE STILL CONTAGIOUS AS LONG AS THEY LIVE.
AND WHAT THE HELL ARE YOU SUPPOSED TO BE?
SHUNK!
THE INFECTION MAY PASS FROM SKIN TO SKIN. AND OTHER WAYS. YOU MUST BURN EVERYTHING. EVEN THE BLOOD THEY LEAVE ON THE GROUND.
AAAAARGH!

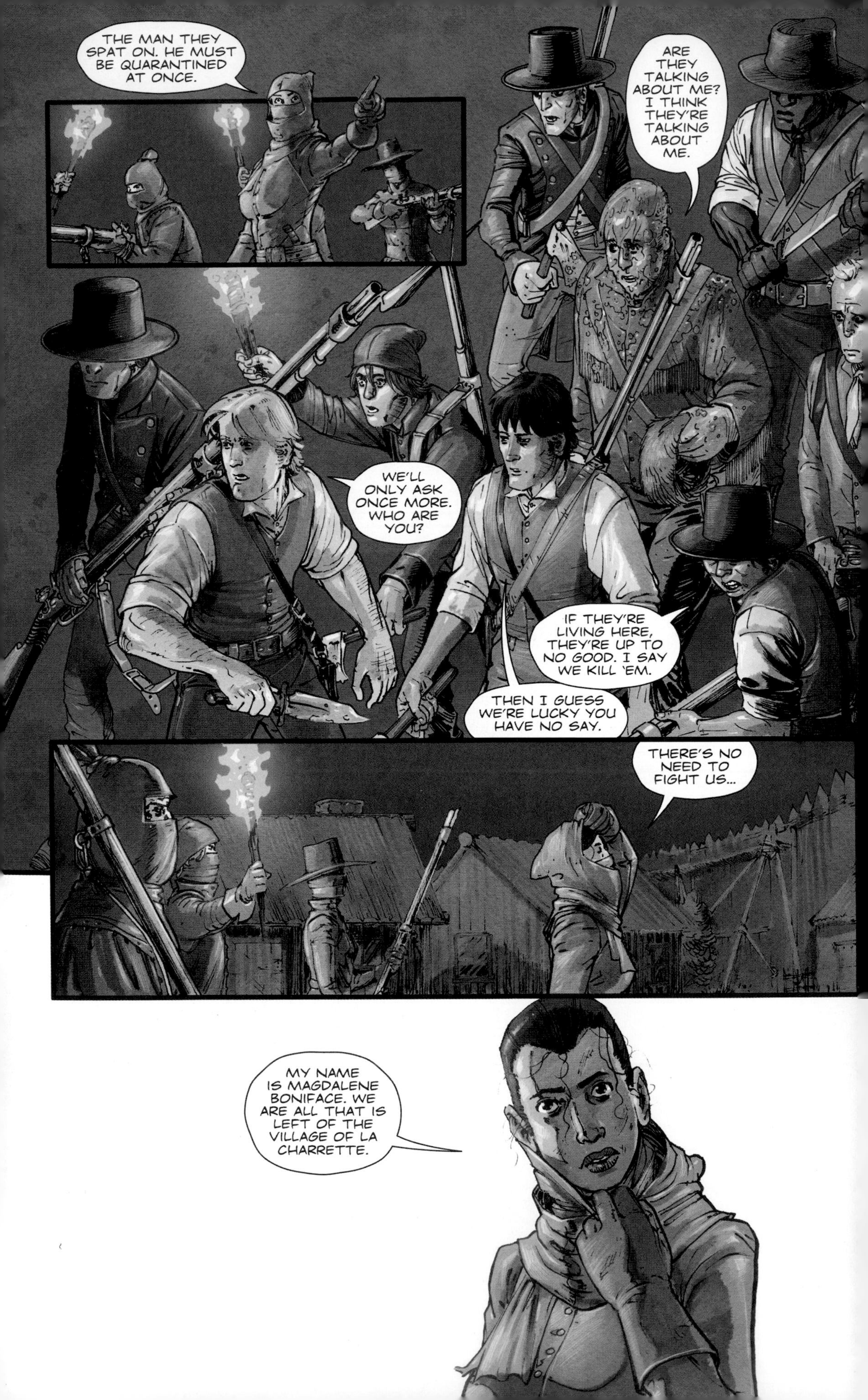
THE MAN THEY SPAT ON. HE MUST BE QUARANTINED AT ONCE.
ARE THEY TALKING ABOUT ME? I THINK THEY'RE TALKING ABOUT ME.
WE'LL ONLY ASK ONCE MORE. WHO ARE YOU?
IF THEY'RE LIVING HERE, THEY'RE UP TO NO GOOD. I SAY WE KILL 'EM.
THEN I GUESS WE'RE LUCKY YOU HAVE NO SAY.
THERE'S NO NEED TO FIGHT US...
MY NAME IS MAGDALENE BONIFACE. WE ARE ALL THAT IS LEFT OF THE VILLAGE OF LA CHARRETTE.

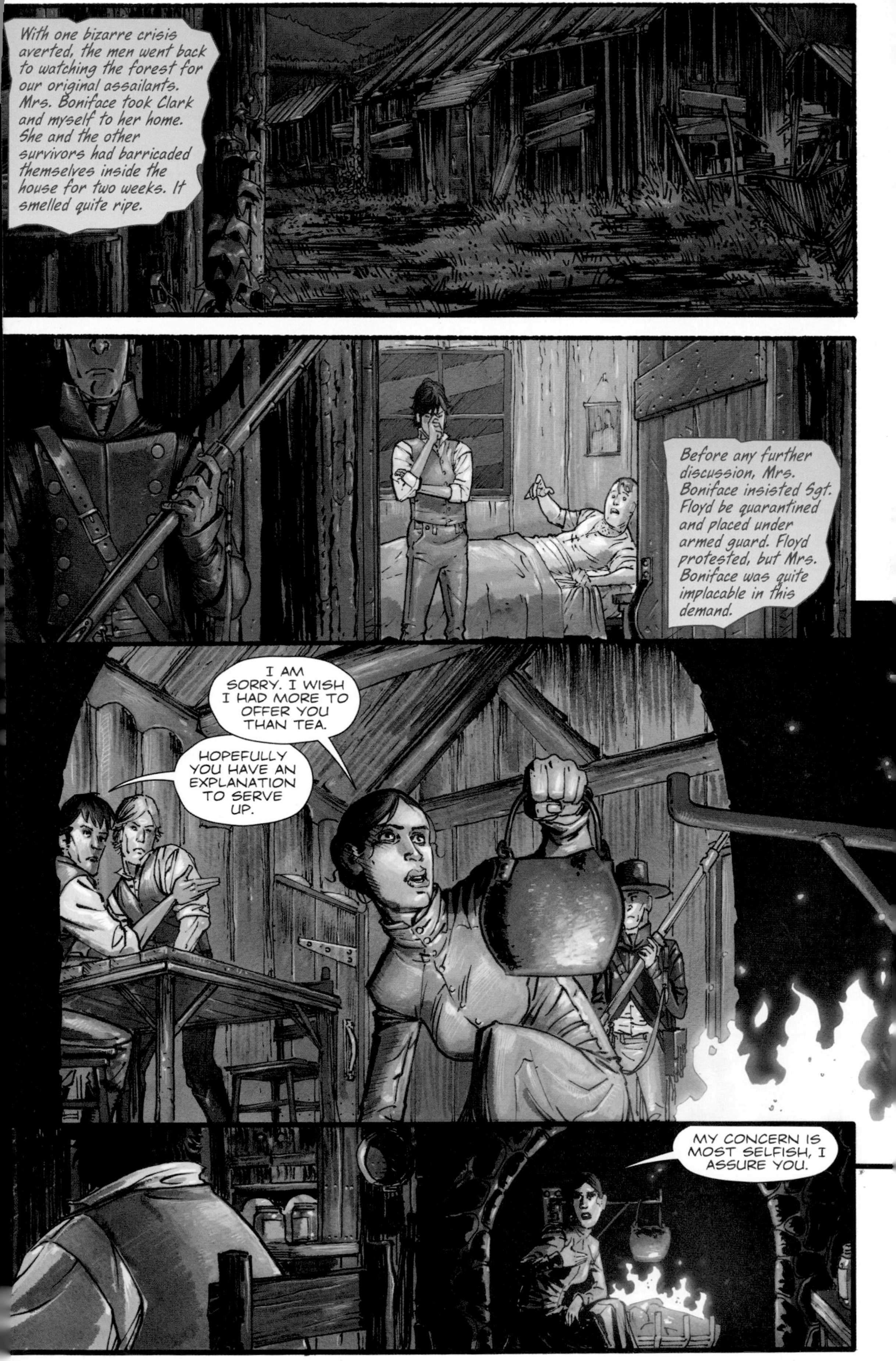
With one bizarre crisis averted, the men went back to watching the forest for our original assailants. Mrs. Boniface took Clark and myself to her home. She and the other survivors had barricaded themselves inside the house for two weeks. It smelled quite ripe.
Before any further discussion, Mrs. Boniface insisted Sgt. Floyd be quarantined and placed under armed guard. Floyd protested, but Mrs. Boniface was quite implacable in this demand.
I AM SORRY. I WISH I HAD MORE TO OFFER YOU THAN TEA.
HOPEFULLY YOU HAVE AN EXPLANATION TO SERVE UP.
MY CONCERN IS MOST SELFISH, I ASSURE YOU.

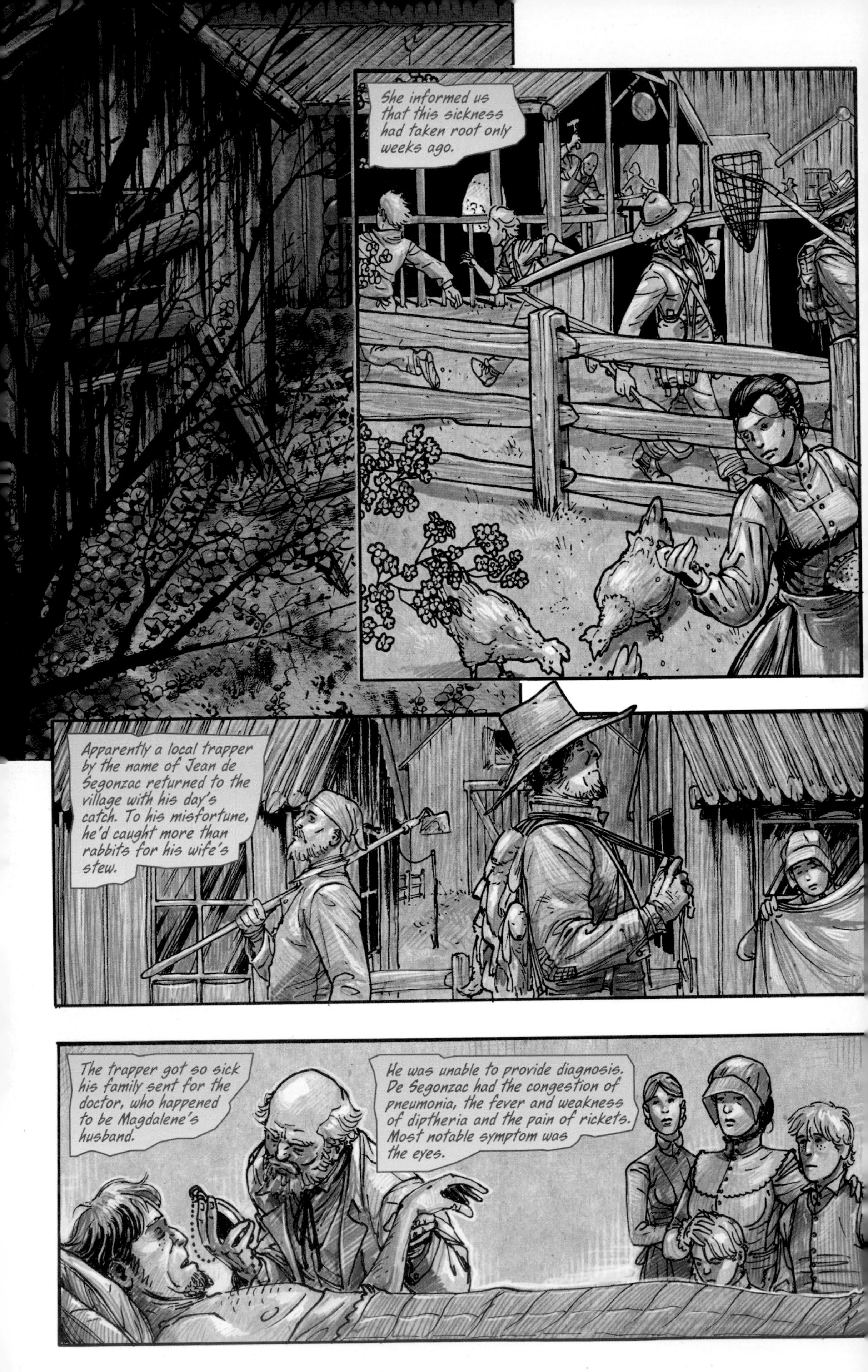
She informed us that this sickness had taken root only weeks ago.
Apparently a local trapper by the name of Jean de Segonzac returned to the village with his day's catch. To his misfortune, he'd caught more than rabbits for his wife's stew.
The trapper got so sick his family sent for the doctor, who happened to be Magdalene's husband.
He was unable to provide diagnosis. De Segonzac had the congestion of pneumonia, the fever and weakness of diptheria and the pain of rickets. Most notable symptom was the eyes.

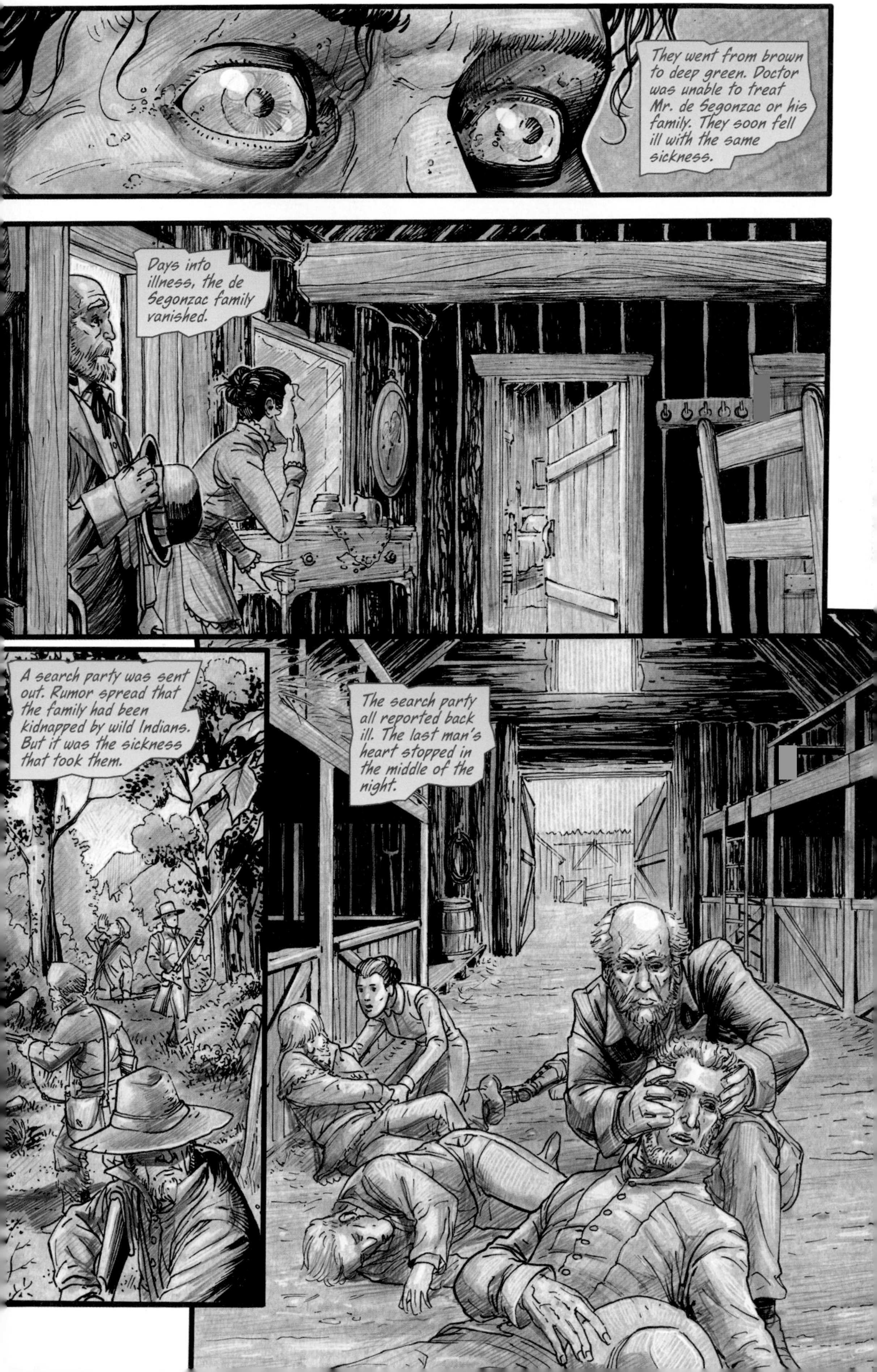
They went from brown to deep green. Doctor was unable to treat Mr. de Segonzac or his family. They soon fell ill with the same sickness.
Days into illness, the de Segonzac family vanished.
A search party was sent out. Rumor spread that the family had been kidnapped by wild Indians. But it was the sickness that took them.
The search party all reported back ill. The last man's heart stopped in the middle of the night.

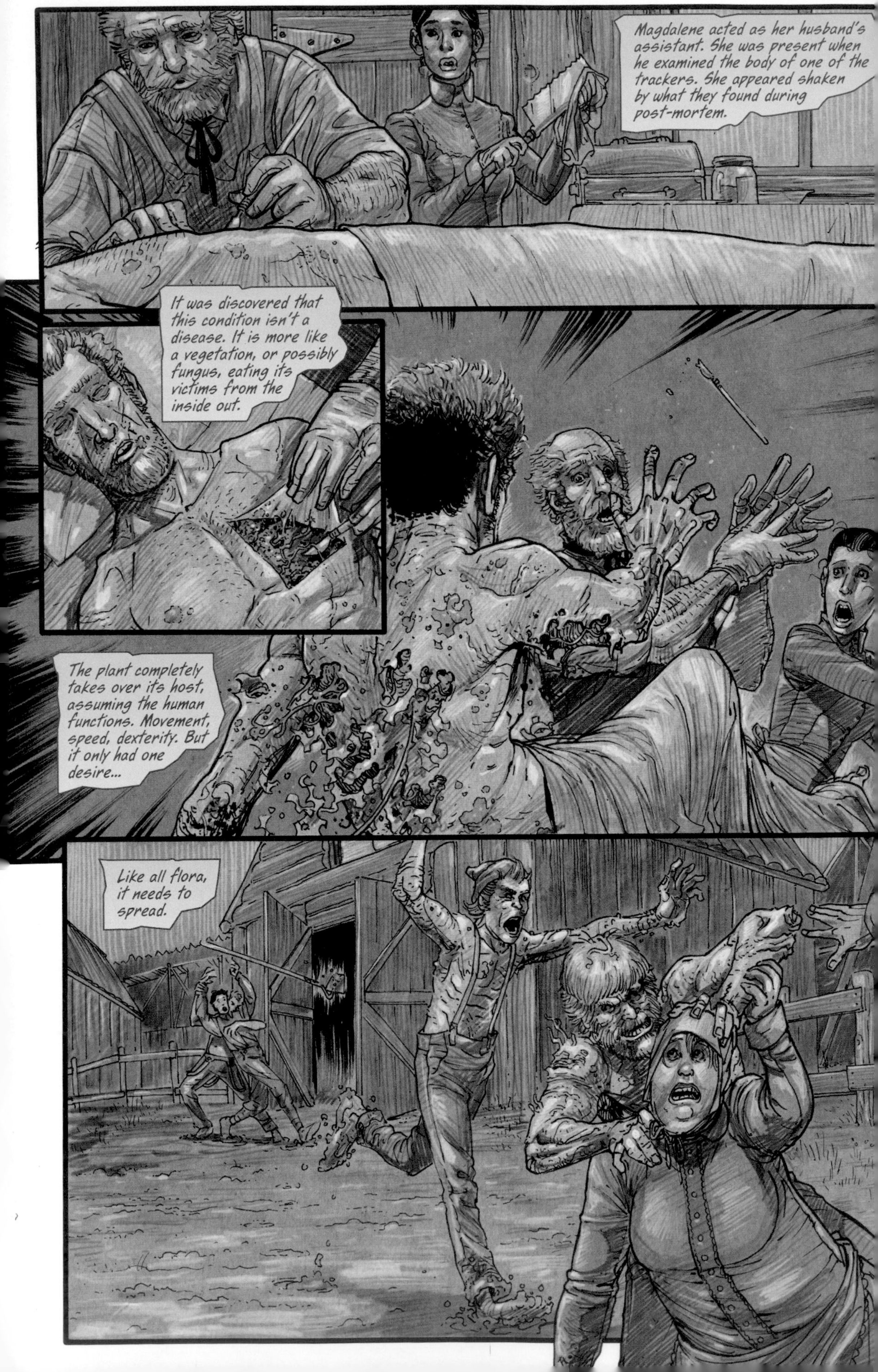
Magdalene acted as her husband's assistant. She was present when he examined the body of one of the trackers. She appeared shaken by what they found during post-mortem.
It was discovered that this condition isn't a disease. It is more like a vegetation, or possibly fungus, eating its victims from the inside out.
The plant completely takes over its host, assuming the human functions. Movement, speed, dexterity. But it only had one desire...
Like all flora, it needs to spread.

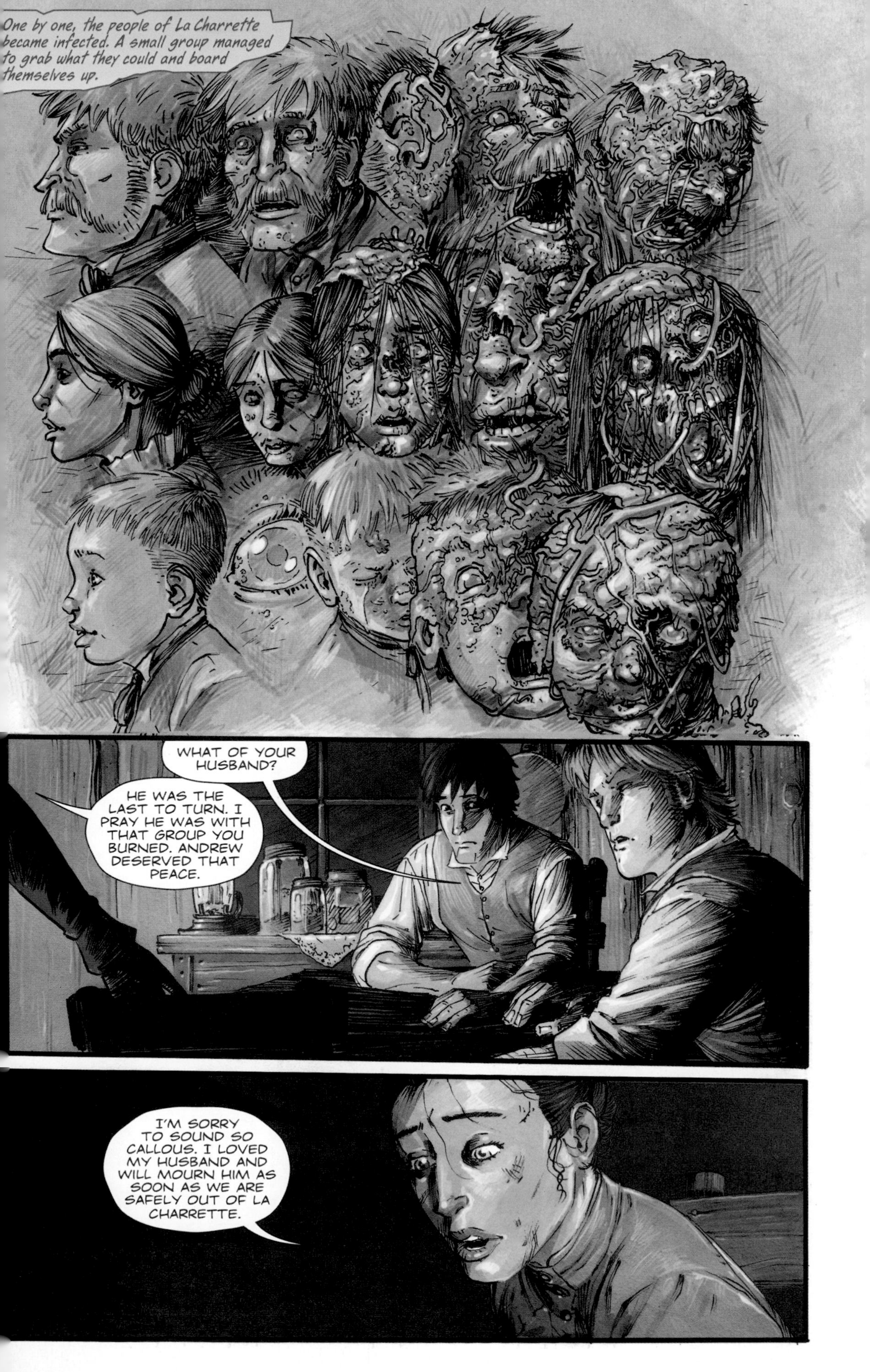
One by one, the people of La Charrette became infected. A small group managed to grab what they could and board themselves up.
WHAT OF YOUR HUSBAND?
HE WAS THE LAST TO TURN. I PRAY HE WAS WITH THAT GROUP YOU BURNED. ANDREW DESERVED THAT PEACE.
I'M SORRY TO SOUND SO CALLOUS. I LOVED MY HUSBAND AND WILL MOURN HIM AS SOON AS WE ARE SAFELY OUT OF LA CHARRETTE.

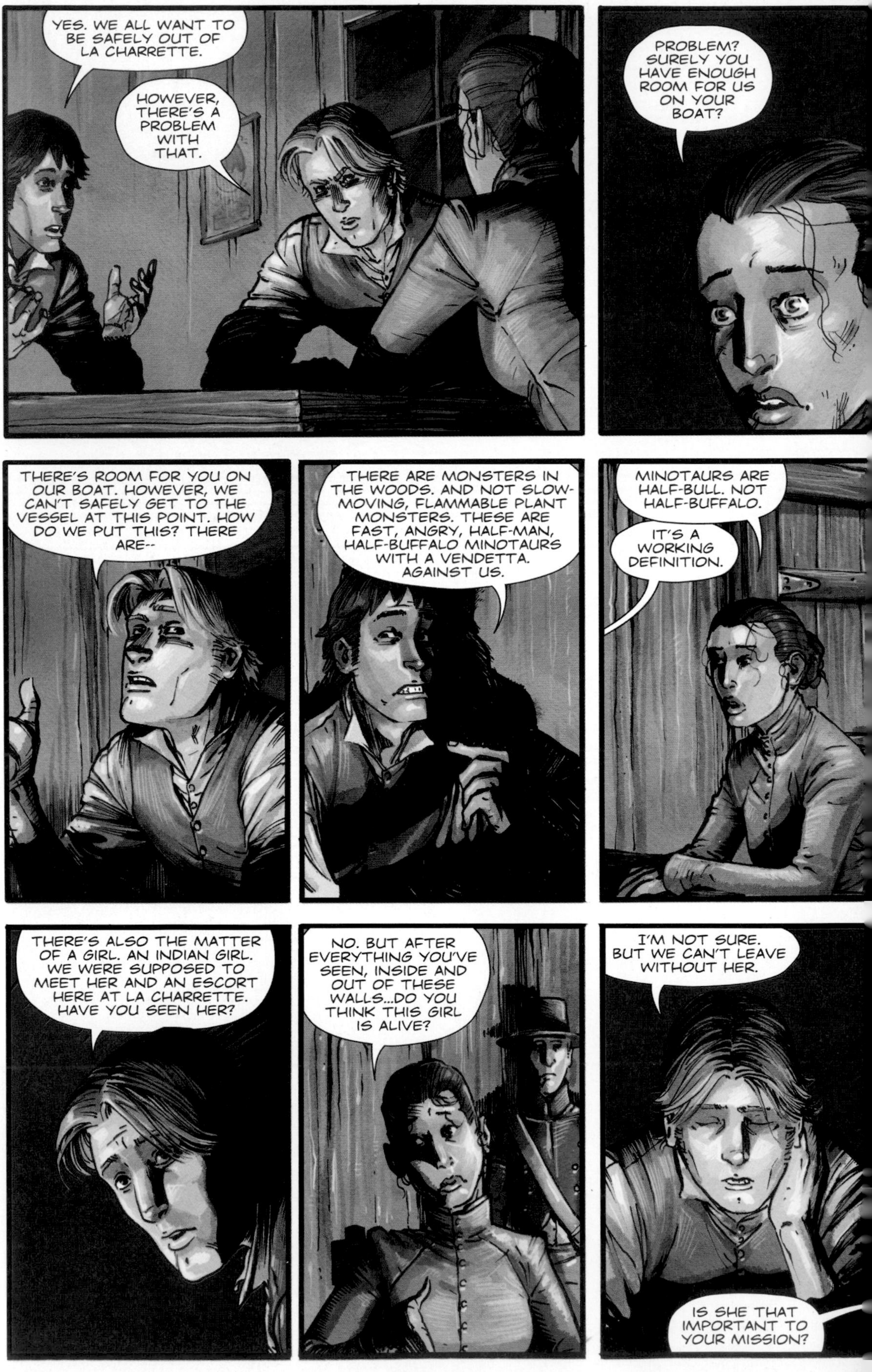
YES. WE ALL WANT TO BE SAFELY OUT OF LA CHARRETTE.
HOWEVER, THERE'S A PROBLEM WITH THAT.
PROBLEM? SURELY YOU HAVE ENOUGH ROOM FOR US ON YOUR BOAT?
THERE'S ROOM FOR YOU ON OUR BOAT. HOWEVER, WE CAN'T SAFELY GET TO THE VESSEL AT THIS POINT. HOW DO WE PUT THIS? THERE ARE--
THERE ARE MONSTERS IN THE WOODS. AND NOT SLOW-MOVING, FLAMMABLE PLANT MONSTERS. THESE ARE FAST, ANGRY, HALF-MAN, HALF-BUFFALO MINOTAURS WITH A VENDETTA. AGAINST US.
MINOTAURS ARE HALF-BULL. NOT HALF-BUFFALO.
IT'S A WORKING DEFINITION.
THERE'S ALSO THE MATTER OF A GIRL. AN INDIAN GIRL. WE WERE SUPPOSED TO MEET HER AND AN ESCORT HERE AT LA CHARRETTE. HAVE YOU SEEN HER?
NO. BUT AFTER EVERYTHING YOU'VE SEEN, INSIDE AND OUT OF THESE WALLS...DO YOU THINK THIS GIRL IS ALIVE?
I'M NOT SURE. BUT WE CAN'T LEAVE WITHOUT HER.
IS SHE THAT IMPORTANT TO YOUR MISSION?

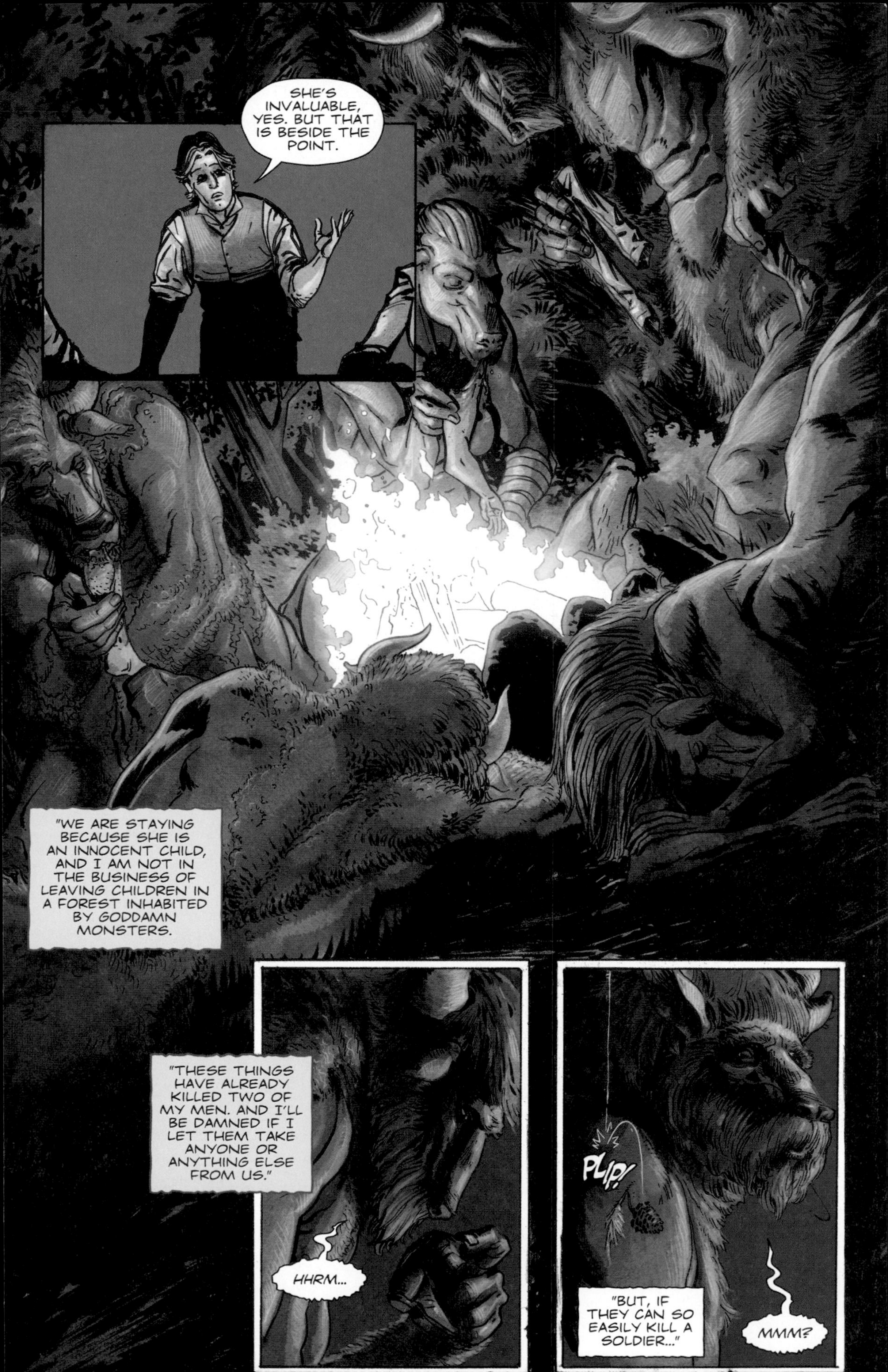
SHE'S INVALUABLE, YES. BUT THAT IS BESIDE THE POINT.
"WE ARE STAYING BECAUSE SHE IS AN INNOCENT CHILD, AND I AM NOT IN THE BUSINESS OF LEAVING CHILDREN IN A FOREST INHABITED BY GODDAMN MONSTERS.
"THESE THINGS HAVE ALREADY KILLED TWO OF MY MEN. AND I'LL BE DAMNED IF I LET THEM TAKE ANYONE OR ANYTHING ELSE FROM US."
HHRM...
PLIP!
"BUT, IF THEY CAN SO EASILY KILL A SOLDIER..."
MMM?

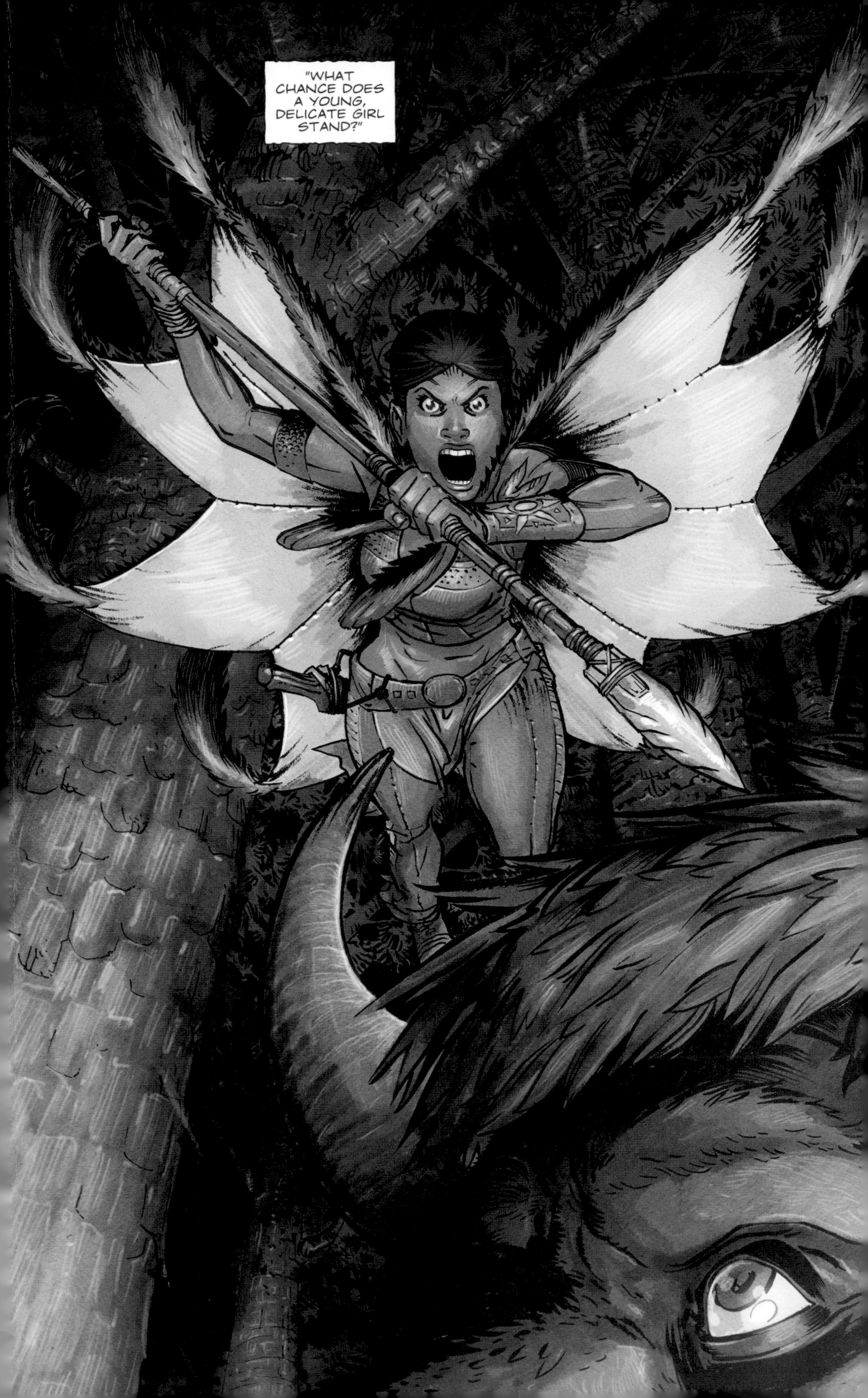
"WHAT CHANCE DOES A YOUNG, DELICATE GIRL STAND?"

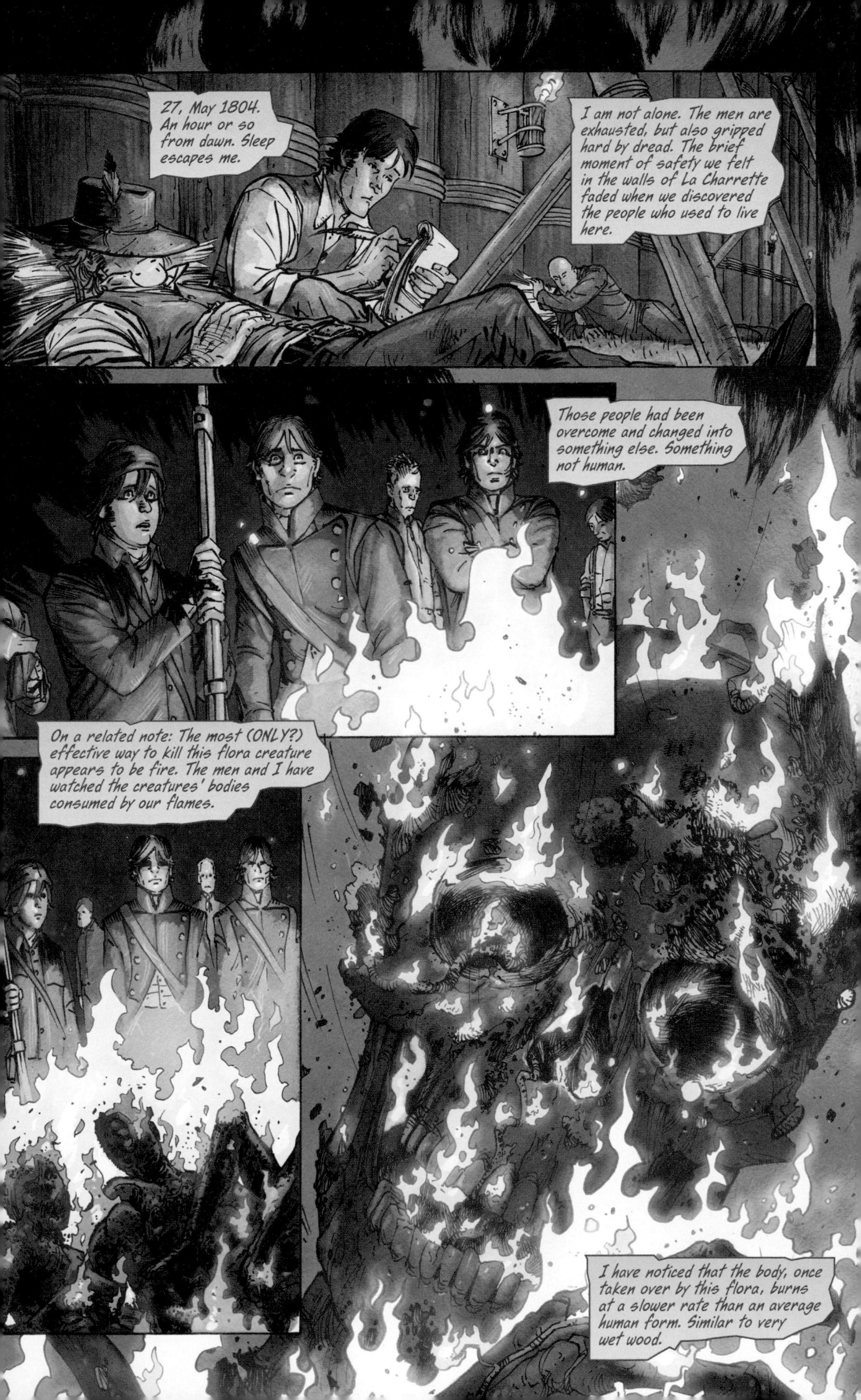
27, May 1804. An hour or so from dawn. Sleep escapes me.
I am not alone. The men are exhausted, but also gripped hard by dread. The brief moment of safety we felt in the walls of La Charrette faded when we discovered the people who used to live here.
Those people had been overcome and changed into something else. Something not human.
On a related note: The most (ONLY?) effective way to kill this flora creature appears to be fire. The men and I have watched the creatures' bodies consumed by our flames.
I have noticed that the body, once taken over by this flora, burns at a slower rate than an average human form. Similar to very wet wood.

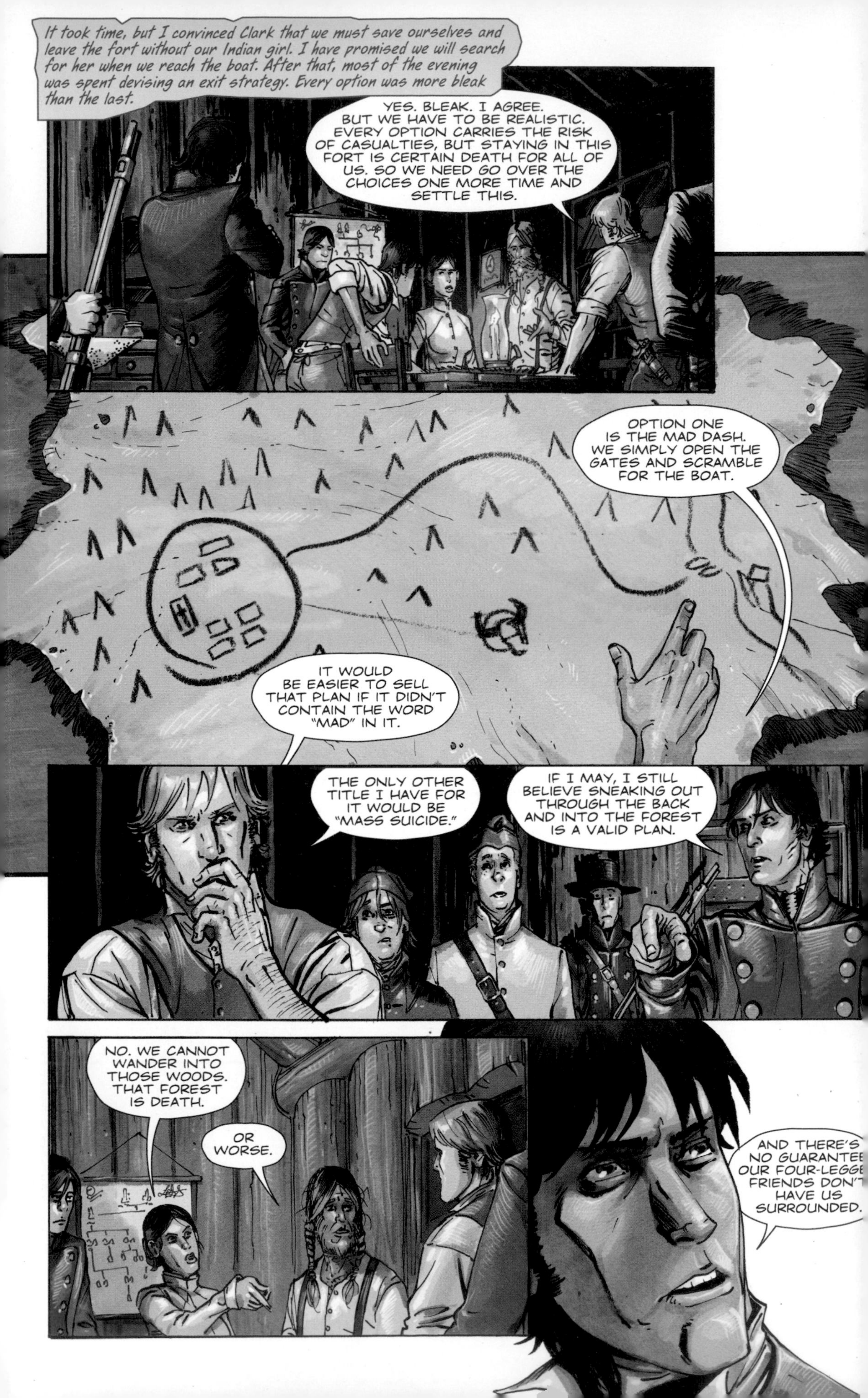
It took time, but I convinced Clark that we must save ourselves and leave the fort without our Indian girl. I have promised we will search for her when we reach the boat. After that, most of the evening was spent devising an exit strategy. Every option was more bleak than the last.
YES. BLEAK. I AGREE. BUT WE HAVE TO BE REALISTIC. EVERY OPTION CARRIES THE RISK OF CASUALTIES, BUT STAYING IN THIS FORT IS CERTAIN DEATH FOR ALL OF US. SO WE NEED GO OVER THE CHOICES ONE MORE TIME AND SETTLE THIS.
OPTION ONE IS THE MAD DASH. WE SIMPLY OPEN THE GATES AND SCRAMBLE FOR THE BOAT.
IT WOULD BE EASIER TO SELL THAT PLAN IF IT DIDN'T CONTAIN THE WORD "MAD" IN IT.
THE ONLY OTHER TITLE I HAVE FOR IT WOULD BE "MASS SUICIDE."
IF I MAY, I STILL BELIEVE SNEAKING OUT THROUGH THE BACK AND INTO THE FOREST IS A VALID PLAN.
NO. WE CANNOT WANDER INTO THOSE WOODS. THAT FOREST IS DEATH.
OR WORSE.
AND THERE'S NO GUARANTEE OUR FOUR-LEGGED FRIENDS DON'T HAVE US SURROUNDED.

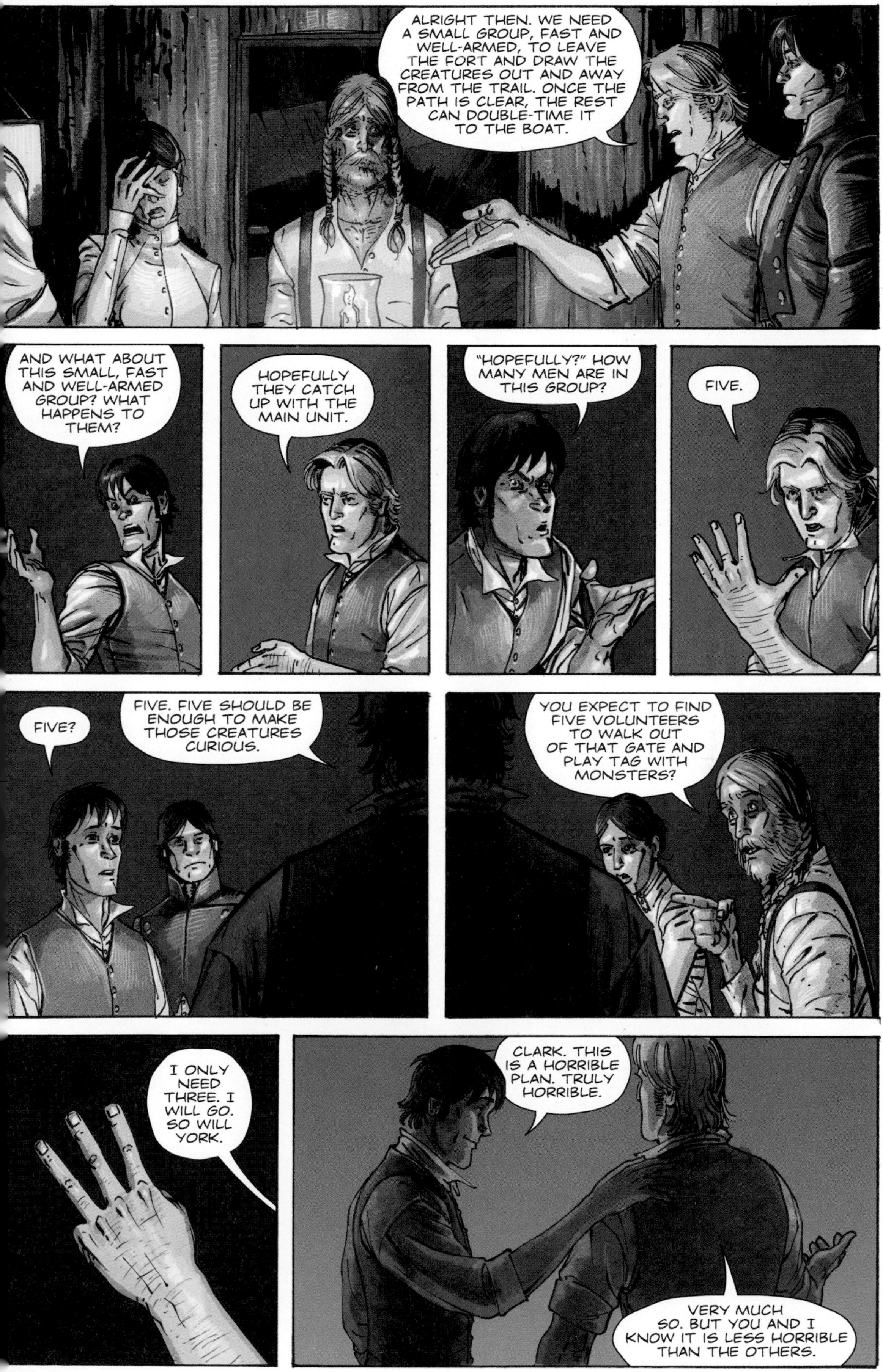
ALRIGHT THEN. WE NEED A SMALL GROUP, FAST AND WELL-ARMED, TO LEAVE THE FORT AND DRAW THE CREATURES OUT AND AWAY FROM THE TRAIL. ONCE THE PATH IS CLEAR, THE REST CAN DOUBLE-TIME IT TO THE BOAT.
AND WHAT ABOUT THIS SMALL, FAST AND WELL-ARMED GROUP? WHAT HAPPENS TO THEM?
HOPEFULLY THEY CATCH UP WITH THE MAIN UNIT.
"HOPEFULLY?" HOW MANY MEN ARE IN THIS GROUP?
FIVE.
FIVE?
FIVE. FIVE SHOULD BE ENOUGH TO MAKE THOSE CREATURES CURIOUS.
YOU EXPECT TO FIND FIVE VOLUNTEERS TO WALK OUT OF THAT GATE AND PLAY TAG WITH MONSTERS?
I ONLY NEED THREE. I WILL GO. SO WILL YORK.
CLARK. THIS IS A HORRIBLE PLAN. TRULY HORRIBLE.
VERY MUCH SO. BUT YOU AND I KNOW IT IS LESS HORRIBLE THAN THE OTHERS.

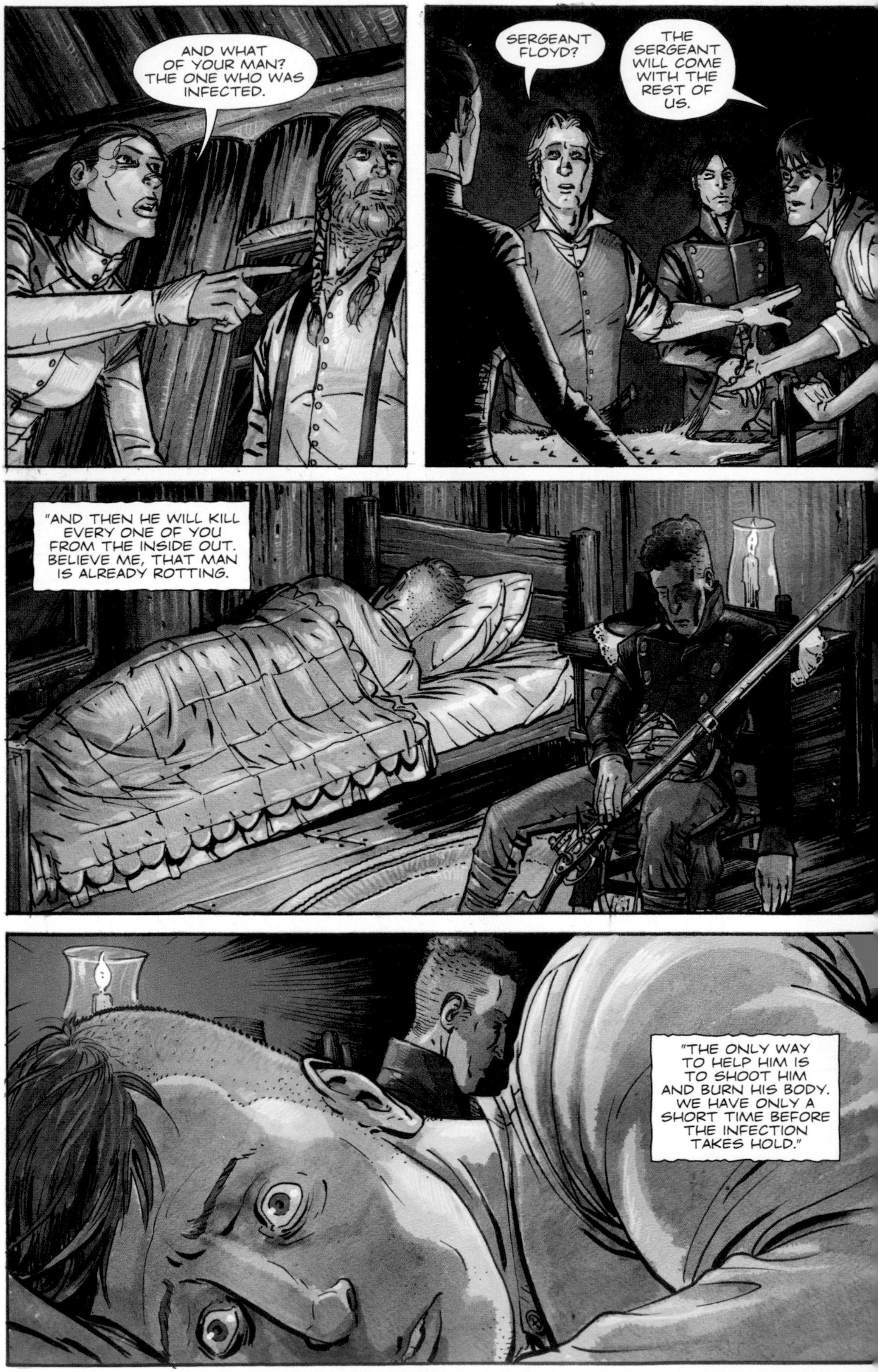
AND WHAT OF YOUR MAN? THE ONE WHO WAS INFECTED.
SERGEANT FLOYD?
THE SERGEANT WILL COME WITH THE REST OF US.
"AND THEN HE WILL KILL EVERY ONE OF YOU FROM THE INSIDE OUT. BELIEVE ME, THAT MAN IS ALREADY ROTTING.
"THE ONLY WAY TO HELP HIM IS TO SHOOT HIM AND BURN HIS BODY. WE HAVE ONLY A SHORT TIME BEFORE THE INFECTION TAKES HOLD."

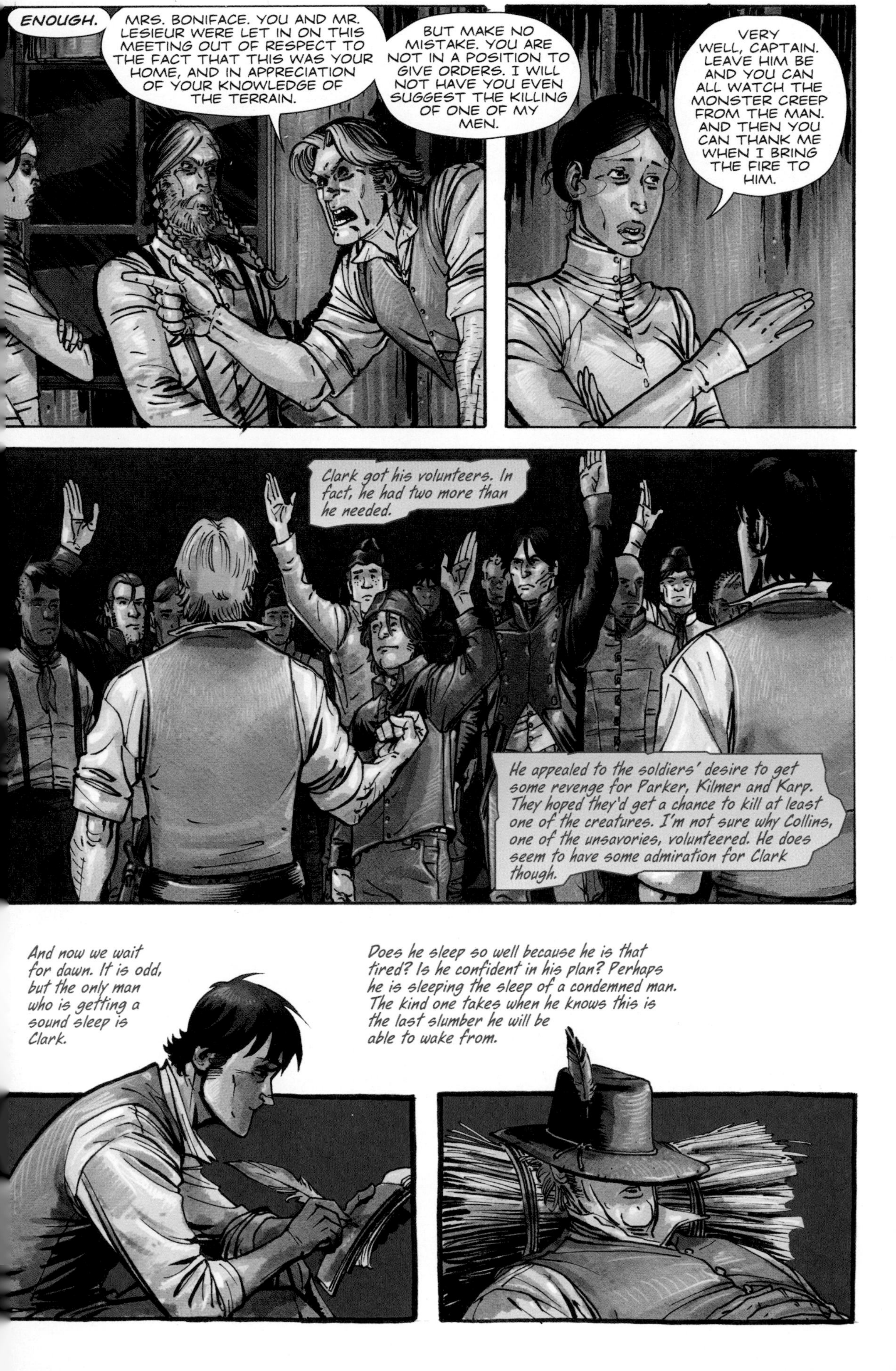
ENOUGH.
MRS. BONIFACE. YOU AND MR. LESIEUR WERE LET IN ON THIS MEETING OUT OF RESPECT TO THE FACT THAT THIS WAS YOUR HOME, AND IN APPRECIATION OF YOUR KNOWLEDGE OF THE TERRAIN.
BUT MAKE NO MISTAKE. YOU ARE NOT IN A POSITION TO GIVE ORDERS. I WILL NOT HAVE YOU EVEN SUGGEST THE KILLING OF ONE OF MY MEN.
VERY WELL, CAPTAIN. LEAVE HIM BE AND YOU CAN ALL WATCH THE MONSTER CREEP FROM THE MAN. AND THEN YOU CAN THANK ME WHEN I BRING THE FIRE TO HIM.
Clark got his volunteers. In fact, he had two more than he needed.
He appealed to the soldiers' desire to get some revenge for Parker, Kilmer and Karp. They hoped they'd get a chance to kill at least one of the creatures. I'm not sure why Collins, one of the unsavories, volunteered. He does seem to have some admiration for Clark though.
And now we wait for dawn. It is odd, but the only man who is getting a sound sleep is Clark.
Does he sleep so well because he is that tired? Is he confident in his plan? Perhaps he is sleeping the sleep of a condemned man. The kind one takes when he knows this is the last slumber he will be able to wake from.

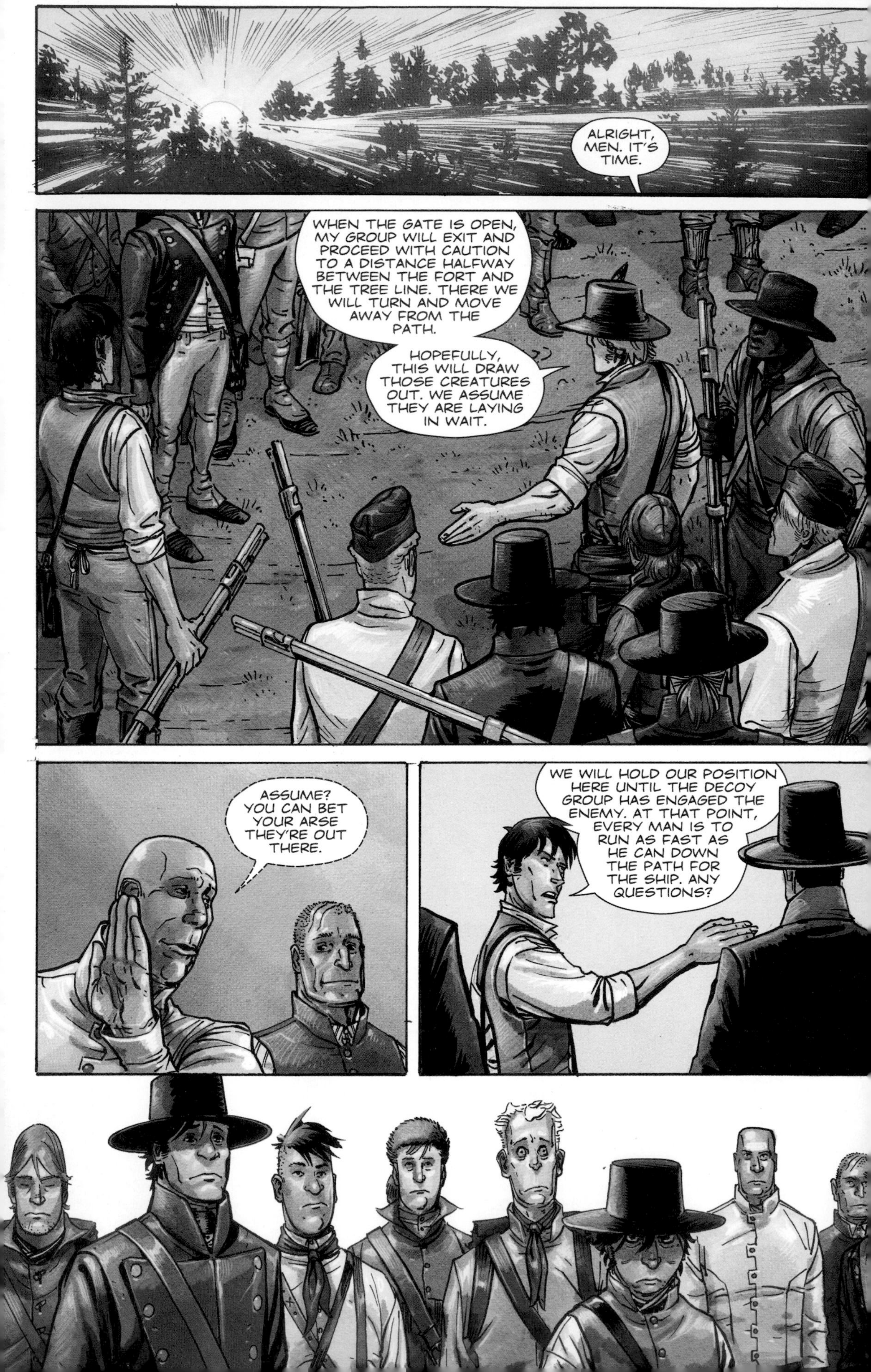
ALRIGHT, MEN. IT'S TIME.
WHEN THE GATE IS OPEN, MY GROUP WILL EXIT AND PROCEED WITH CAUTION TO A DISTANCE HALFWAY BETWEEN THE FORT AND THE TREE LINE. THERE WE WILL TURN AND MOVE AWAY FROM THE PATH.
HOPEFULLY, THIS WILL DRAW THOSE CREATURES OUT. WE ASSUME THEY ARE LAYING IN WAIT.
ASSUME? YOU CAN BET YOUR ARSE THEY'RE OUT THERE.
WE WILL HOLD OUR POSITION HERE UNTIL THE DECOY GROUP HAS ENGAGED THE ENEMY. AT THAT POINT, EVERY MAN IS TO RUN AS FAST AS HE CAN DOWN THE PATH FOR THE SHIP. ANY QUESTIONS?

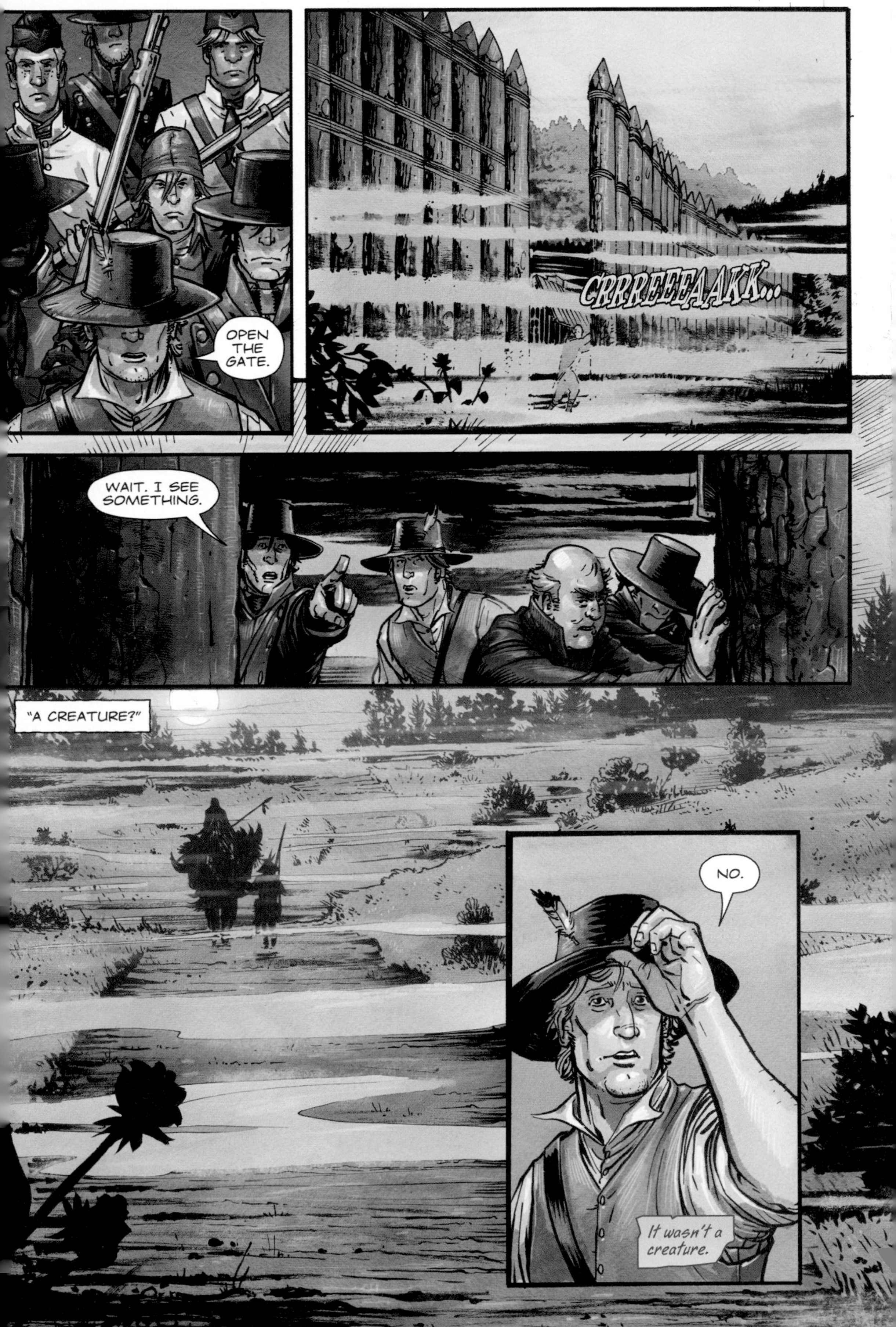
OPEN THE GATE.
CRRREEEAAKK...
WAIT. I SEE SOMETHING.
"A CREATURE?"
NO.
It wasn't a creature.

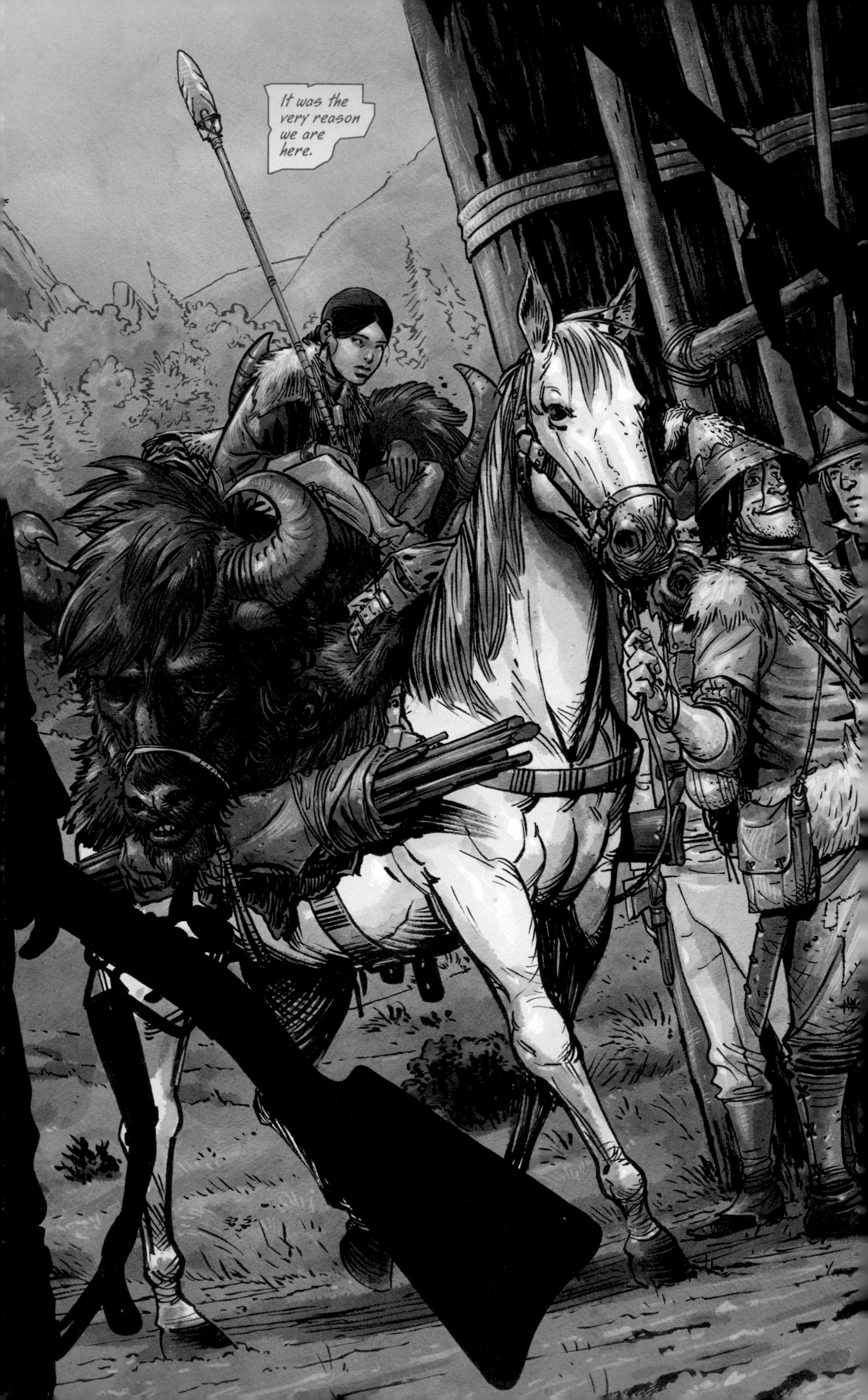
It was the very reason we are here.

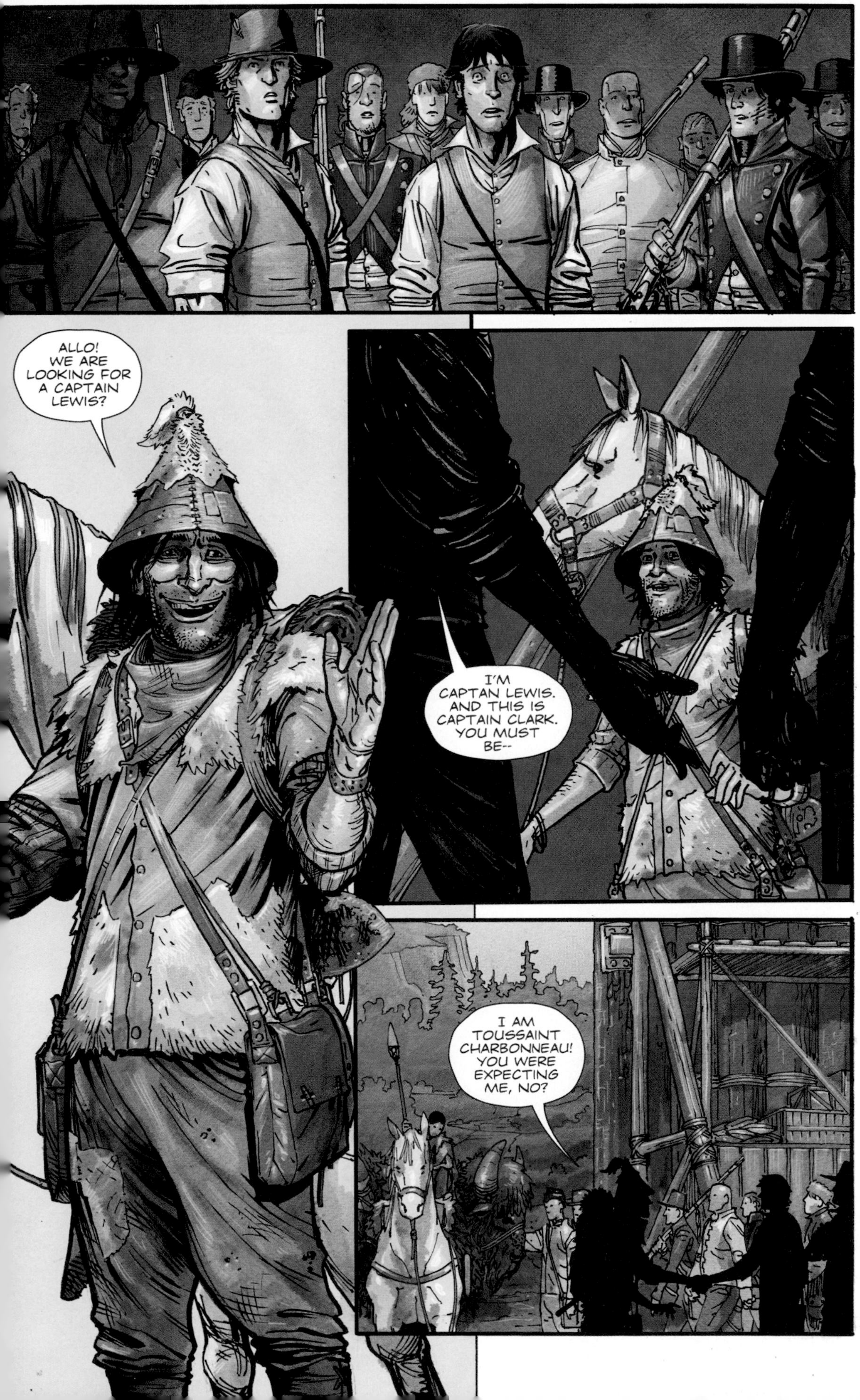
ALLO! WE ARE LOOKING FOR A CAPTAIN LEWIS?
I'M CAPTAN LEWIS. AND THIS IS CAPTAIN CLARK. YOU MUST BE--
I AM TOUSSAINT CHARBONNEAU! YOU WERE EXPECTING ME, NO?

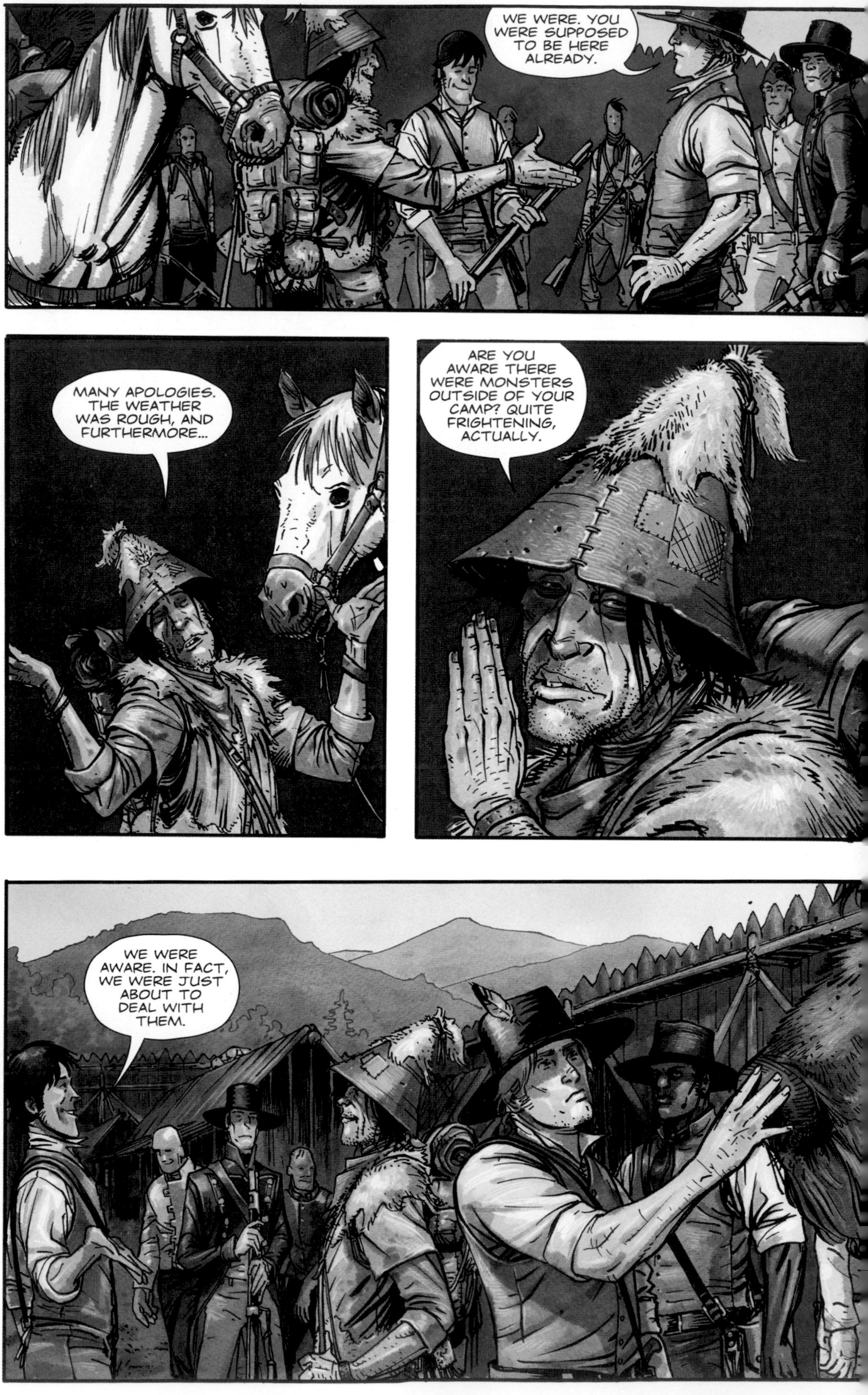
WE WERE. YOU WERE SUPPOSED TO BE HERE ALREADY.
MANY APOLOGIES. THE WEATHER WAS ROUGH, AND FURTHERMORE...
ARE YOU AWARE THERE WERE MONSTERS OUTSIDE OF YOUR CAMP? QUITE FRIGHTENING, ACTUALLY.
WE WERE AWARE. IN FACT, WE WERE JUST ABOUT TO DEAL WITH THEM.

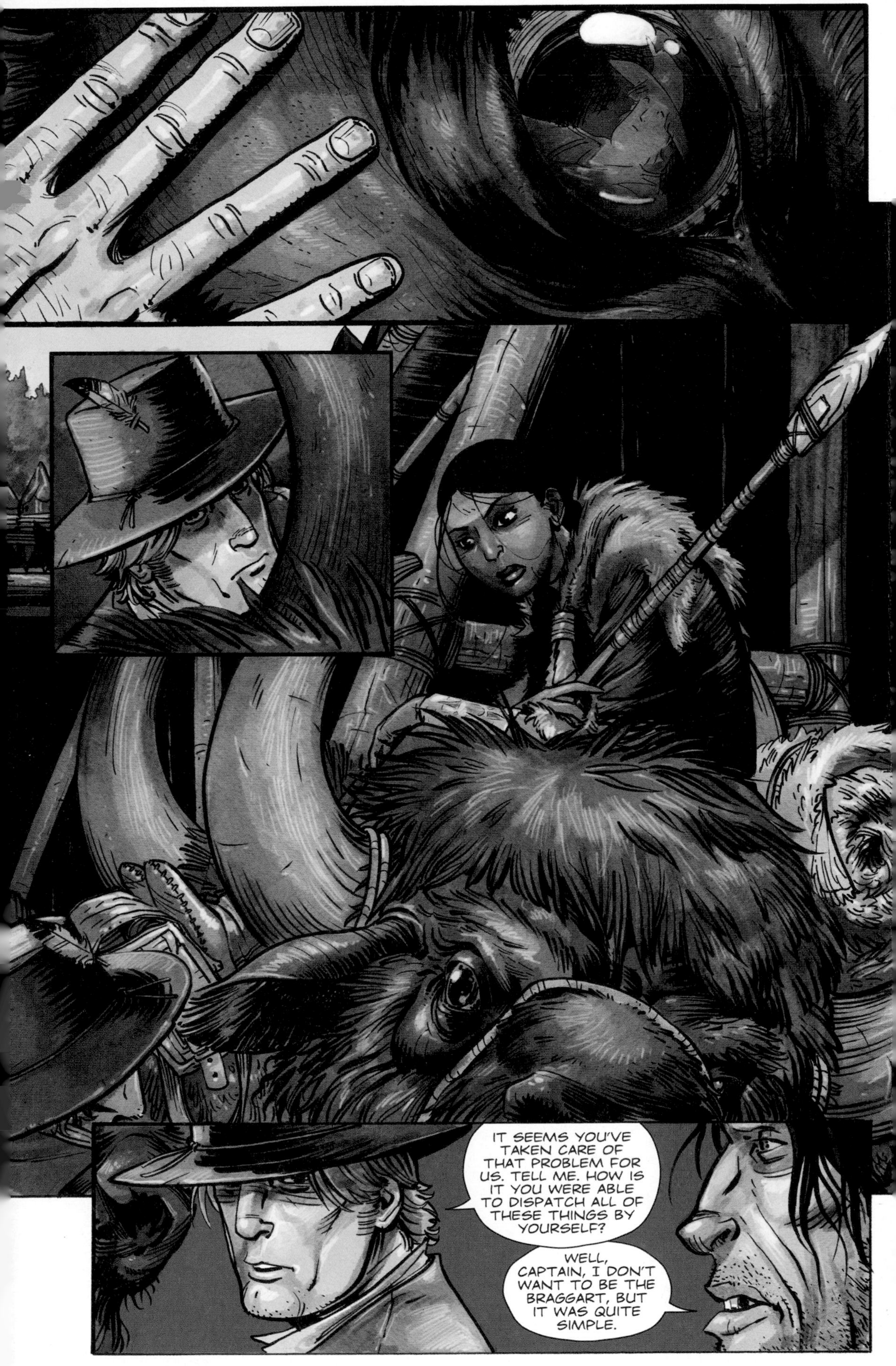
IT SEEMS YOU'VE TAKEN CARE OF THAT PROBLEM FOR US. TELL ME. HOW IS IT YOU WERE ABLE TO DISPATCH ALL OF THESE THINGS BY YOURSELF?
WELL, CAPTAIN, I DON'T WANT TO BE THE BRAGGART, BUT IT WAS QUITE SIMPLE.

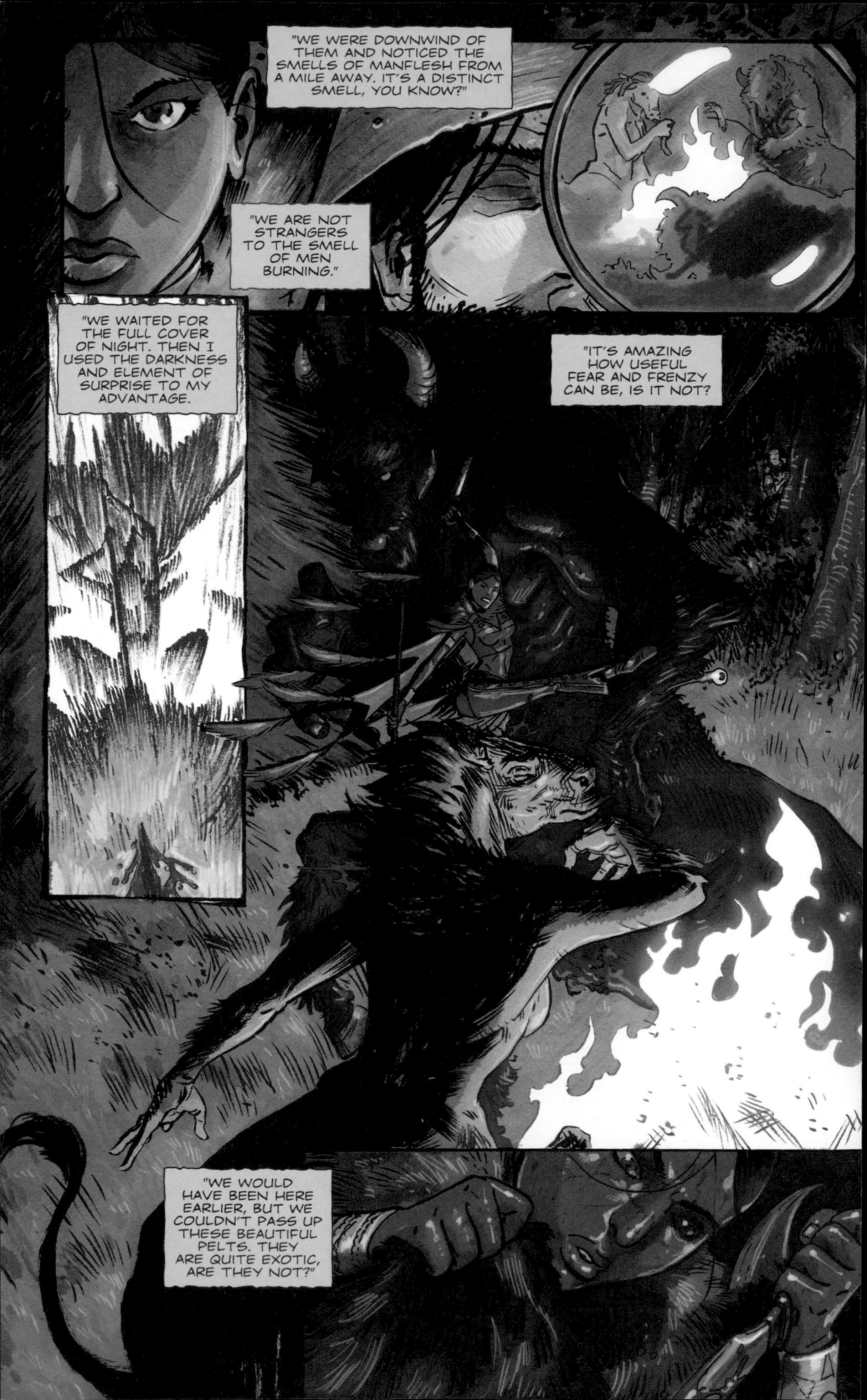
"WE WERE DOWNWIND OF THEM AND NOTICED THE SMELLS OF MANFLESH FROM A MILE AWAY. IT'S A DISTINCT SMELL, YOU KNOW?"
"WE ARE NOT STRANGERS TO THE SMELL OF MEN BURNING."
"WE WAITED FOR THE FULL COVER OF NIGHT. THEN I USED THE DARKNESS AND ELEMENT OF SURPRISE TO MY ADVANTAGE.
"IT'S AMAZING HOW USEFUL FEAR AND FRENZY CAN BE, IS IT NOT?
"WE WOULD HAVE BEEN HERE EARLIER, BUT WE COULDN'T PASS UP THESE BEAUTIFUL PELTS. THEY ARE QUITE EXOTIC, ARE THEY NOT?"

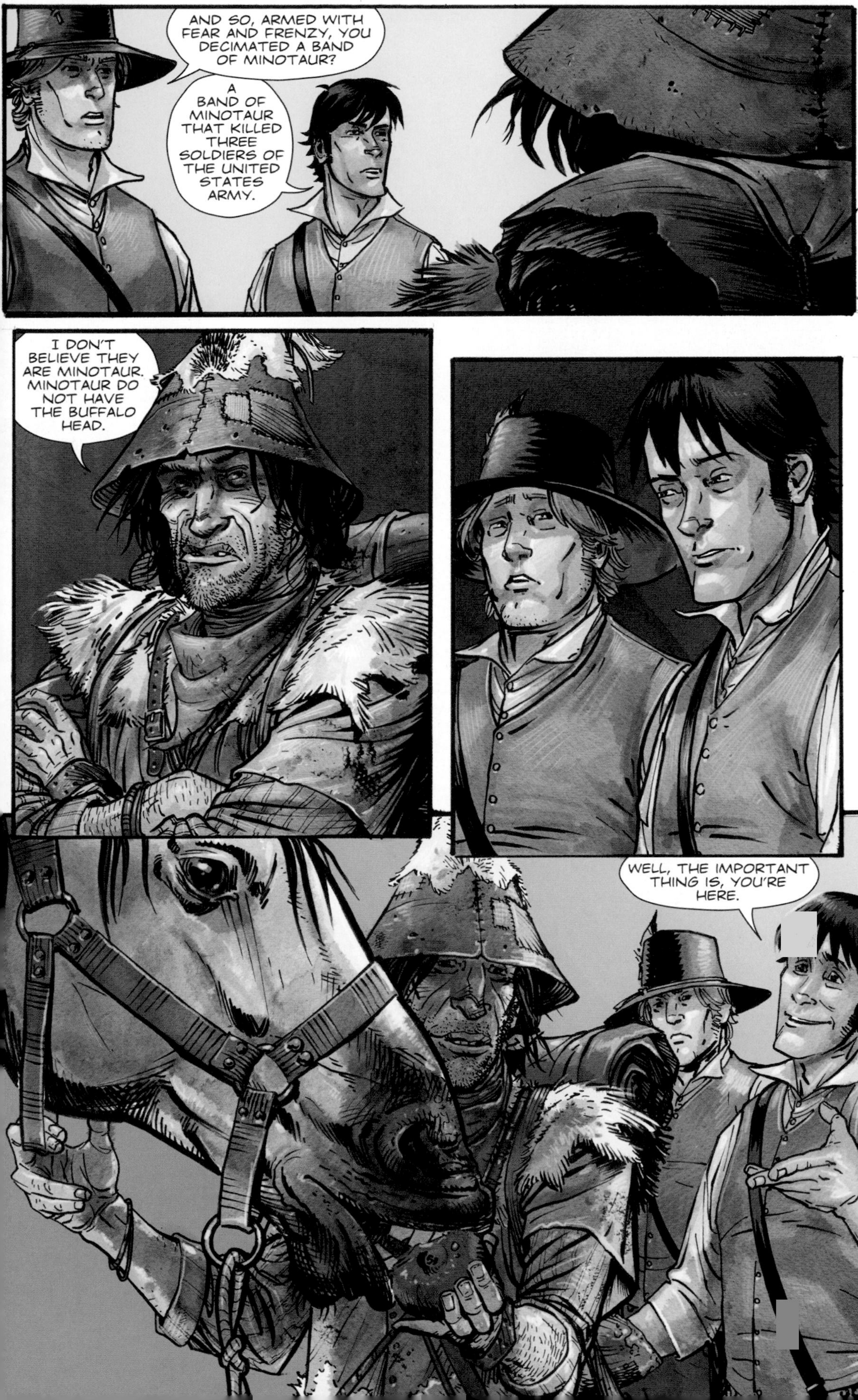
AND SO, ARMED WITH FEAR AND FRENZY, YOU DECIMATED A BAND OF MINOTAUR?
A BAND OF MINOTAUR THAT KILLED THREE SOLDIERS OF THE UNITED STATES ARMY.
I DON'T BELIEVE THEY ARE MINOTAUR. MINOTAUR DO NOT HAVE THE BUFFALO HEAD.
WELL, THE IMPORTANT THING IS, YOU'RE HERE.

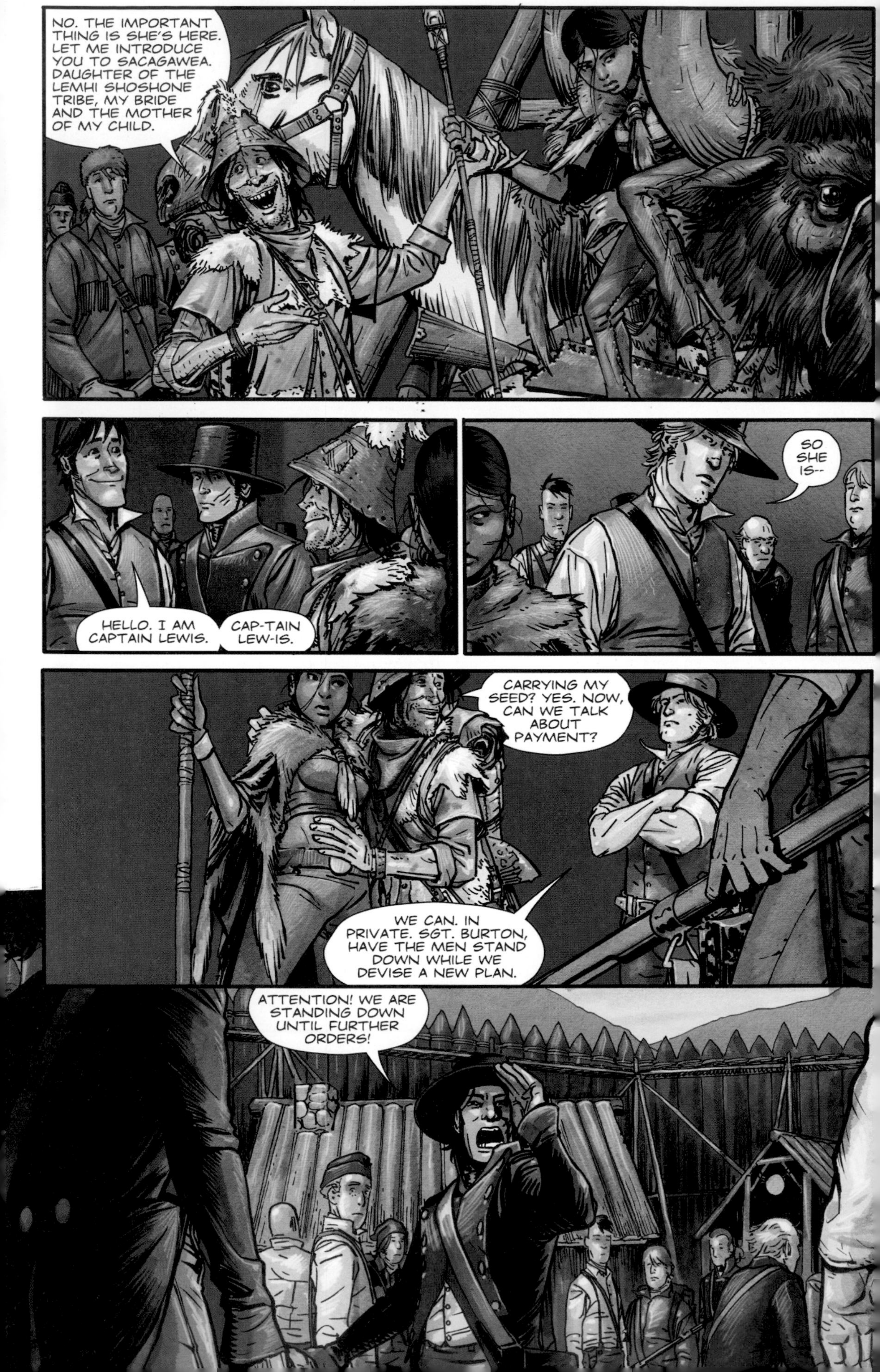
NO. THE IMPORTANT THING IS SHE'S HERE. LET ME INTRODUCE YOU TO SACAGAWEA. DAUGHTER OF THE LEMHI SHOSHONE TRIBE, MY BRIDE AND THE MOTHER OF MY CHILD.
HELLO. I AM CAPTAIN LEWIS.
CAP-TAIN LEW-IS.
SO SHE IS--
CARRYING MY SEED? YES. NOW, CAN WE TALK ABOUT PAYMENT?
WE CAN. IN PRIVATE. SGT. BURTON, HAVE THE MEN STAND DOWN WHILE WE DEVISE A NEW PLAN.
ATTENTION! WE ARE STANDING DOWN UNTIL FURTHER ORDERS!

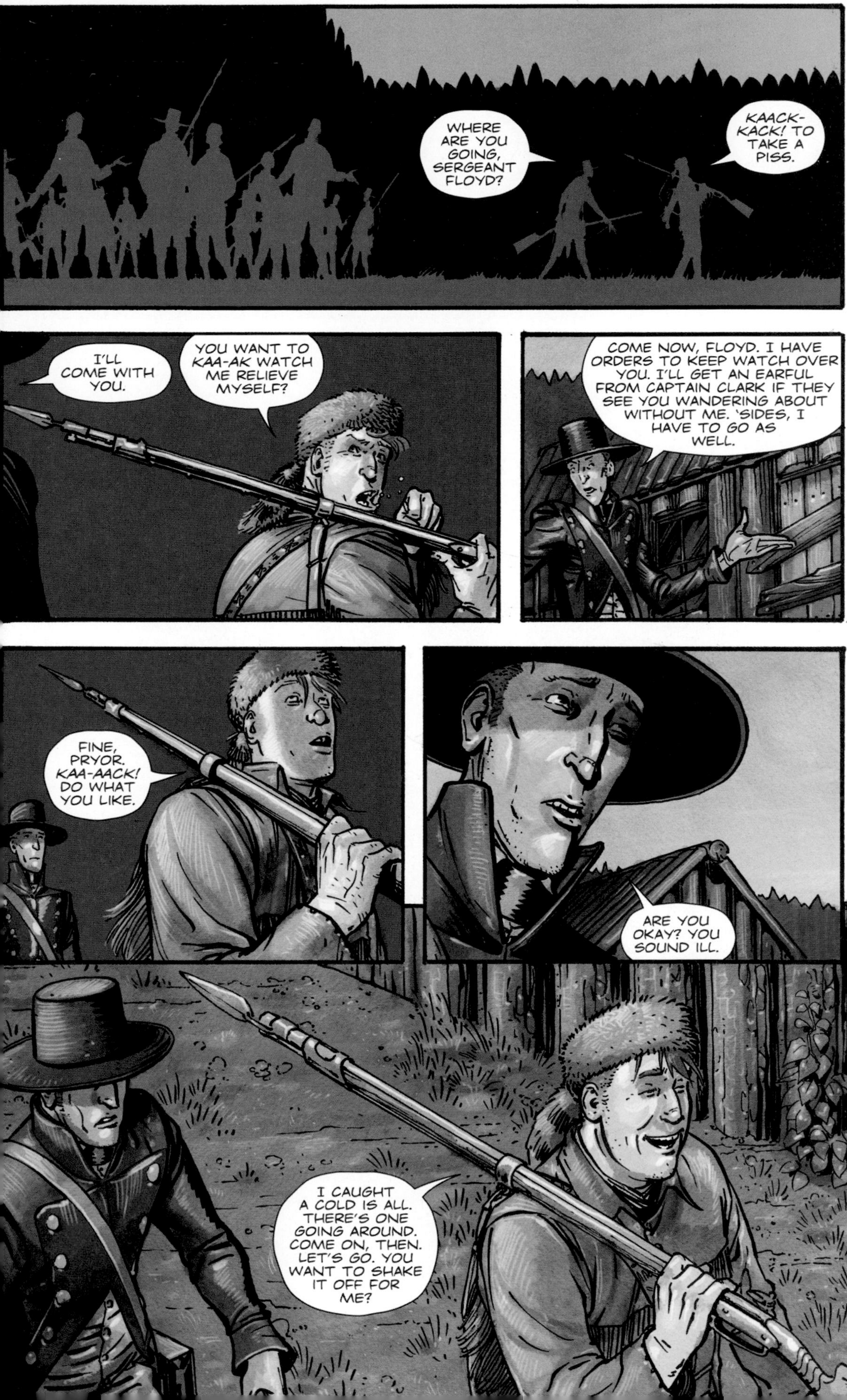
WHERE ARE YOU GOING, SERGEANT FLOYD?
KAACK-KACK! TO TAKE A PISS.
I'LL COME WITH YOU.
YOU WANT TO KAA-AK WATCH ME RELIEVE MYSELF?
COME NOW, FLOYD. I HAVE ORDERS TO KEEP WATCH OVER YOU. I'LL GET AN EARFUL FROM CAPTAIN CLARK IF THEY SEE YOU WANDERING ABOUT WITHOUT ME. 'SIDES, I HAVE TO GO AS WELL.
FINE, PRYOR. KAA-AACK! DO WHAT YOU LIKE.
ARE YOU OKAY? YOU SOUND ILL.
I CAUGHT A COLD IS ALL. THERE'S ONE GOING AROUND. COME ON, THEN. LET'S GO. YOU WANT TO SHAKE IT OFF FOR ME?

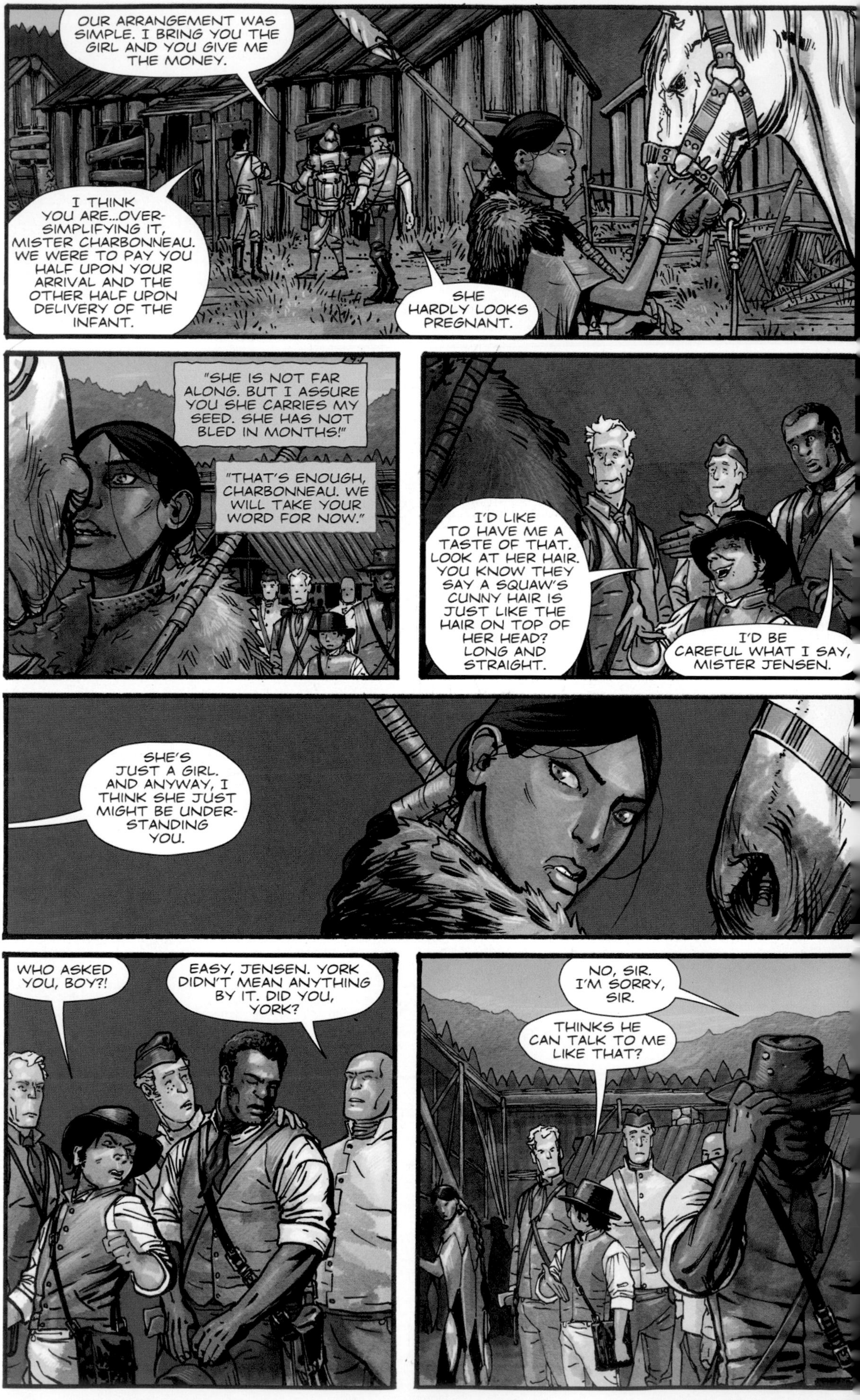
OUR ARRANGEMENT WAS SIMPLE. I BRING YOU THE GIRL AND YOU GIVE ME THE MONEY.
I THINK YOU ARE...OVER-SIMPLIFYING IT, MISTER CHARBONNEAU. WE WERE TO PAY YOU HALF UPON YOUR ARRIVAL AND THE OTHER HALF UPON DELIVERY OF THE INFANT.
SHE HARDLY LOOKS PREGNANT.
"SHE IS NOT FAR ALONG. BUT I ASSURE YOU SHE CARRIES MY SEED. SHE HAS NOT BLED IN MONTHS!"
"THAT'S ENOUGH, CHARBONNEAU. WE WILL TAKE YOUR WORD FOR NOW."
I'D LIKE TO HAVE ME A TASTE OF THAT. LOOK AT HER HAIR. YOU KNOW THEY SAY A SQUAW'S CUNNY HAIR IS JUST LIKE THE HAIR ON TOP OF HER HEAD? LONG AND STRAIGHT.
I'D BE CAREFUL WHAT I SAY, MISTER JENSEN.
SHE'S JUST A GIRL. AND ANYWAY, I THINK SHE JUST MIGHT BE UNDER-STANDING YOU.
WHO ASKED YOU, BOY?!
EASY, JENSEN. YORK DIDN'T MEAN ANYTHING BY IT. DID YOU, YORK?
NO, SIR. I'M SORRY, SIR.
THINKS HE CAN TALK TO ME LIKE THAT?

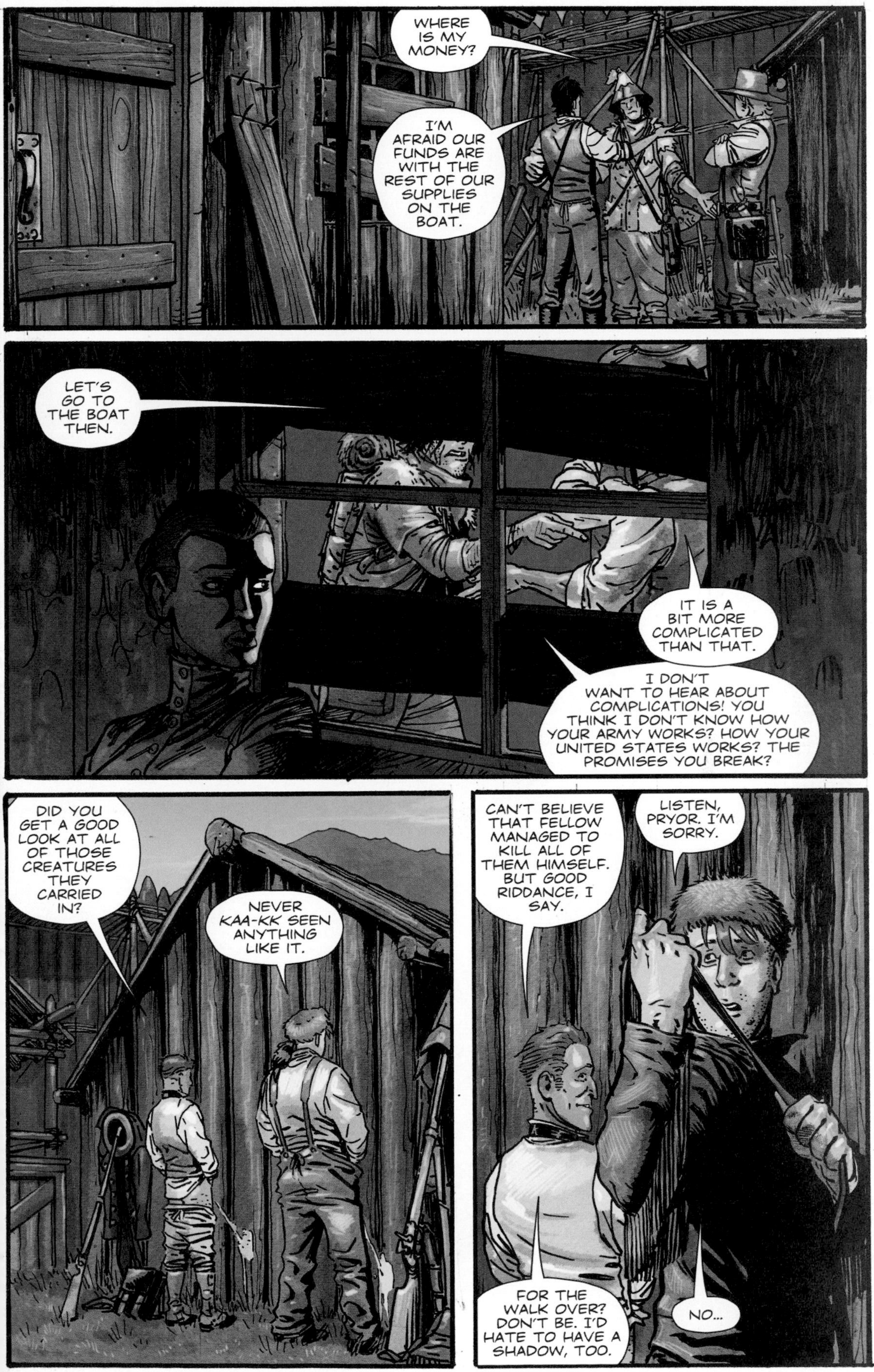
WHERE IS MY MONEY?
I'M AFRAID OUR FUNDS ARE WITH THE REST OF OUR SUPPLIES ON THE BOAT.
LET'S GO TO THE BOAT THEN.
IT IS A BIT MORE COMPLICATED THAN THAT.
I DON'T WANT TO HEAR ABOUT COMPLICATIONS! YOU THINK I DON'T KNOW HOW YOUR ARMY WORKS? HOW YOUR UNITED STATES WORKS? THE PROMISES YOU BREAK?
DID YOU GET A GOOD LOOK AT ALL OF THOSE CREATURES THEY CARRIED IN?
NEVER KAA-KK SEEN ANYTHING LIKE IT.
CAN'T BELIEVE THAT FELLOW MANAGED TO KILL ALL OF THEM HIMSELF. BUT GOOD RIDDANCE, I SAY.
LISTEN, PRYOR. I'M SORRY.
FOR THE WALK OVER? DON'T BE. I'D HATE TO HAVE A SHADOW, TOO.
NO...

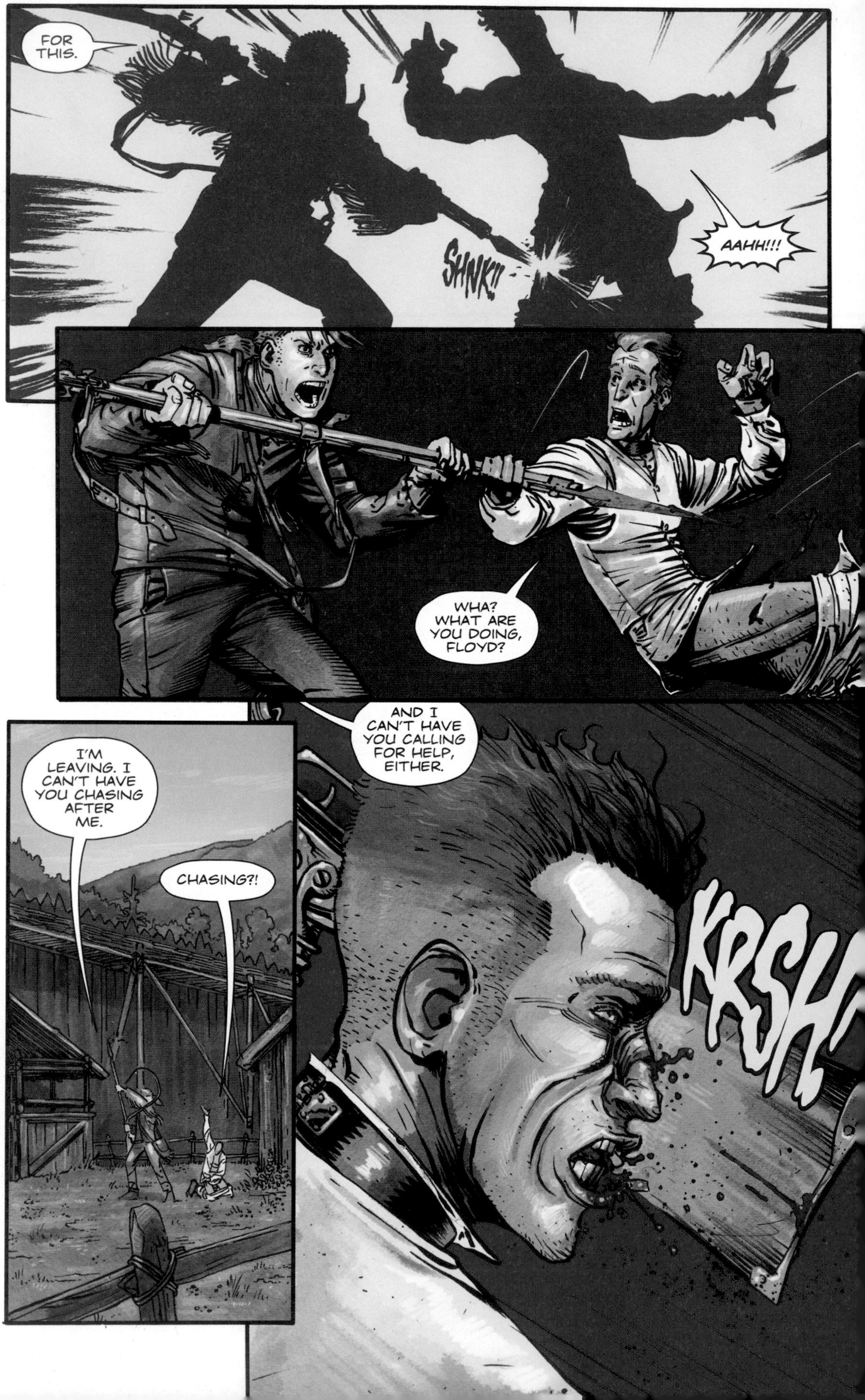
FOR THIS.
SHNK!!
AAHH!!!
WHA? WHAT ARE YOU DOING, FLOYD?
I'M LEAVING. I CAN'T HAVE YOU CHASING AFTER ME.
CHASING?!
AND I CAN'T HAVE YOU CALLING FOR HELP, EITHER.

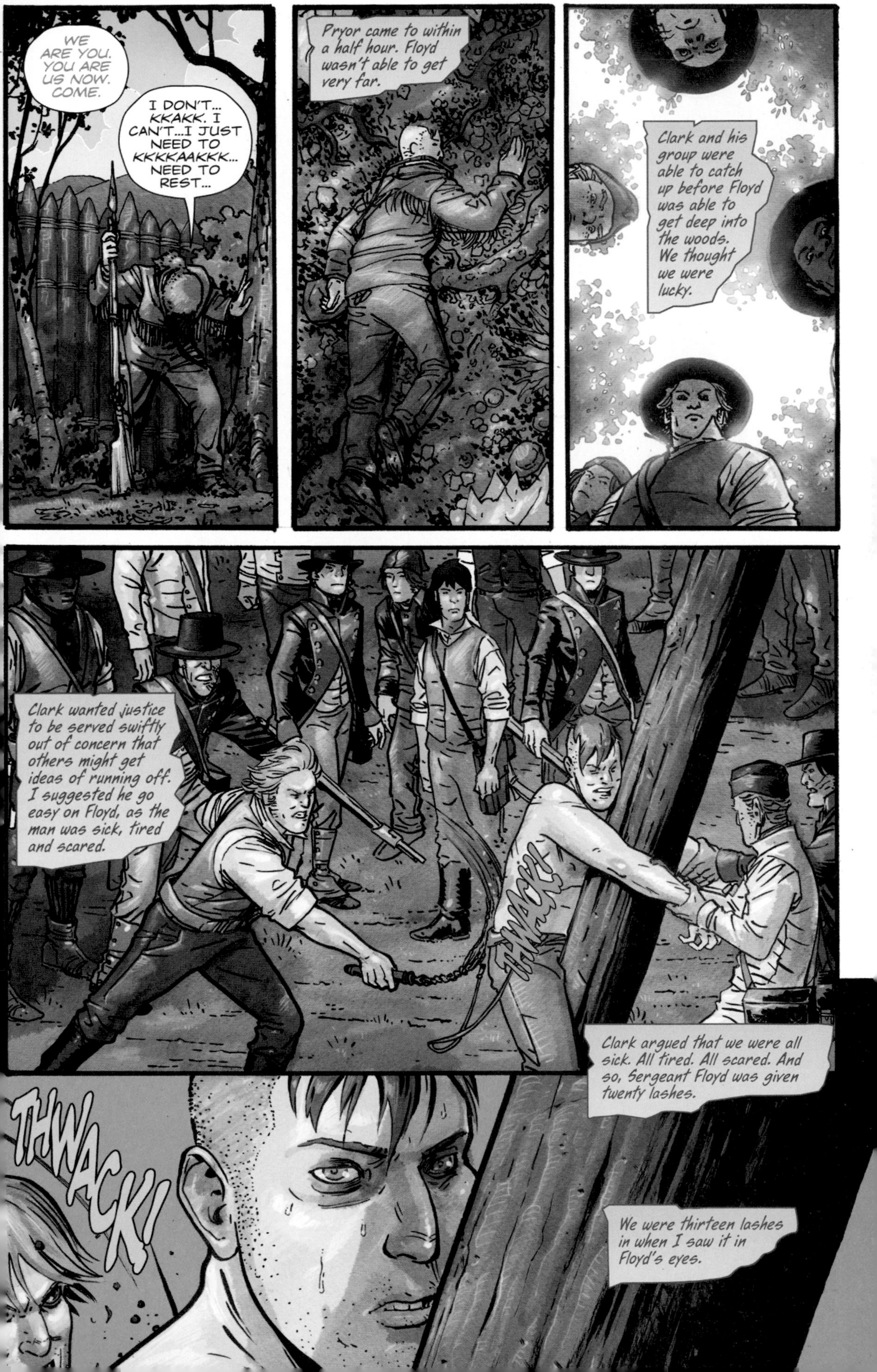
WE ARE YOU. YOU ARE US NOW. COME.
I DON'T... KKAKK. I CAN'T...I JUST NEED TO KKKKAAKKK... NEED TO REST...
Pryor came to within a half hour. Floyd wasn't able to get very far.
Clark and his group were able to catch up before Floyd was able to get deep into the woods. We thought we were lucky.
Clark wanted justice to be served swiftly out of concern that others might get ideas of running off. I suggested he go easy on Floyd, as the man was sick, tired and scared.
THWACK!
Clark argued that we were all sick. All tired. All scared. And so, Sergeant Floyd was given twenty lashes.
THWACK!
We were thirteen lashes in when I saw it in Floyd's eyes.

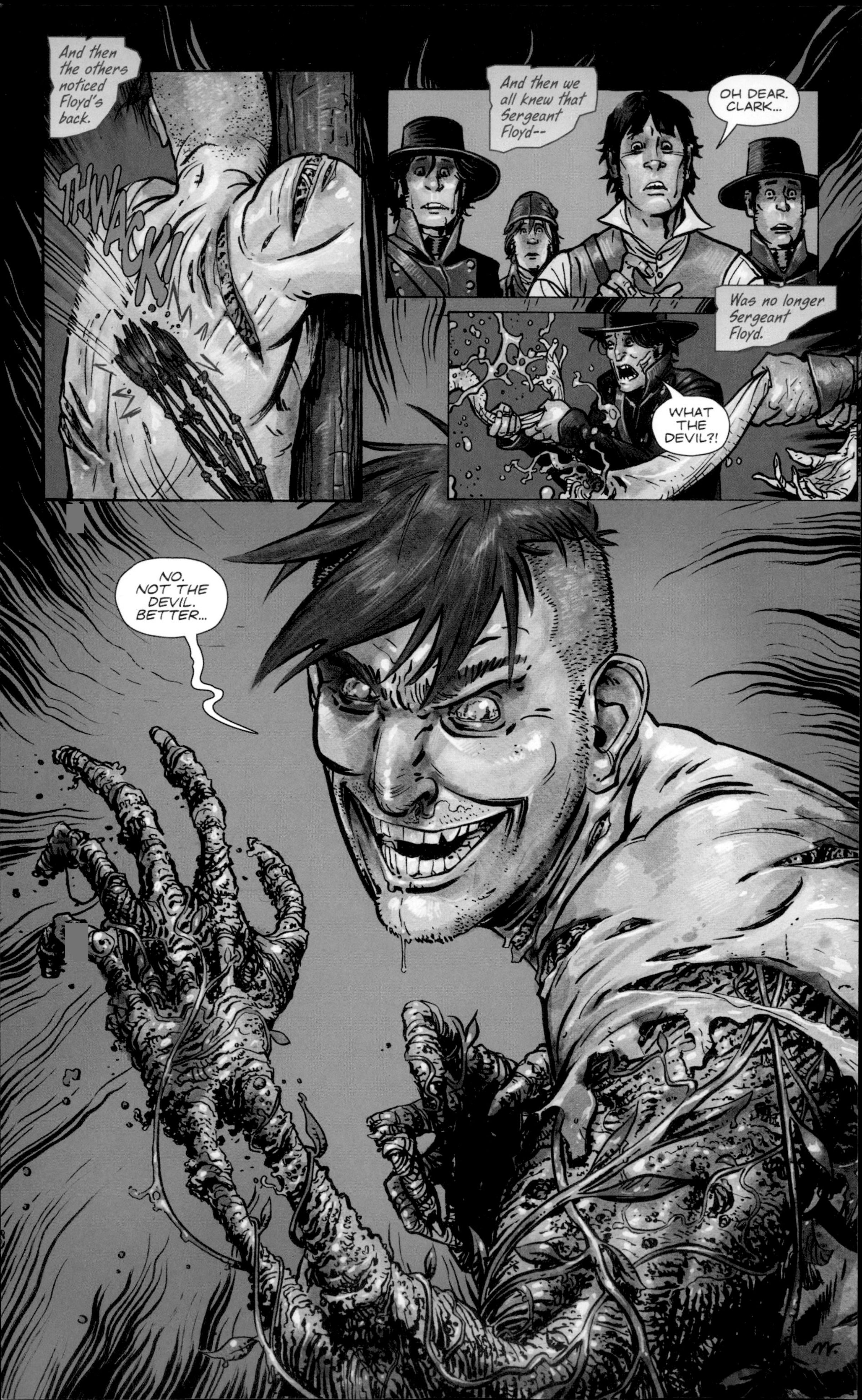
And then the others noticed Floyd's back.
THWACK!
And then we all knew that Sergeant Floyd--
OH DEAR. CLARK...
Was no longer Sergeant Floyd.
WHAT THE DEVIL?!
NO. NOT THE DEVIL. BETTER...

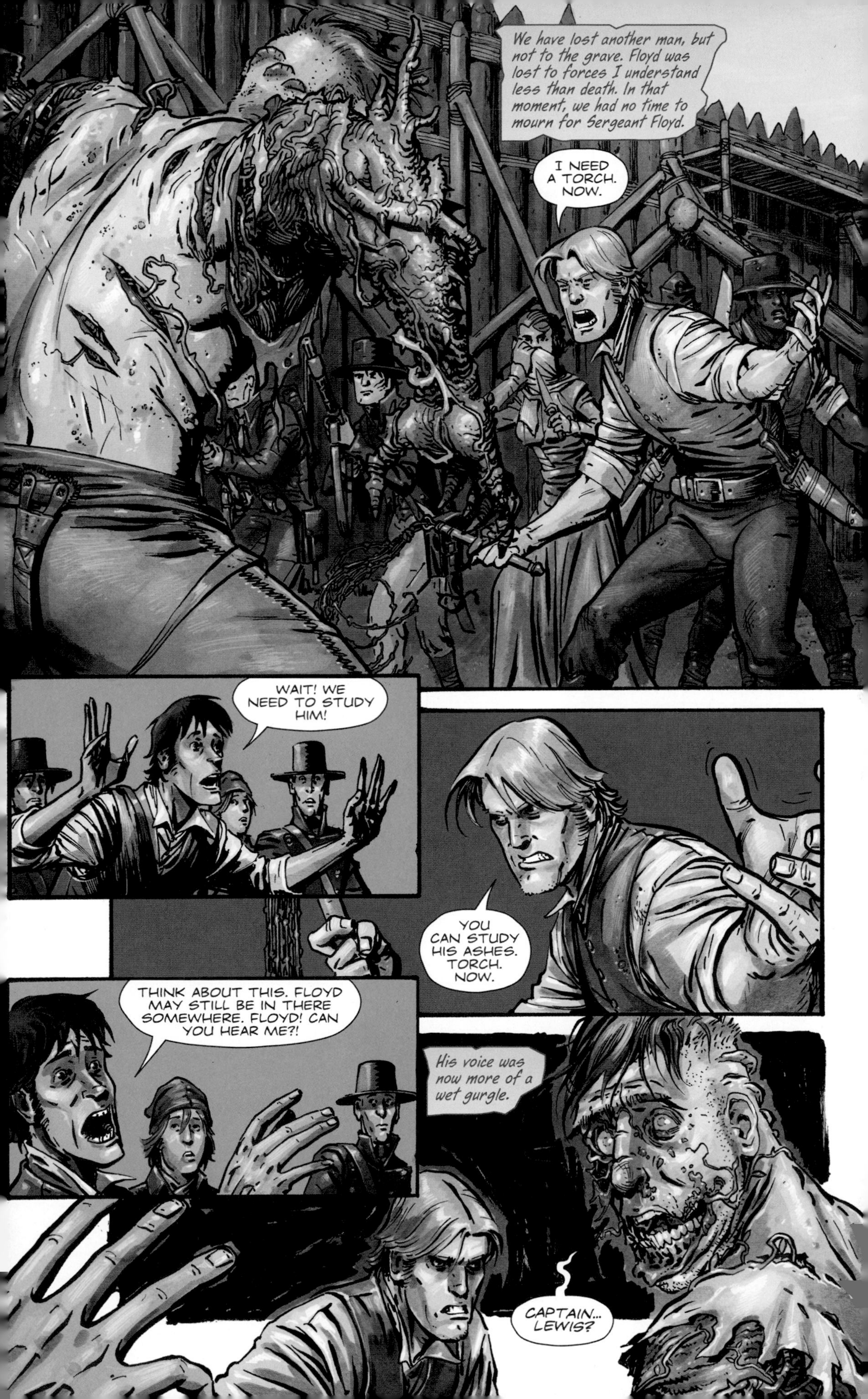
We have lost another man, but not to the grave. Floyd was lost to forces I understand less than death. In that moment, we had no time to mourn for Sergeant Floyd.
I NEED A TORCH. NOW.
WAIT! WE NEED TO STUDY HIM!
YOU CAN STUDY HIS ASHES. TORCH. NOW.
THINK ABOUT THIS. FLOYD MAY STILL BE IN THERE SOMEWHERE. FLOYD! CAN YOU HEAR ME?!
His voice was now more of a wet gurgle.
CAPTAIN... LEWIS?

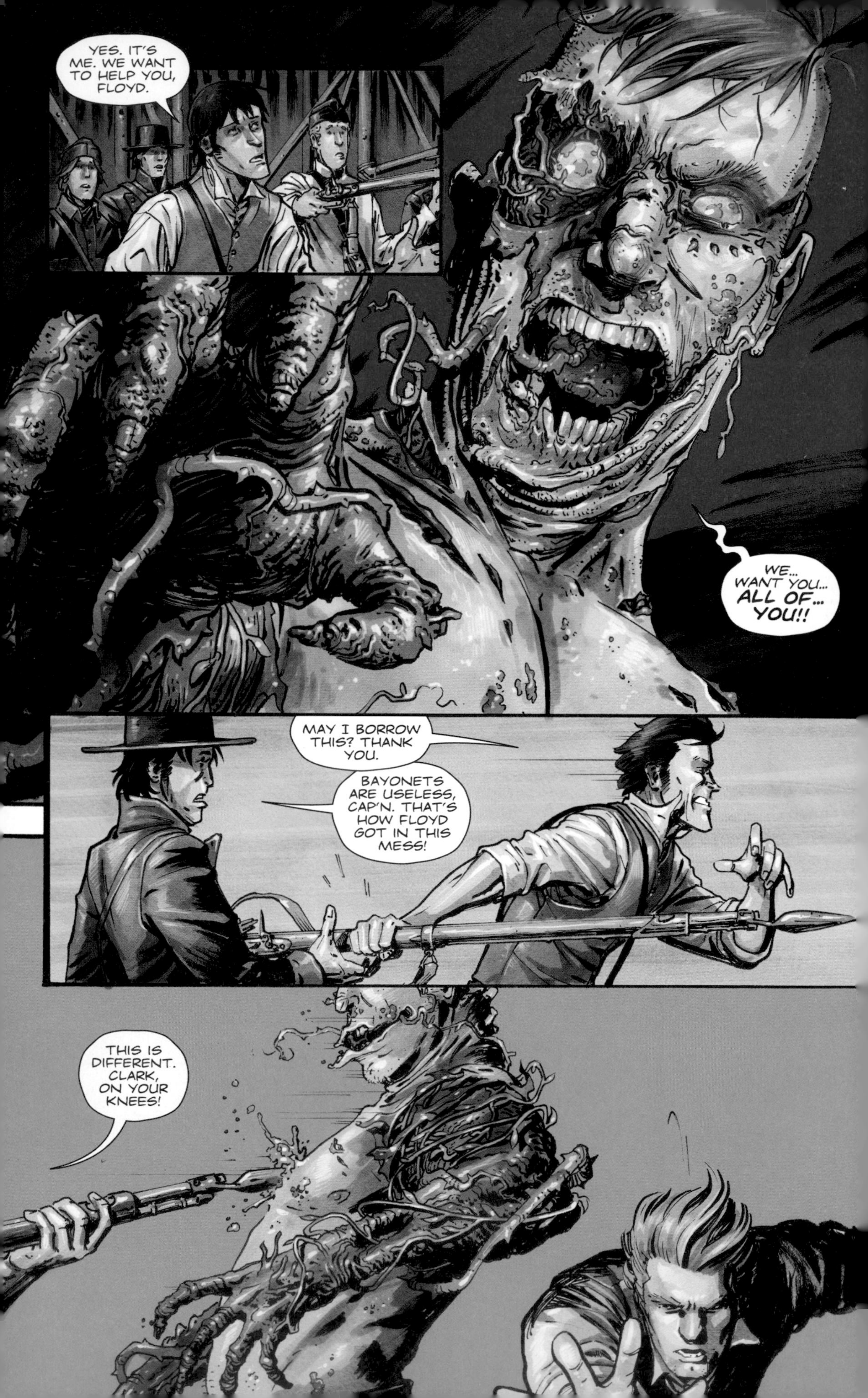
YES. IT'S ME. WE WANT TO HELP YOU, FLOYD.
WE... WANT YOU... ALL OF... YOU!!
MAY I BORROW THIS? THANK YOU.
BAYONETS ARE USELESS, CAP'N. THAT'S HOW FLOYD GOT IN THIS MESS!
THIS IS DIFFERENT. CLARK, ON YOUR KNEES!

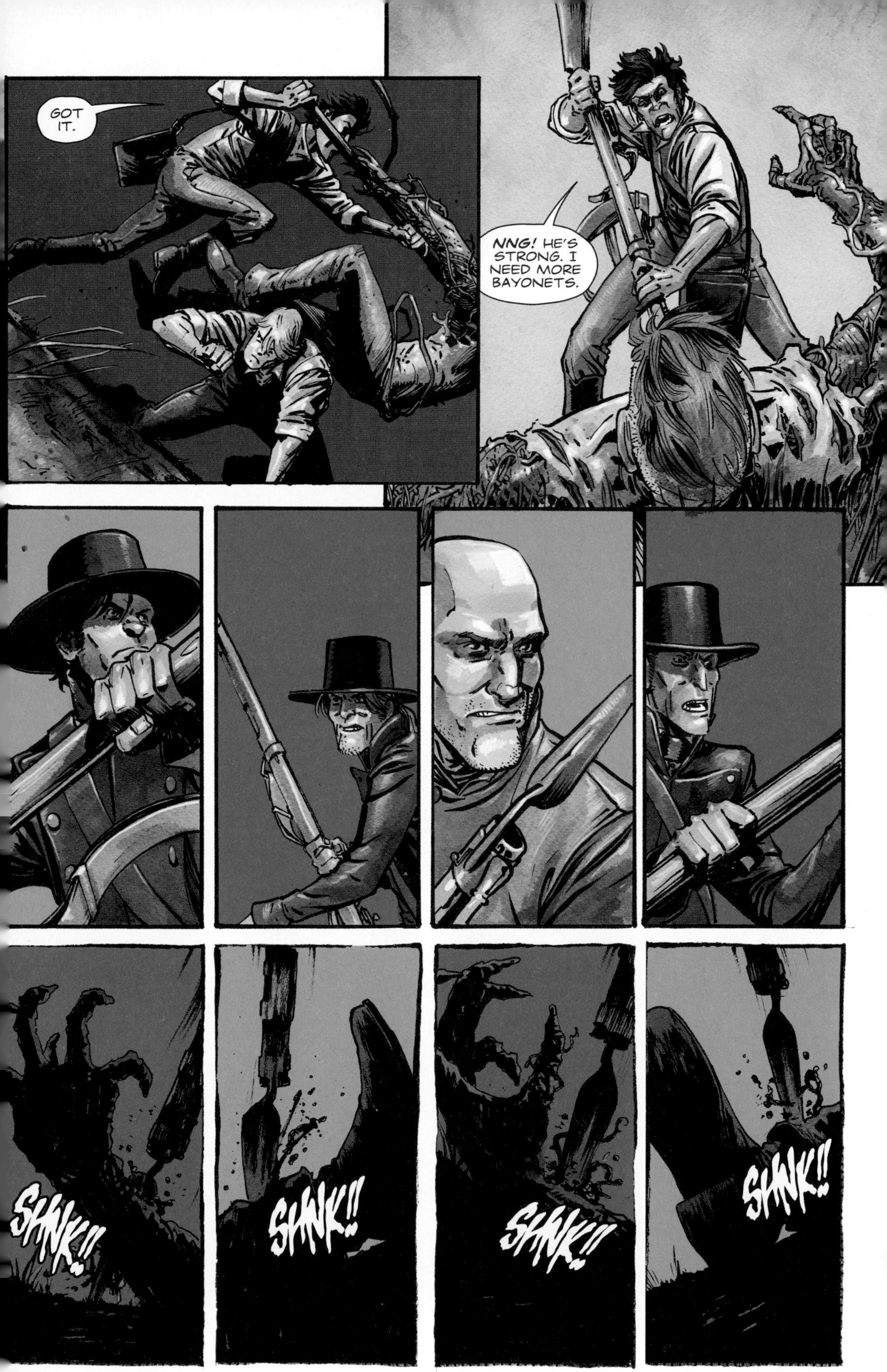
GOT IT.
NNG! HE'S STRONG. I NEED MORE BAYONETS.
SHNK!!
SHNK!!
SHNK!!
SHNK!!

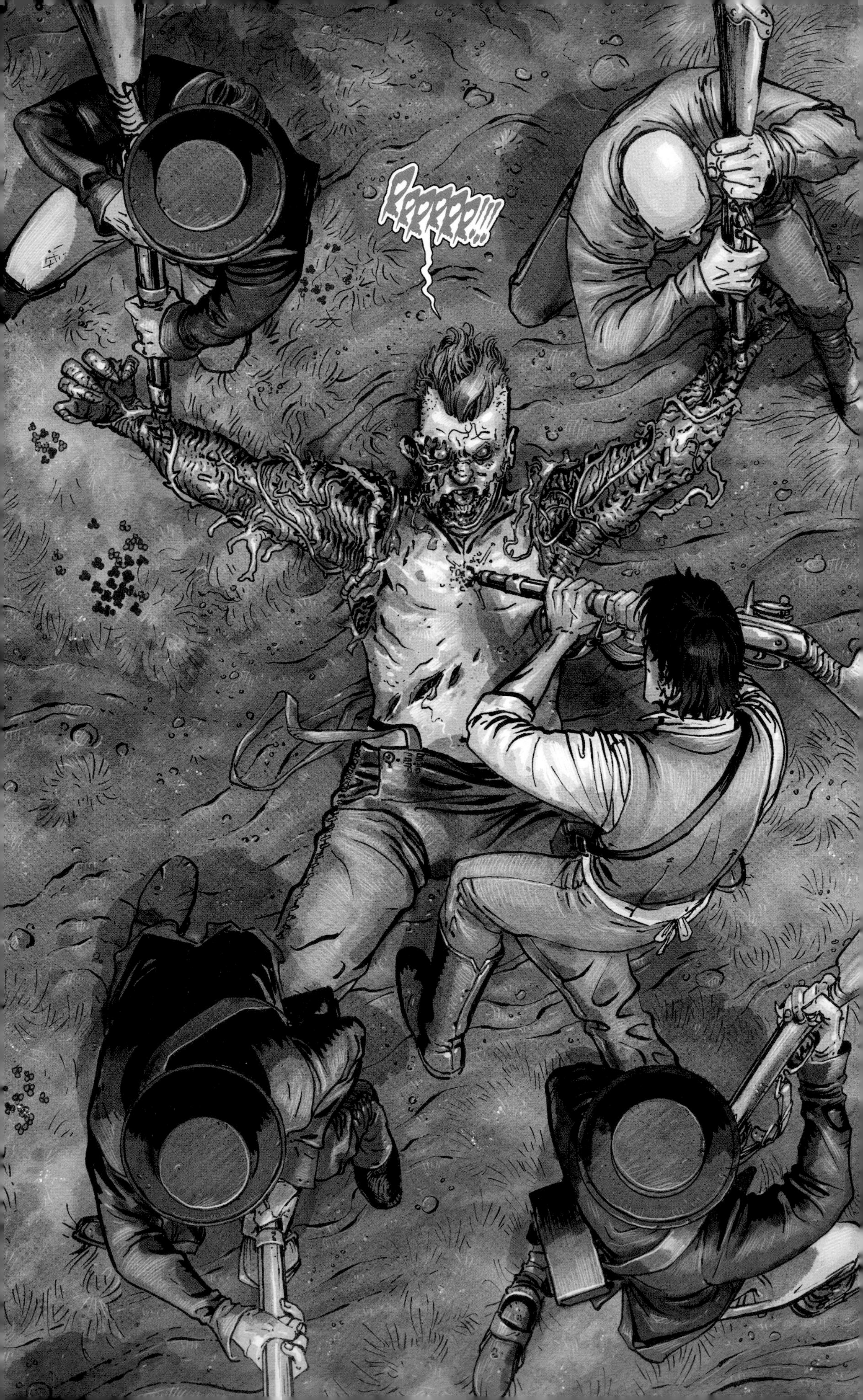
RRRRRR!!!

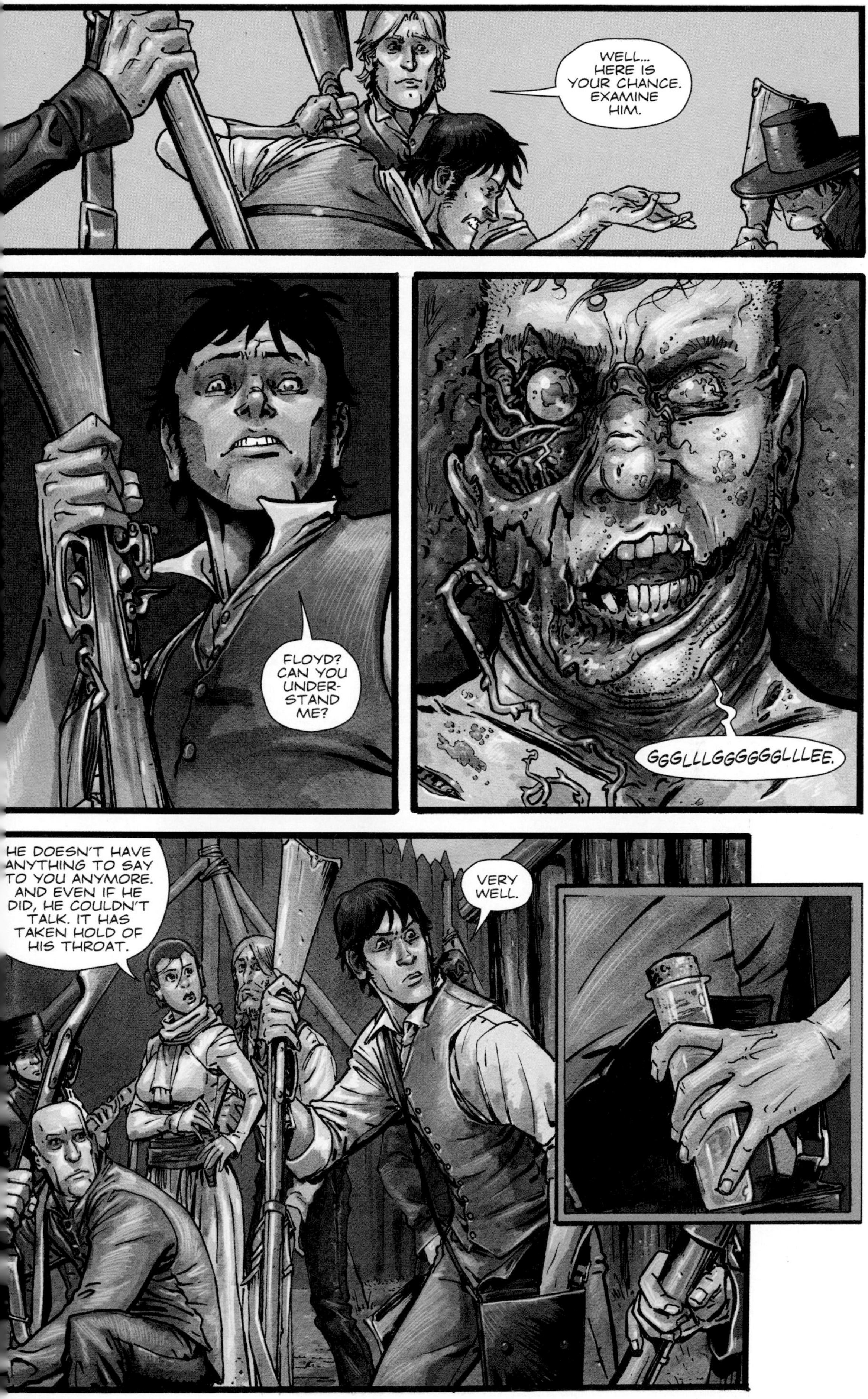
WELL... HERE IS YOUR CHANCE. EXAMINE HIM.
FLOYD? CAN YOU UNDER- STAND ME?
GGGLLLGGGGGLLLEE.
HE DOESN'T HAVE ANYTHING TO SAY TO YOU ANYMORE. AND EVEN IF HE DID, HE COULDN'T TALK. IT HAS TAKEN HOLD OF HIS THROAT.
VERY WELL.

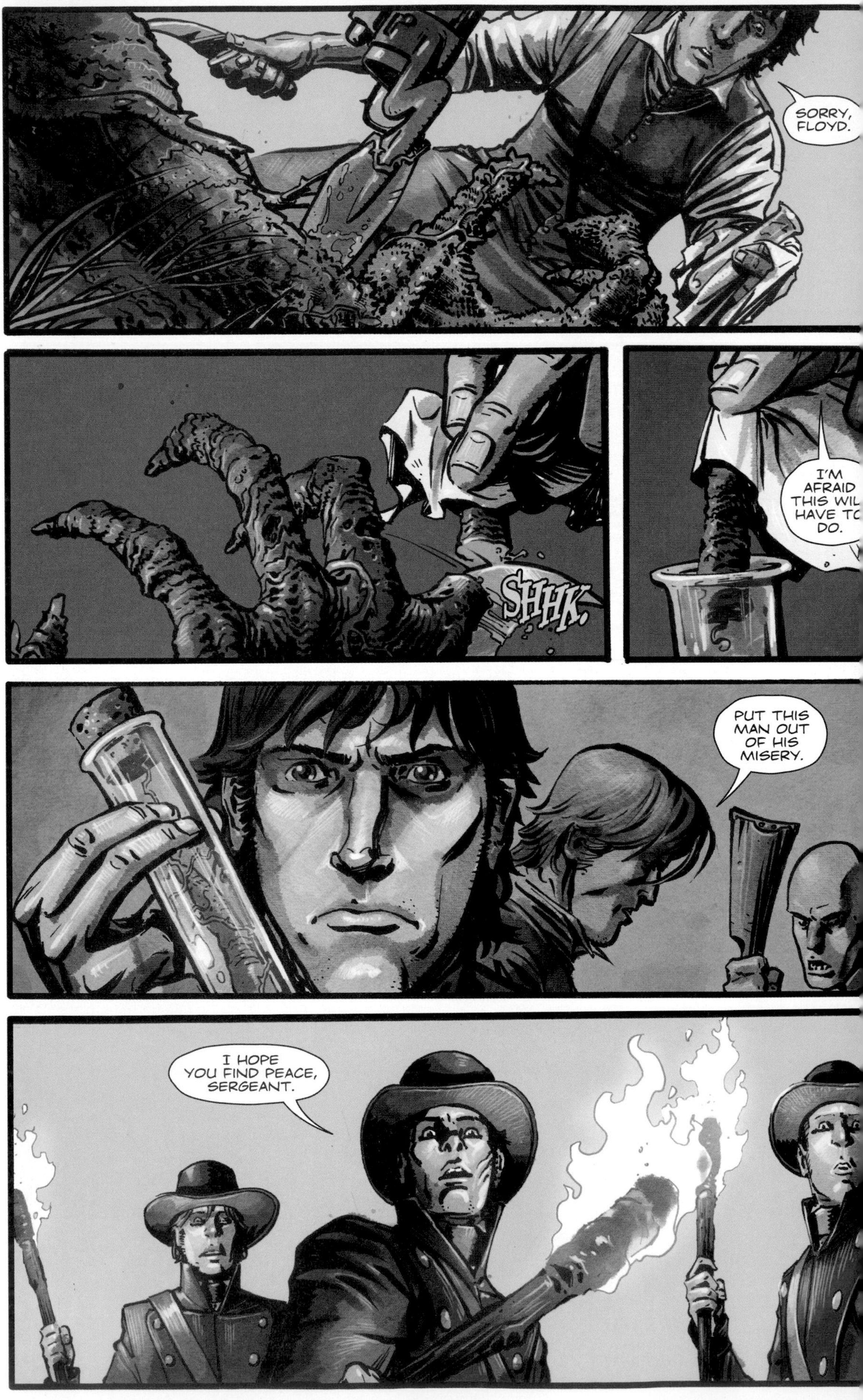
SORRY, FLOYD.
SHHK.
I'M AFRAID THIS WIL HAVE TO DO.
PUT THIS MAN OUT OF HIS MISERY.
I HOPE YOU FIND PEACE, SERGEANT.

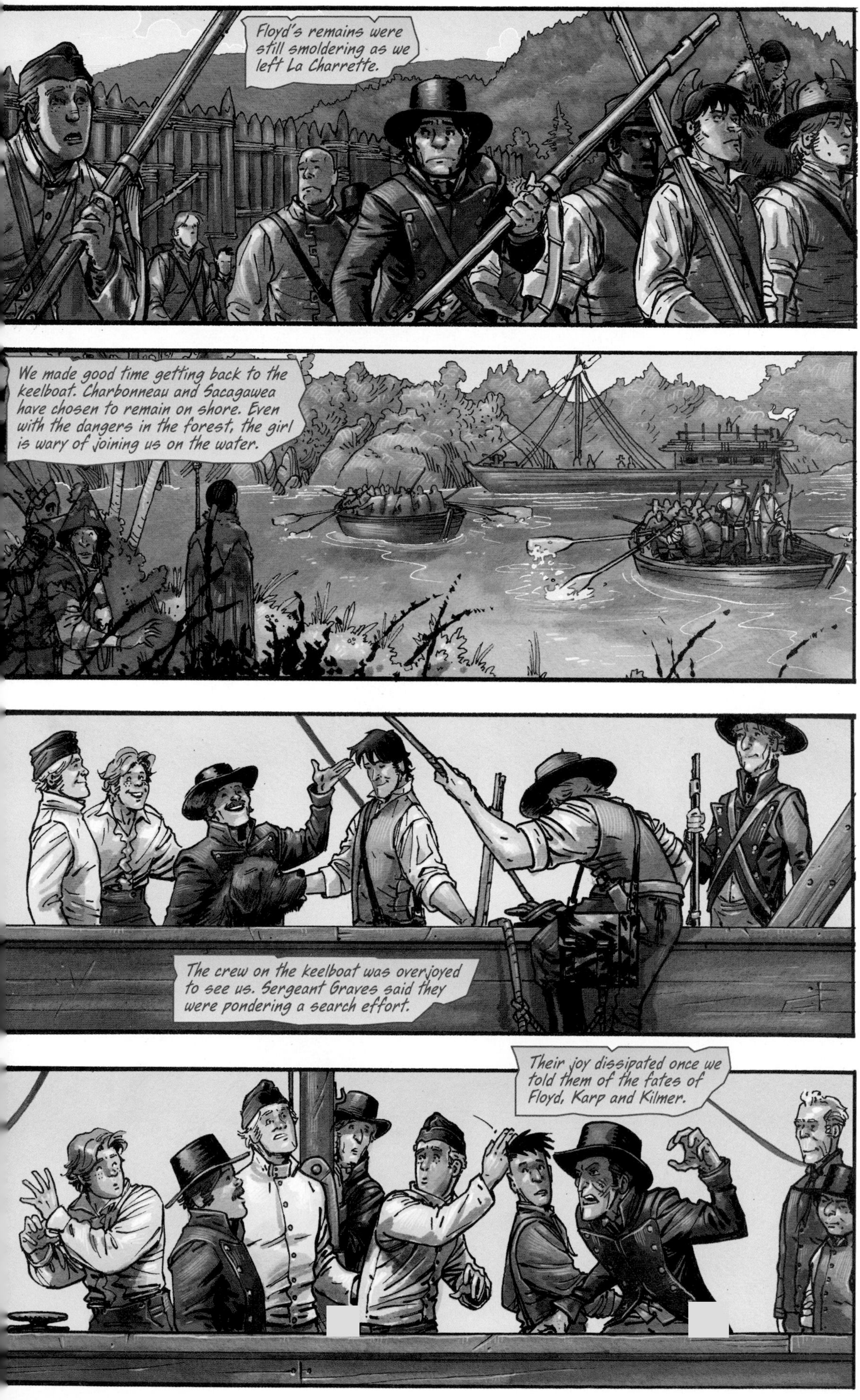
Floyd's remains were still smoldering as we left La Charrette.
We made good time getting back to the keelboat. Charbonneau and Sacagawea have chosen to remain on shore. Even with the dangers in the forest, the girl is wary of joining us on the water.
The crew on the keelboat was overjoyed to see us. Sergeant Graves said they were pondering a search effort.
Their joy dissipated once we told them of the fates of Floyd, Karp and Kilmer.

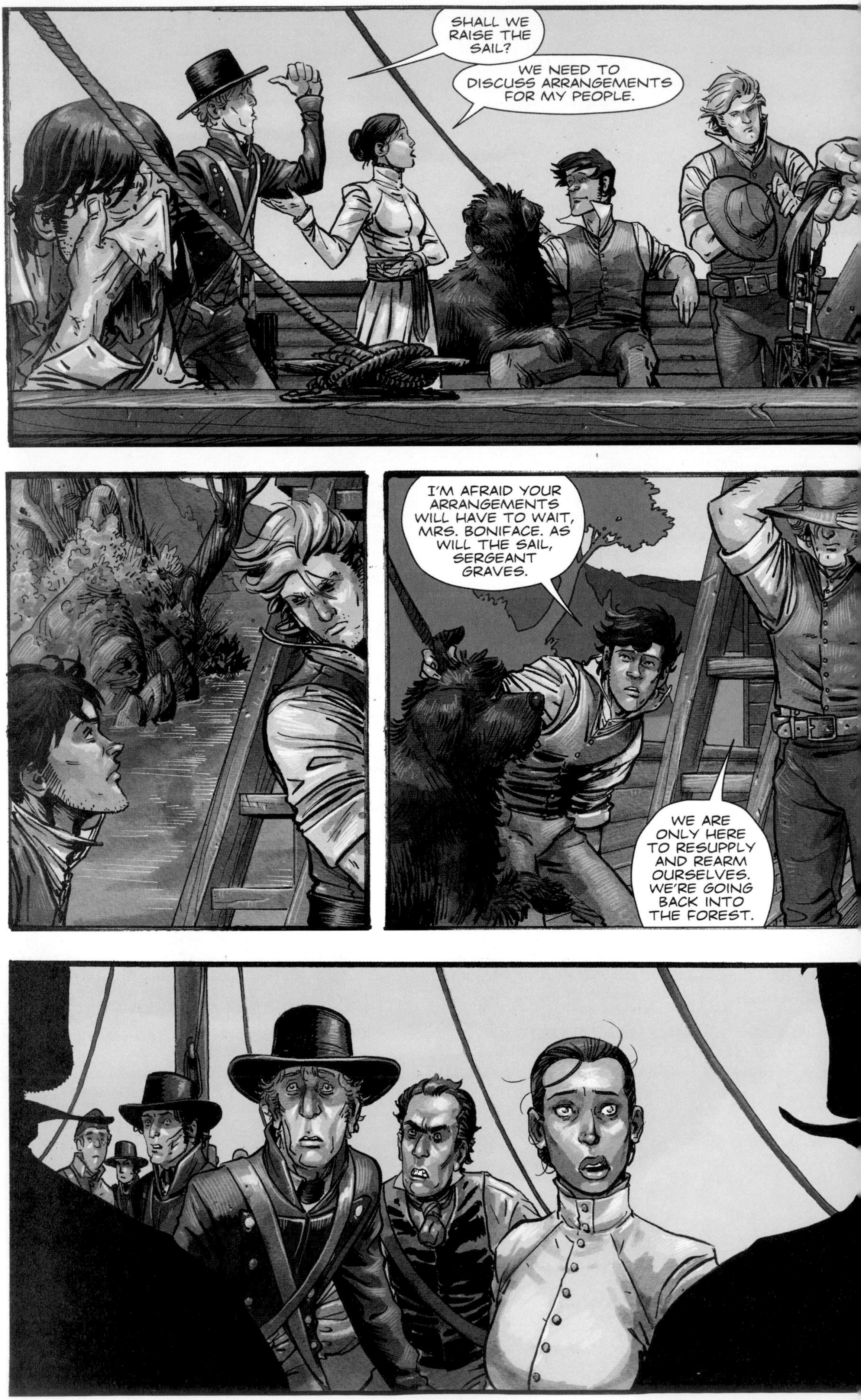
SHALL WE RAISE THE SAIL?
WE NEED TO DISCUSS ARRANGEMENTS FOR MY PEOPLE.
I'M AFRAID YOUR ARRANGEMENTS WILL HAVE TO WAIT, MRS. BONIFACE. AS WILL THE SAIL, SERGEANT GRAVES.
WE ARE ONLY HERE TO RESUPPLY AND REARM OURSELVES. WE'RE GOING BACK INTO THE FOREST.

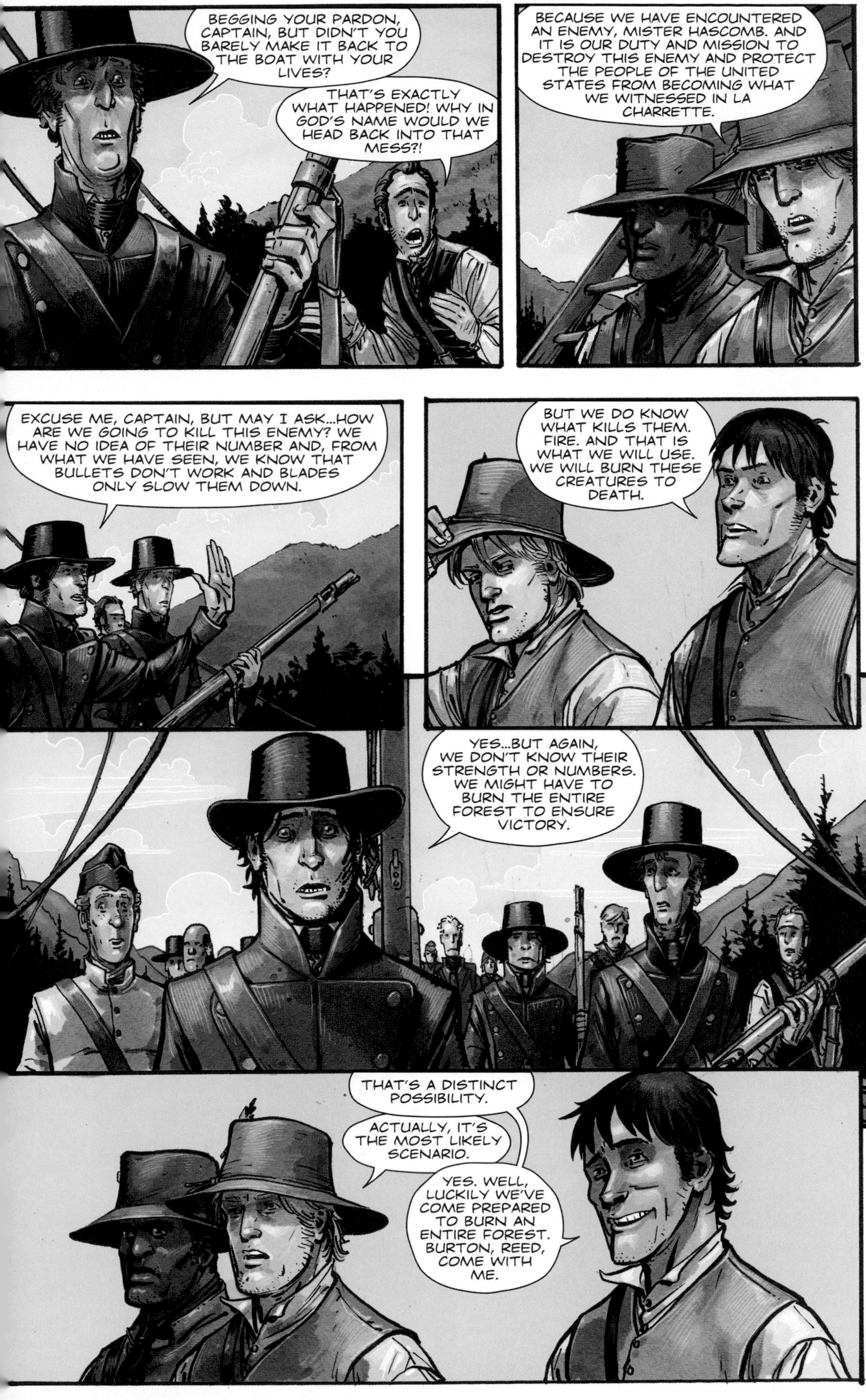
BEGGING YOUR PARDON, CAPTAIN, BUT DIDN'T YOU BARELY MAKE IT BACK TO THE BOAT WITH YOUR LIVES?
THAT'S EXACTLY WHAT HAPPENED! WHY IN GOD'S NAME WOULD WE HEAD BACK INTO THAT MESS?!
BECAUSE WE HAVE ENCOUNTERED AN ENEMY, MISTER HASCOMB. AND IT IS OUR DUTY AND MISSION TO DESTROY THIS ENEMY AND PROTECT THE PEOPLE OF THE UNITED STATES FROM BECOMING WHAT WE WITNESSED IN LA CHARRETTE.
EXCUSE ME, CAPTAIN, BUT MAY I ASK...HOW ARE WE GOING TO KILL THIS ENEMY? WE HAVE NO IDEA OF THEIR NUMBER AND, FROM WHAT WE HAVE SEEN, WE KNOW THAT BULLETS DON'T WORK AND BLADES ONLY SLOW THEM DOWN.
BUT WE DO KNOW WHAT KILLS THEM. FIRE. AND THAT IS WHAT WE WILL USE. WE WILL BURN THESE CREATURES TO DEATH.
YES...BUT AGAIN, WE DON'T KNOW THEIR STRENGTH OR NUMBERS. WE MIGHT HAVE TO BURN THE ENTIRE FOREST TO ENSURE VICTORY.
THAT'S A DISTINCT POSSIBILITY.
ACTUALLY, IT'S THE MOST LIKELY SCENARIO.
YES. WELL, LUCKILY WE'VE COME PREPARED TO BURN AN ENTIRE FOREST. BURTON, REED, COME WITH ME.

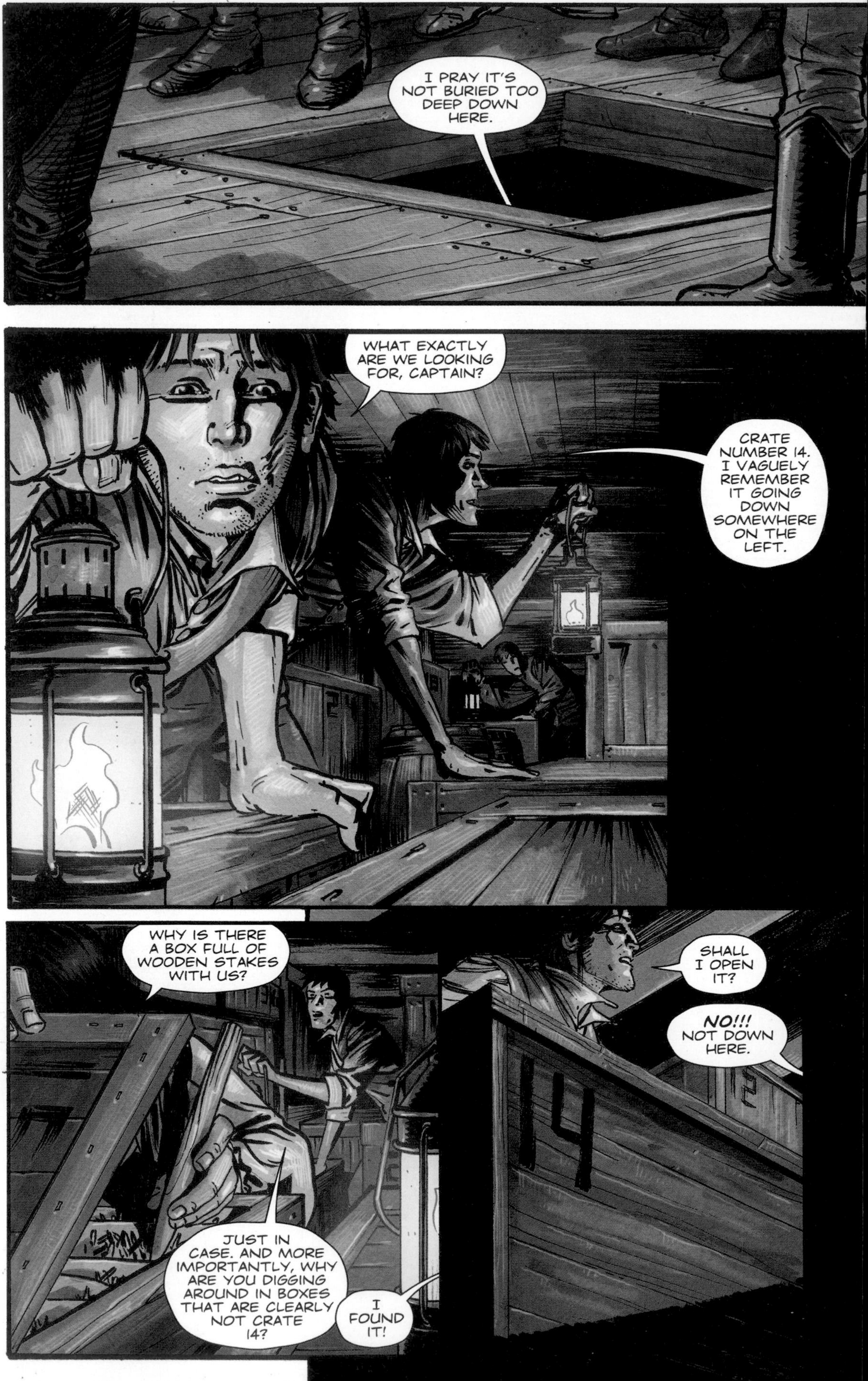
I PRAY IT'S NOT BURIED TOO DEEP DOWN HERE.
WHAT EXACTLY ARE WE LOOKING FOR, CAPTAIN?
CRATE NUMBER 14. I VAGUELY REMEMBER IT GOING DOWN SOMEWHERE ON THE LEFT.
WHY IS THERE A BOX FULL OF WOODEN STAKES WITH US?
JUST IN CASE. AND MORE IMPORTANTLY, WHY ARE YOU DIGGING AROUND IN BOXES THAT ARE CLEARLY NOT CRATE 14?
I FOUND IT!
SHALL I OPEN IT?
NO!!! NOT DOWN HERE.

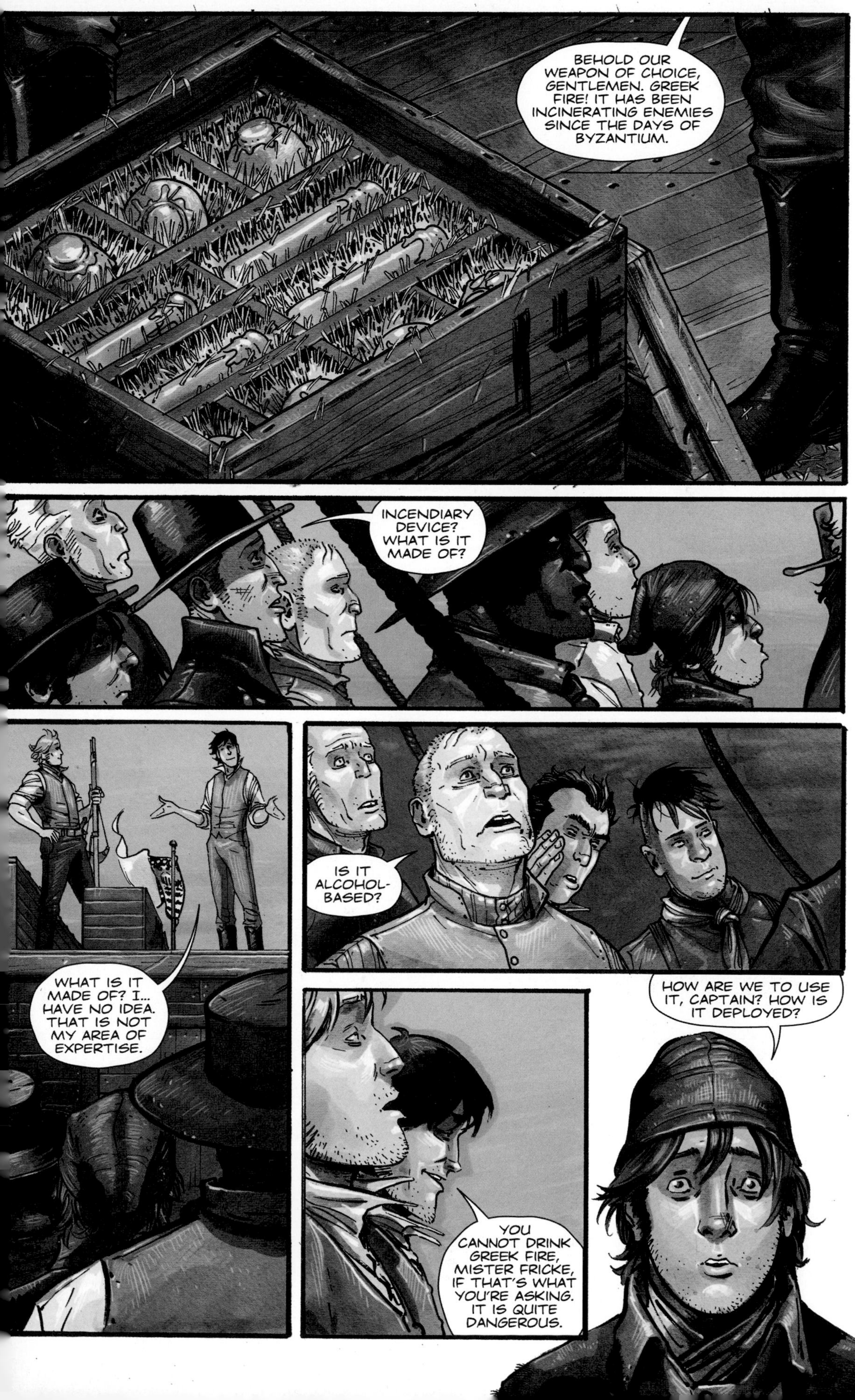
BEHOLD OUR WEAPON OF CHOICE, GENTLEMEN. GREEK FIRE! IT HAS BEEN INCINERATING ENEMIES SINCE THE DAYS OF BYZANTIUM.
INCENDIARY DEVICE? WHAT IS IT MADE OF?
WHAT IS IT MADE OF? I... HAVE NO IDEA. THAT IS NOT MY AREA OF EXPERTISE.
IS IT ALCOHOL-BASED?
YOU CANNOT DRINK GREEK FIRE, MISTER FRICKE, IF THAT'S WHAT YOU'RE ASKING. IT IS QUITE DANGEROUS.
HOW ARE WE TO USE IT, CAPTAIN? HOW IS IT DEPLOYED?

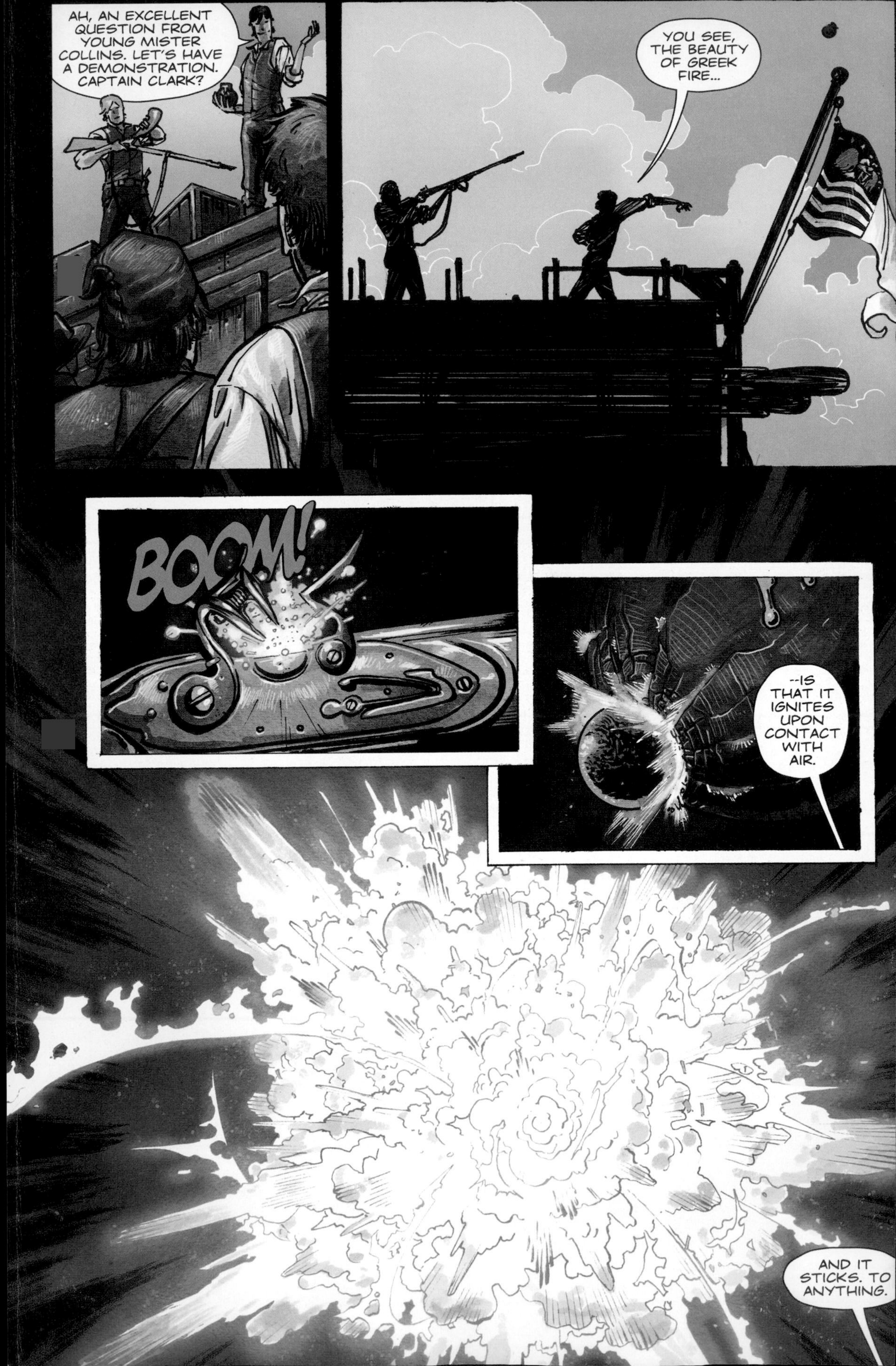
AH, AN EXCELLENT QUESTION FROM YOUNG MISTER COLLINS. LET'S HAVE A DEMONSTRATION. CAPTAIN CLARK?
YOU SEE, THE BEAUTY OF GREEK FIRE...
BOOM!
--IS THAT IT IGNITES UPON CONTACT WITH AIR.
AND IT STICKS. TO ANYTHING.

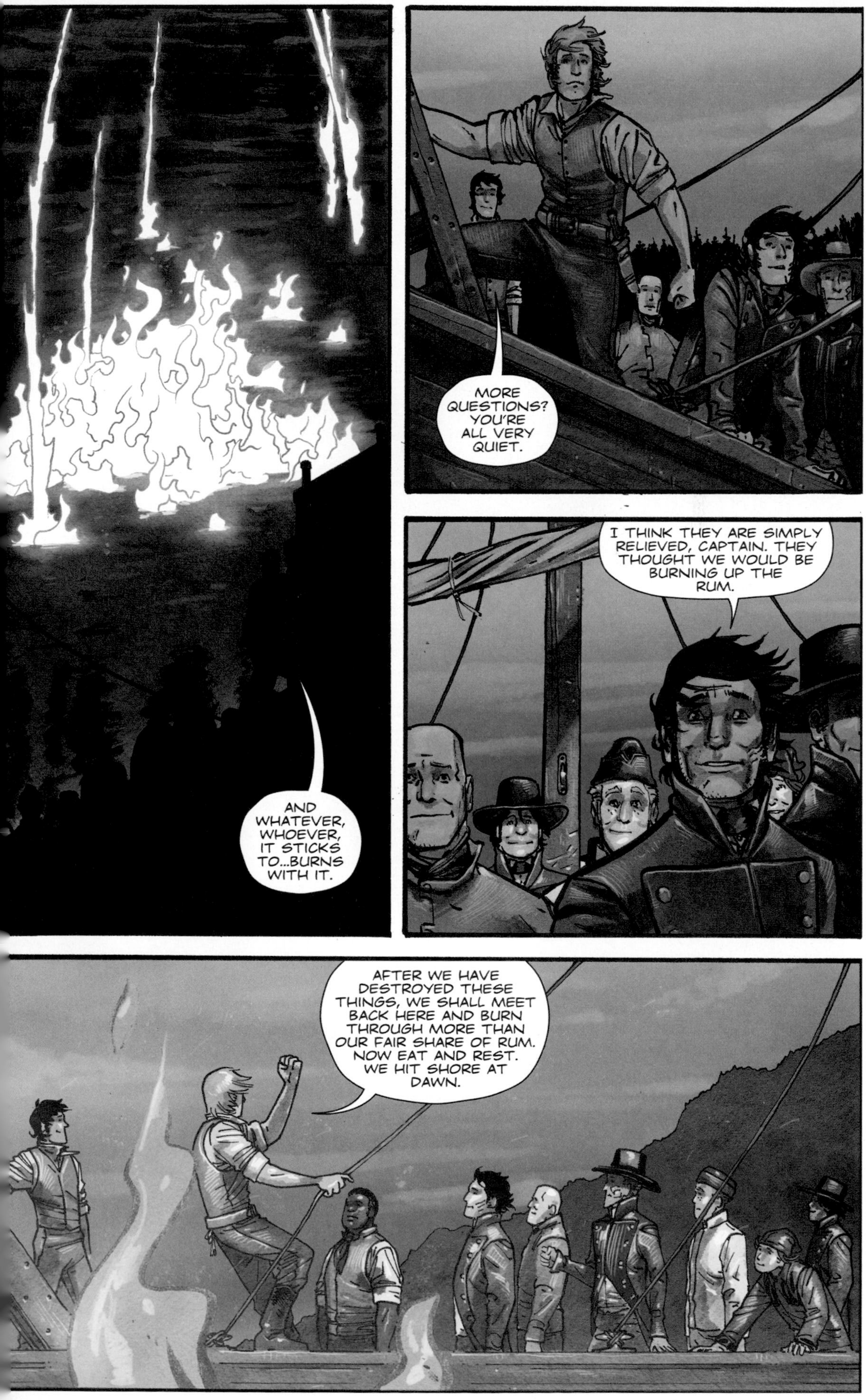
MORE QUESTIONS? YOU'RE ALL VERY QUIET.
AND WHATEVER, WHOEVER, IT STICKS TO...BURNS WITH IT.
I THINK THEY ARE SIMPLY RELIEVED, CAPTAIN. THEY THOUGHT WE WOULD BE BURNING UP THE RUM.
AFTER WE HAVE DESTROYED THESE THINGS, WE SHALL MEET BACK HERE AND BURN THROUGH MORE THAN OUR FAIR SHARE OF RUM. NOW EAT AND REST. WE HIT SHORE AT DAWN.

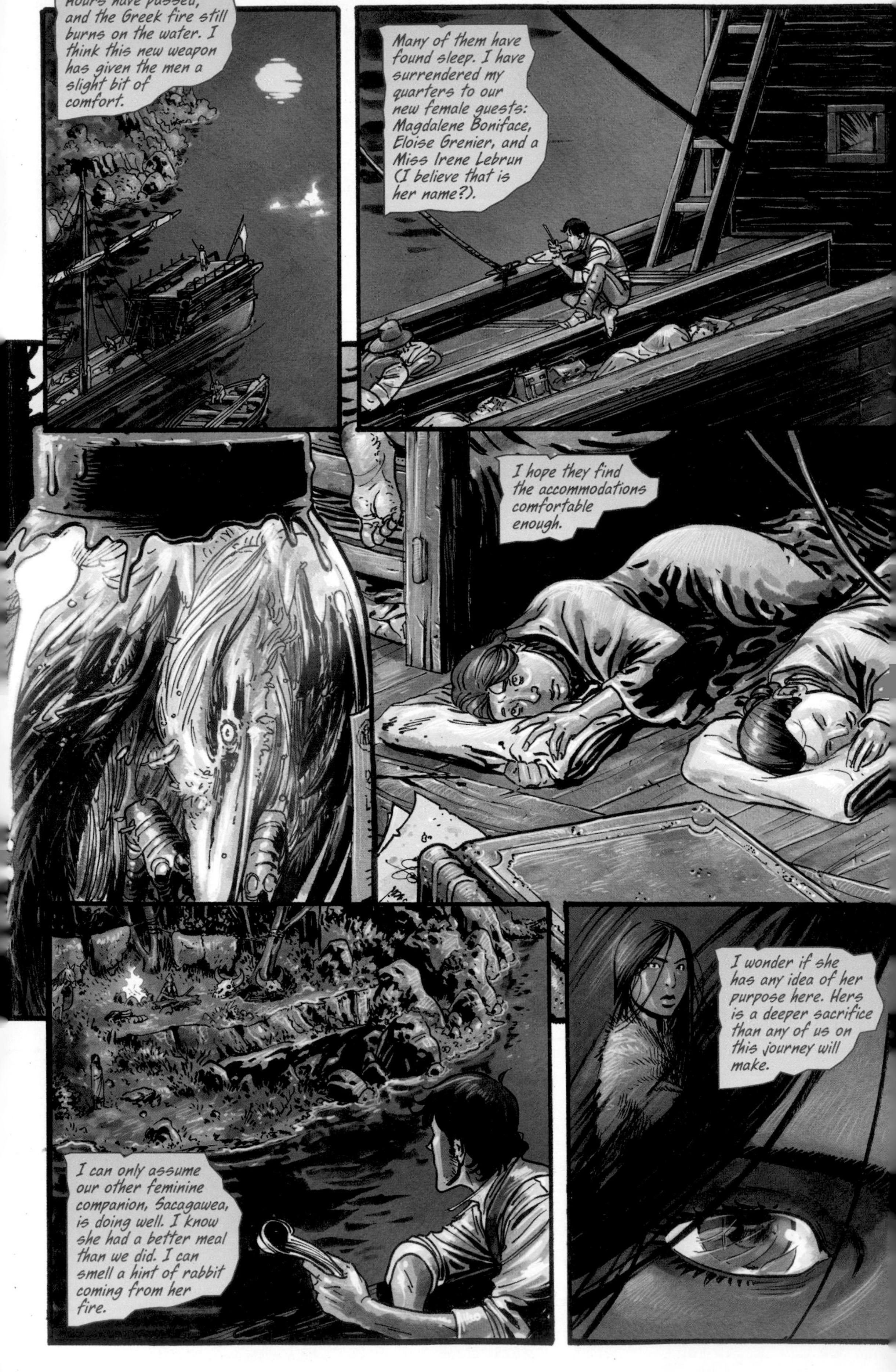
Hours have passed, and the Greek fire still burns on the water. I think this new weapon has given the men a slight bit of comfort.
Many of them have found sleep. I have surrendered my quarters to our new female guests: Magdalene Boniface, Eloise Grenier, and a Miss Irene Lebrun (I believe that is her name?).
I hope they find the accommodations comfortable enough.
I can only assume our other feminine companion, Sacagawea, is doing well. I know she had a better meal than we did. I can smell a hint of rabbit coming from her fire.
I wonder if she has any idea of her purpose here. Hers is a deeper sacrifice than any of us on this journey will make.

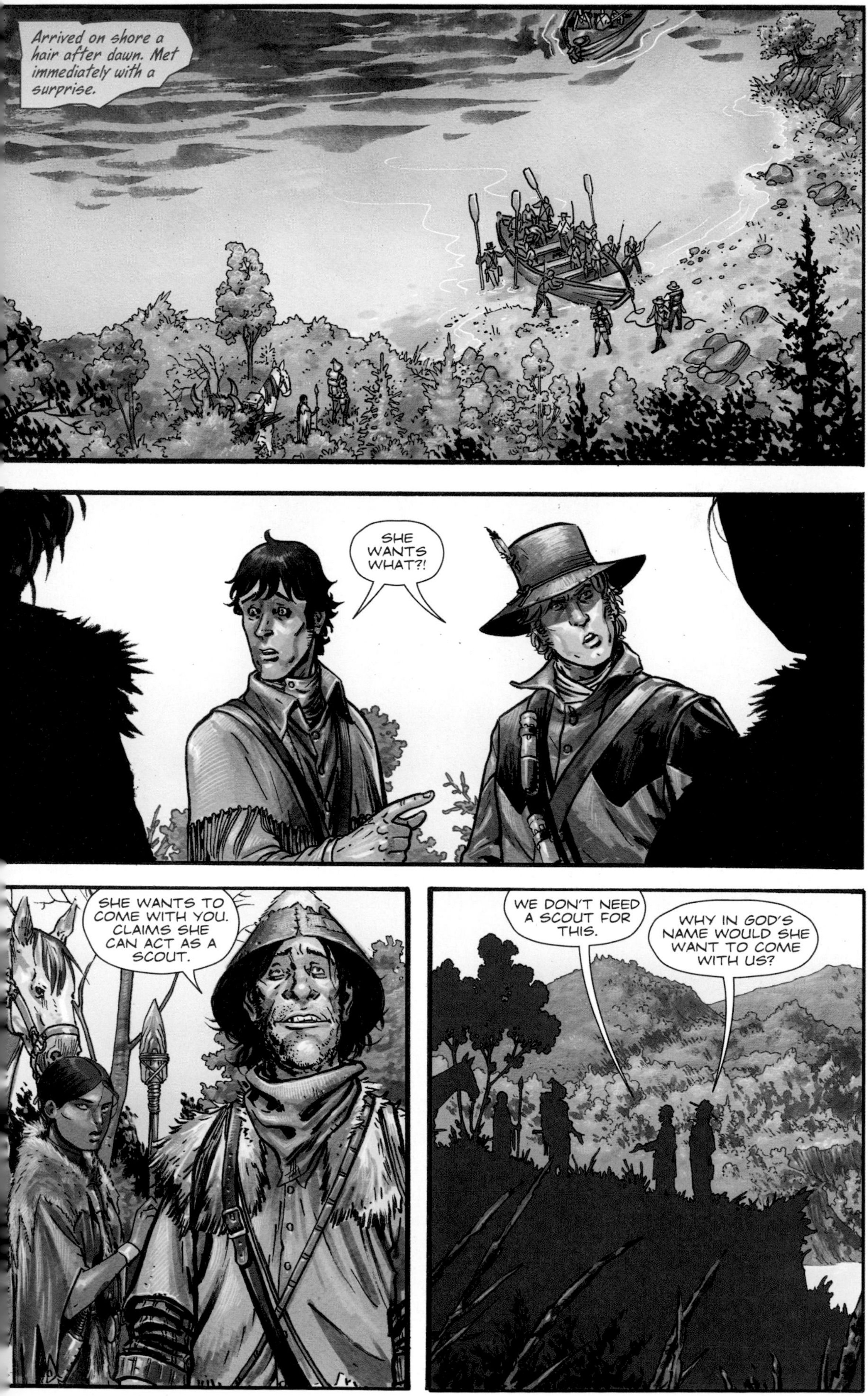
Arrived on shore a hair after dawn. Met immediately with a surprise.
SHE WANTS WHAT?!
SHE WANTS TO COME WITH YOU. CLAIMS SHE CAN ACT AS A SCOUT.
WE DON'T NEED A SCOUT FOR THIS.
WHY IN GOD'S NAME WOULD SHE WANT TO COME WITH US?

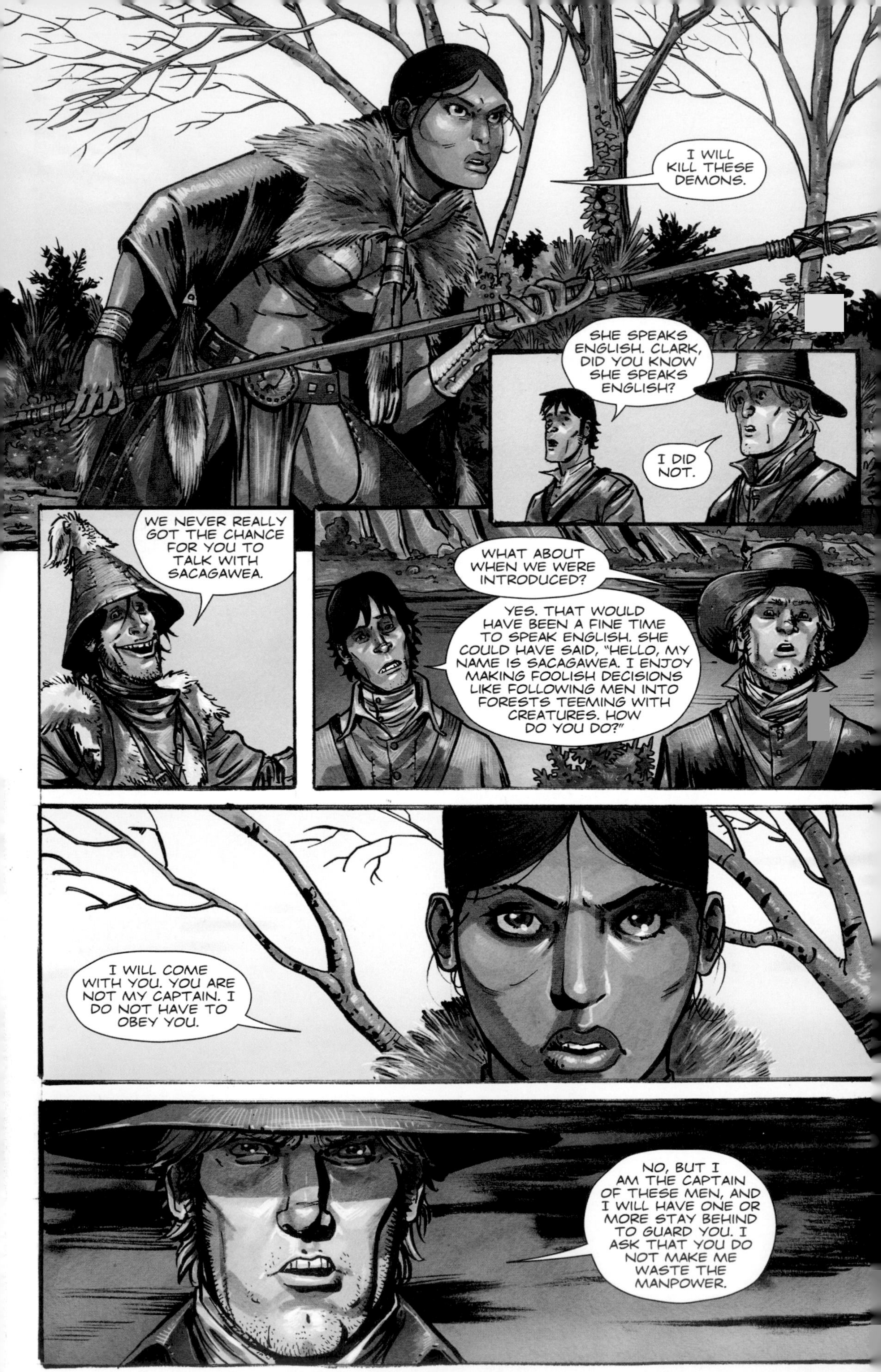
I WILL KILL THESE DEMONS.
SHE SPEAKS ENGLISH. CLARK, DID YOU KNOW SHE SPEAKS ENGLISH?
I DID NOT.
WE NEVER REALLY GOT THE CHANCE FOR YOU TO TALK WITH SACAGAWEA.
WHAT ABOUT WHEN WE WERE INTRODUCED?
YES. THAT WOULD HAVE BEEN A FINE TIME TO SPEAK ENGLISH. SHE COULD HAVE SAID, "HELLO, MY NAME IS SACAGAWEA. I ENJOY MAKING FOOLISH DECISIONS LIKE FOLLOWING MEN INTO FORESTS TEEMING WITH CREATURES. HOW DO YOU DO?"
I WILL COME WITH YOU. YOU ARE NOT MY CAPTAIN. I DO NOT HAVE TO OBEY YOU.
NO, BUT I AM THE CAPTAIN OF THESE MEN, AND I WILL HAVE ONE OR MORE STAY BEHIND TO GUARD YOU. I ASK THAT YOU DO NOT MAKE ME WASTE THE MANPOWER.

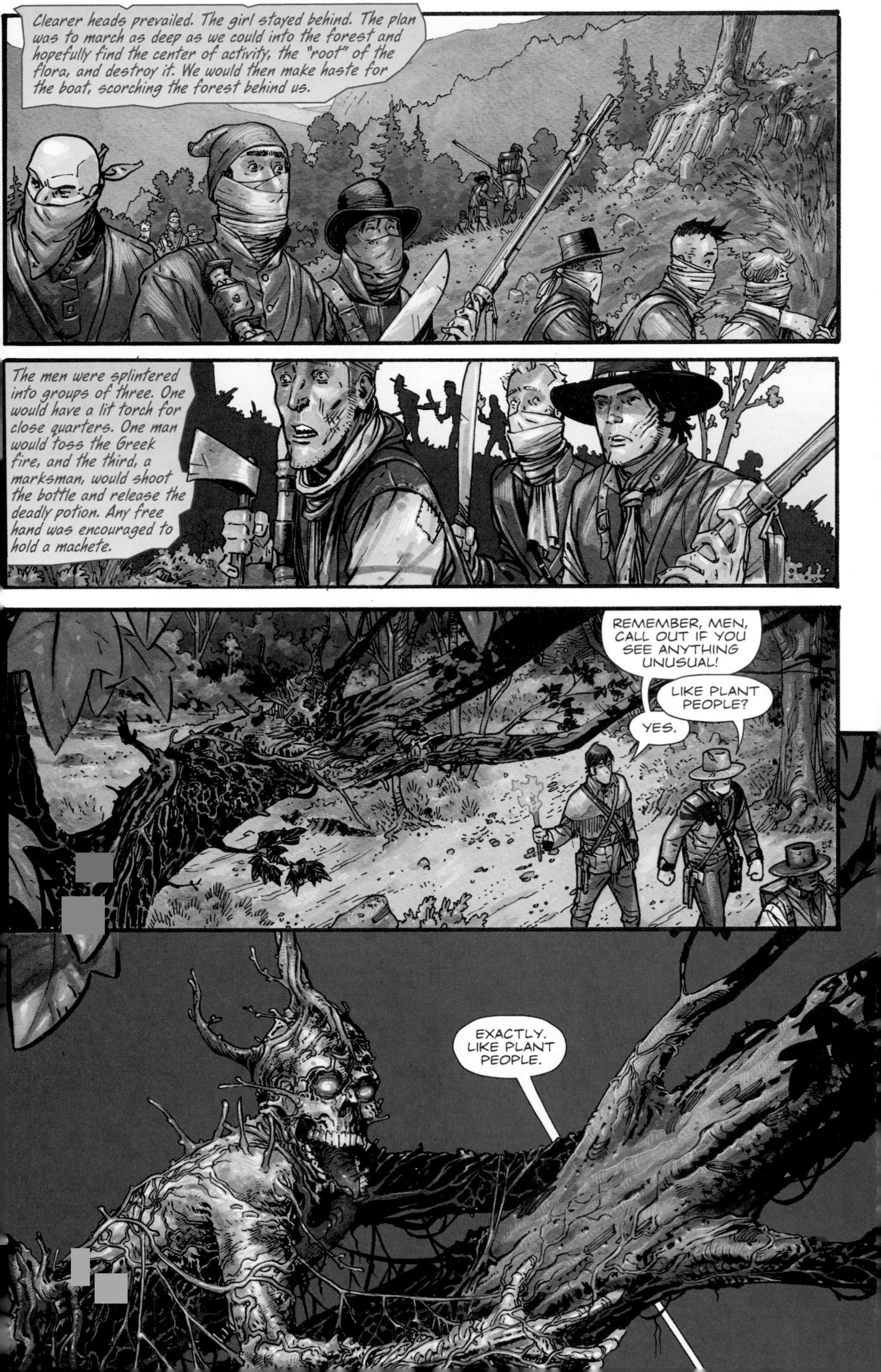
Clearer heads prevailed. The girl stayed behind. The plan was to march as deep as we could into the forest and hopefully find the center of activity, the "root" of the flora, and destroy it. We would then make haste for the boat, scorching the forest behind us.
The men were splintered into groups of three. One would have a lit torch for close quarters. One man would toss the Greek fire, and the third, a marksman, would shoot the bottle and release the deadly potion. Any free hand was encouraged to hold a machete.
REMEMBER, MEN, CALL OUT IF YOU SEE ANYTHING UNUSUAL!
LIKE PLANT PEOPLE?
YES.
EXACTLY. LIKE PLANT PEOPLE.

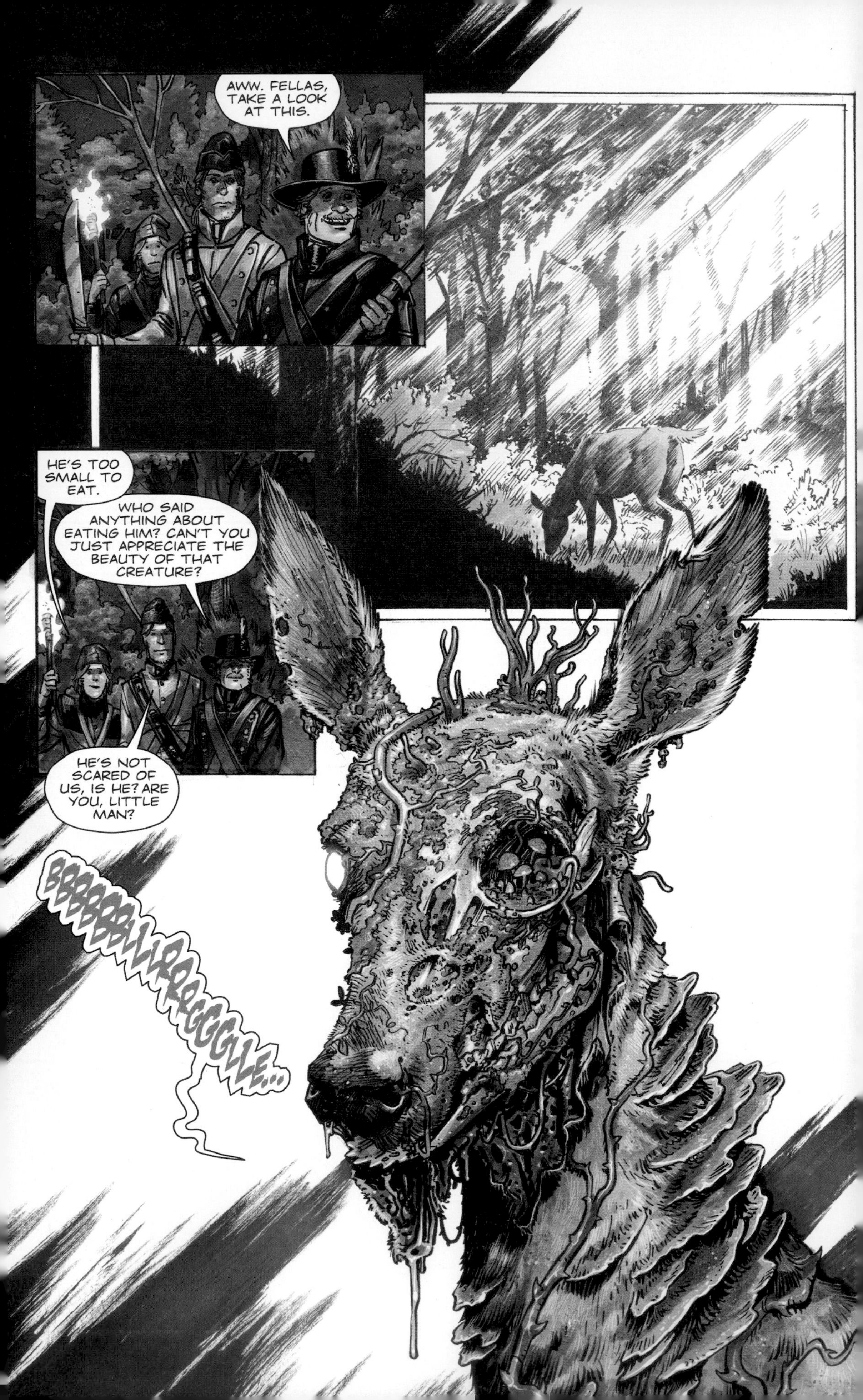
AWW. FELLAS, TAKE A LOOK AT THIS.
HE'S TOO SMALL TO EAT.
WHO SAID ANYTHING ABOUT EATING HIM? CAN'T YOU JUST APPRECIATE THE BEAUTY OF THAT CREATURE?
HE'S NOT SCARED OF US, IS HE? ARE YOU, LITTLE MAN?
BBBBBBLLRRGGGLLE...

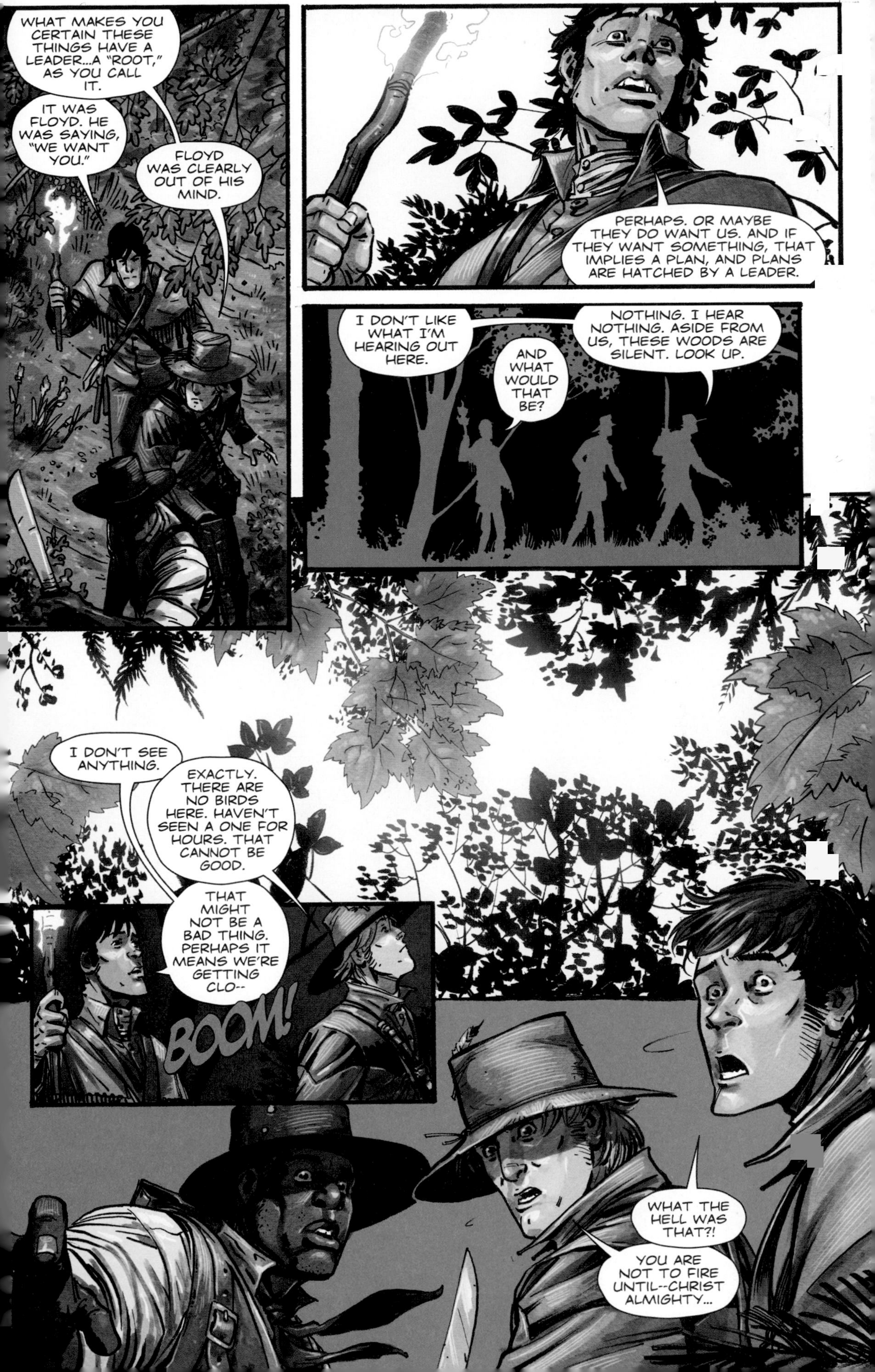
WHAT MAKES YOU CERTAIN THESE THINGS HAVE A LEADER...A "ROOT," AS YOU CALL IT.
IT WAS FLOYD. HE WAS SAYING, "WE WANT YOU."
FLOYD WAS CLEARLY OUT OF HIS MIND.
PERHAPS. OR MAYBE THEY DO WANT US. AND IF THEY WANT SOMETHING, THAT IMPLIES A PLAN, AND PLANS ARE HATCHED BY A LEADER.
I DON'T LIKE WHAT I'M HEARING OUT HERE.
AND WHAT WOULD THAT BE?
NOTHING. I HEAR NOTHING. ASIDE FROM US, THESE WOODS ARE SILENT. LOOK UP.
I DON'T SEE ANYTHING.
EXACTLY. THERE ARE NO BIRDS HERE. HAVEN'T SEEN A ONE FOR HOURS. THAT CANNOT BE GOOD.
THAT MIGHT NOT BE A BAD THING. PERHAPS IT MEANS WE'RE GETTING CLO--
BOOM!
WHAT THE HELL WAS THAT?!
YOU ARE NOT TO FIRE UNTIL--CHRIST ALMIGHTY...

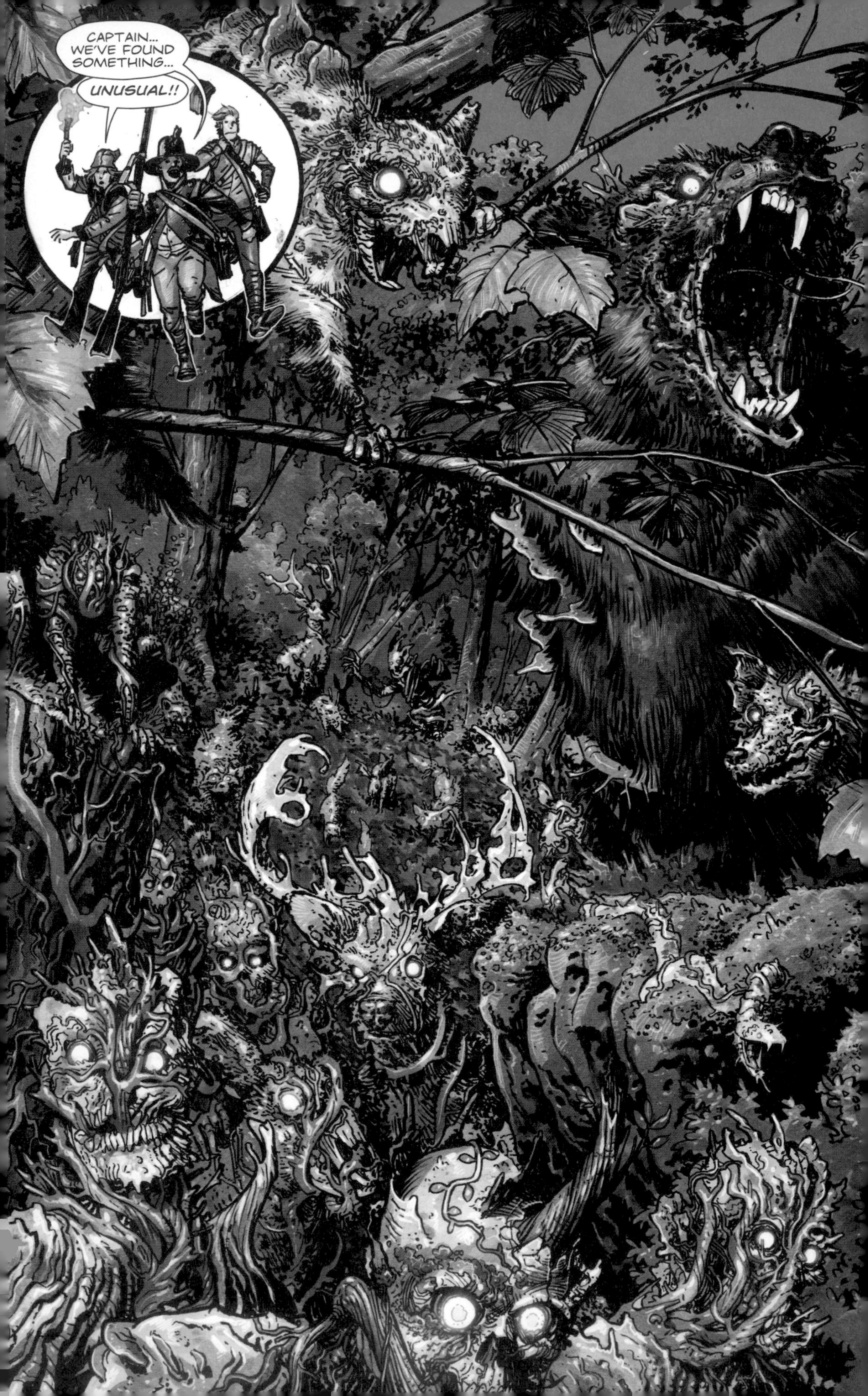
CAPTAIN... WE'VE FOUND SOMETHING...
UNUSUAL!!

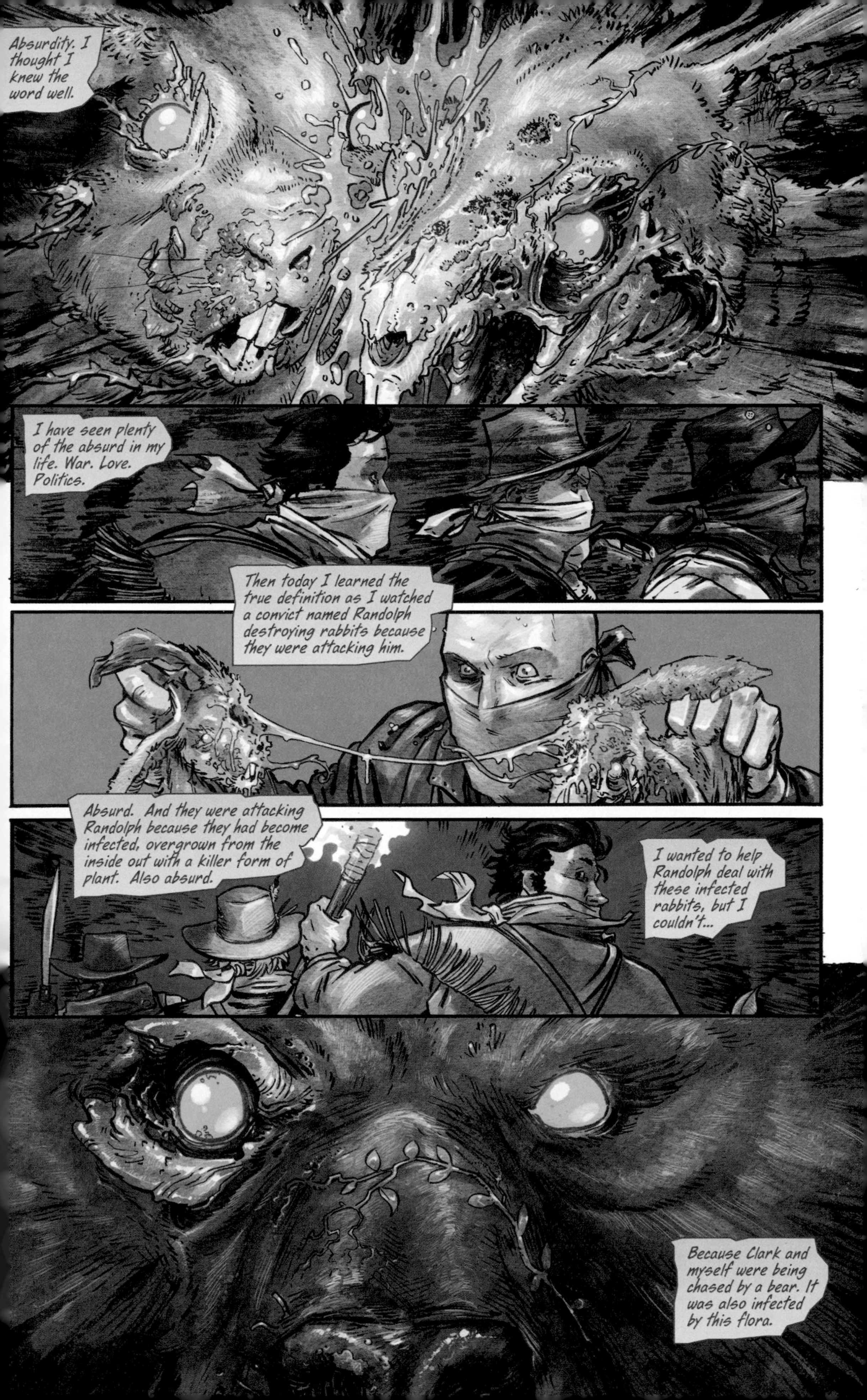
Absurdity. I thought I knew the word well.
I have seen plenty of the absurd in my life. War. Love. Politics.
Then today I learned the true definition as I watched a convict named Randolph destroying rabbits because they were attacking him.
Absurd. And they were attacking Randolph because they had become infected, overgrown from the inside out with a killer form of plant. Also absurd.
I wanted to help Randolph deal with these infected rabbits, but I couldn't...
Because Clark and myself were being chased by a bear. It was also infected by this flora.

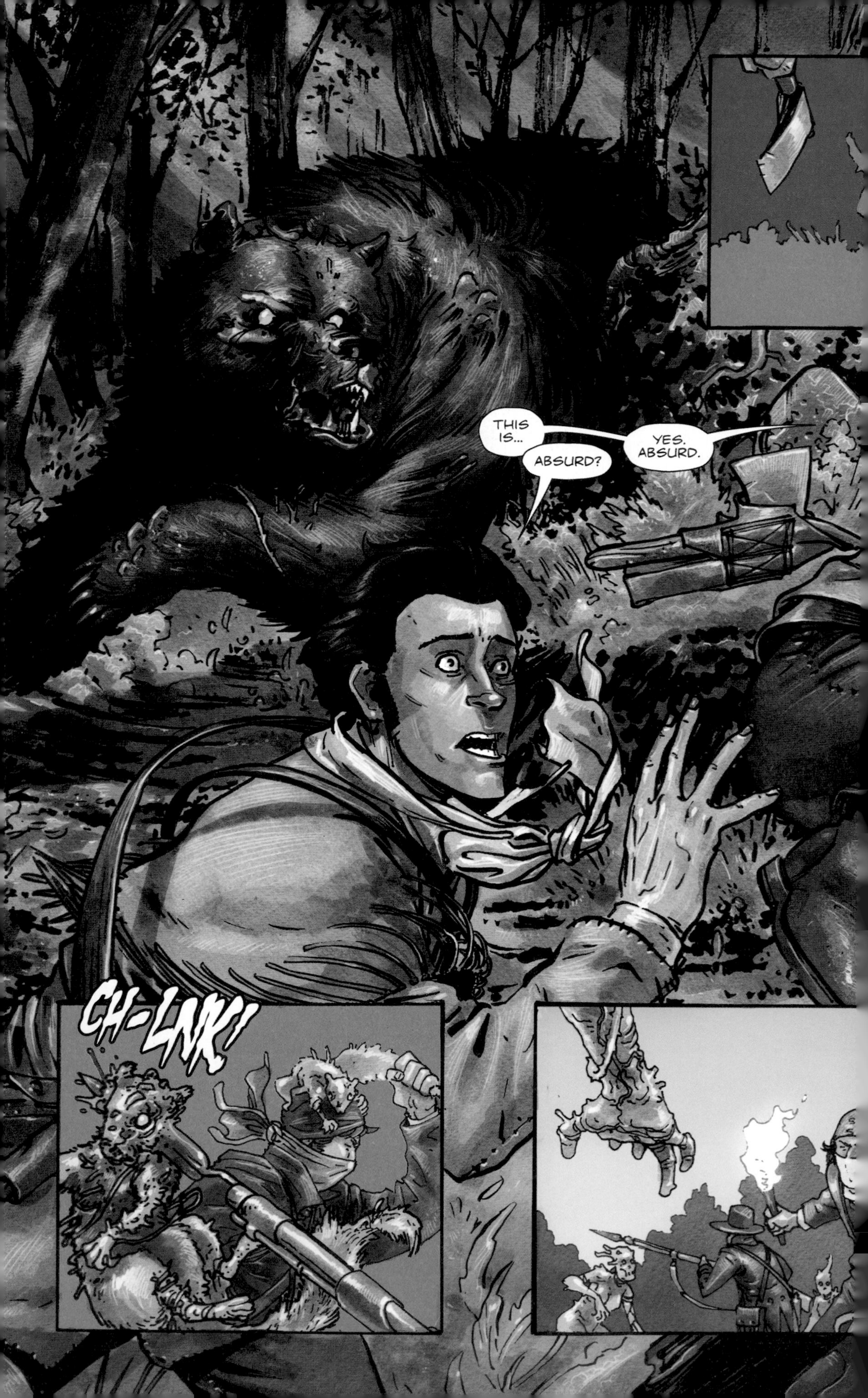
THIS IS...
ABSURD?
YES. ABSURD.
CH-LNK!

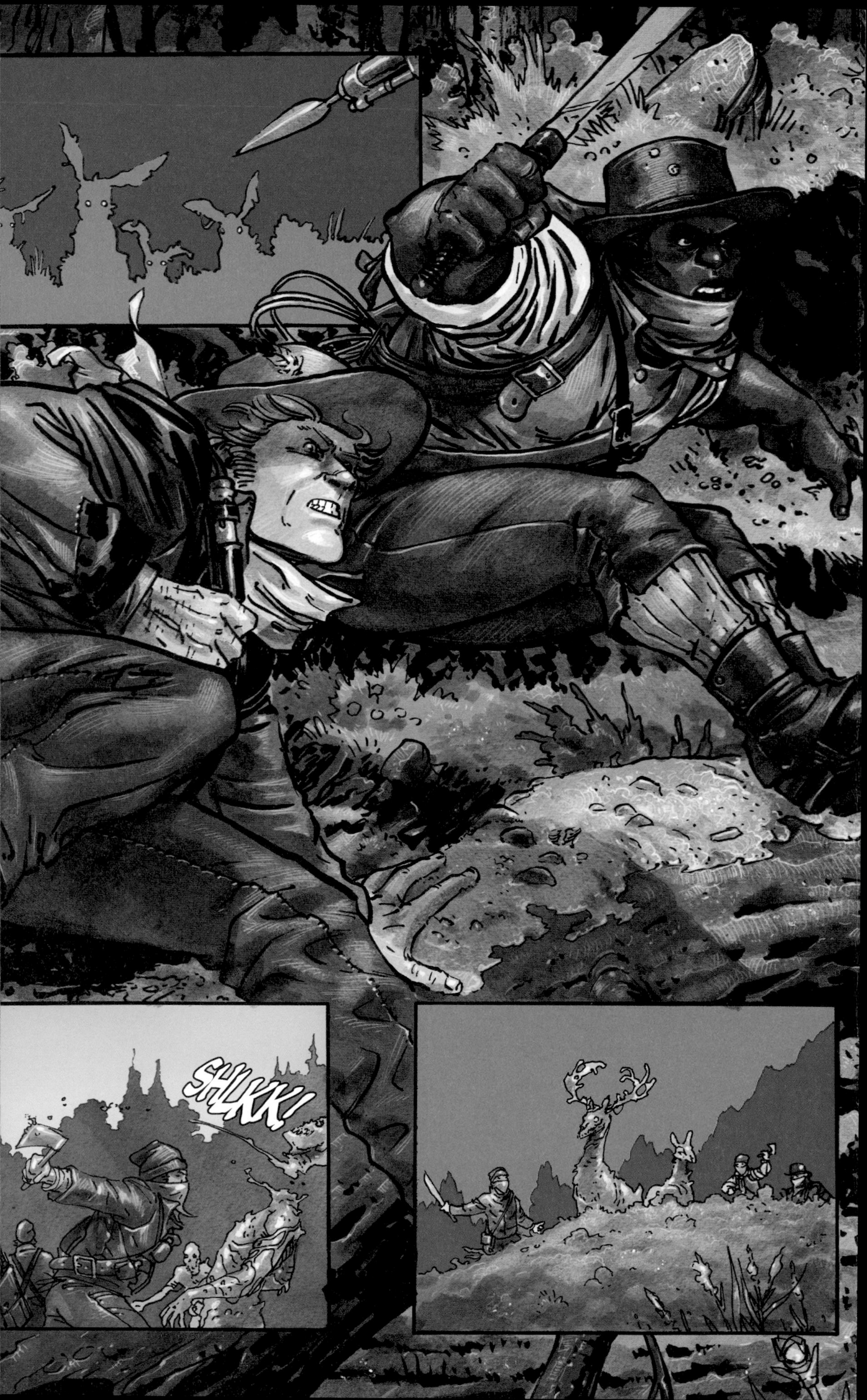
SHLKK!

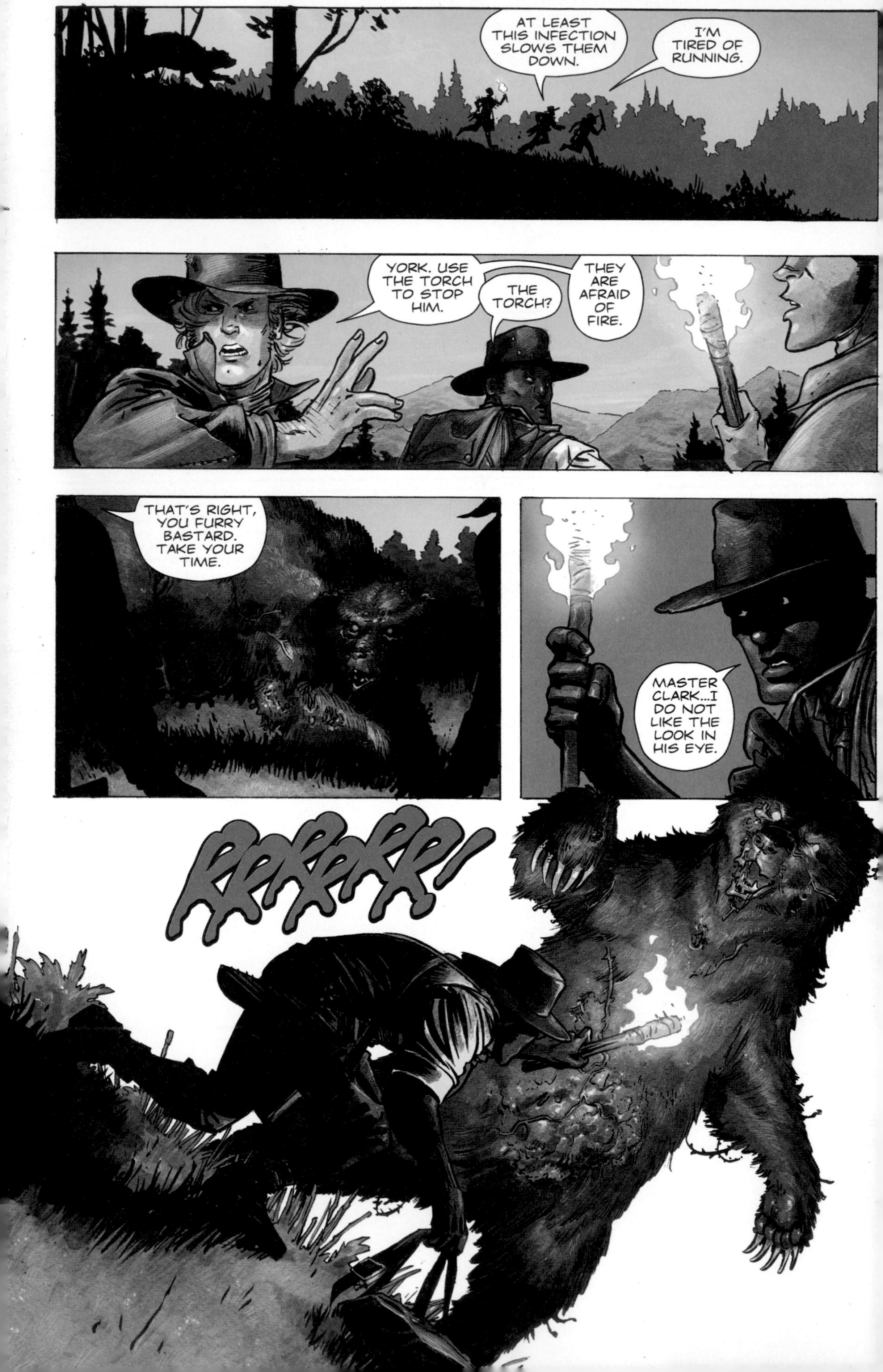
AT LEAST THIS INFECTION SLOWS THEM DOWN.
I'M TIRED OF RUNNING.
YORK. USE THE TORCH TO STOP HIM.
THE TORCH?
THEY ARE AFRAID OF FIRE.
THAT'S RIGHT, YOU FURRY BASTARD. TAKE YOUR TIME.
MASTER CLARK...I DO NOT LIKE THE LOOK IN HIS EYE.
RRRRRR!

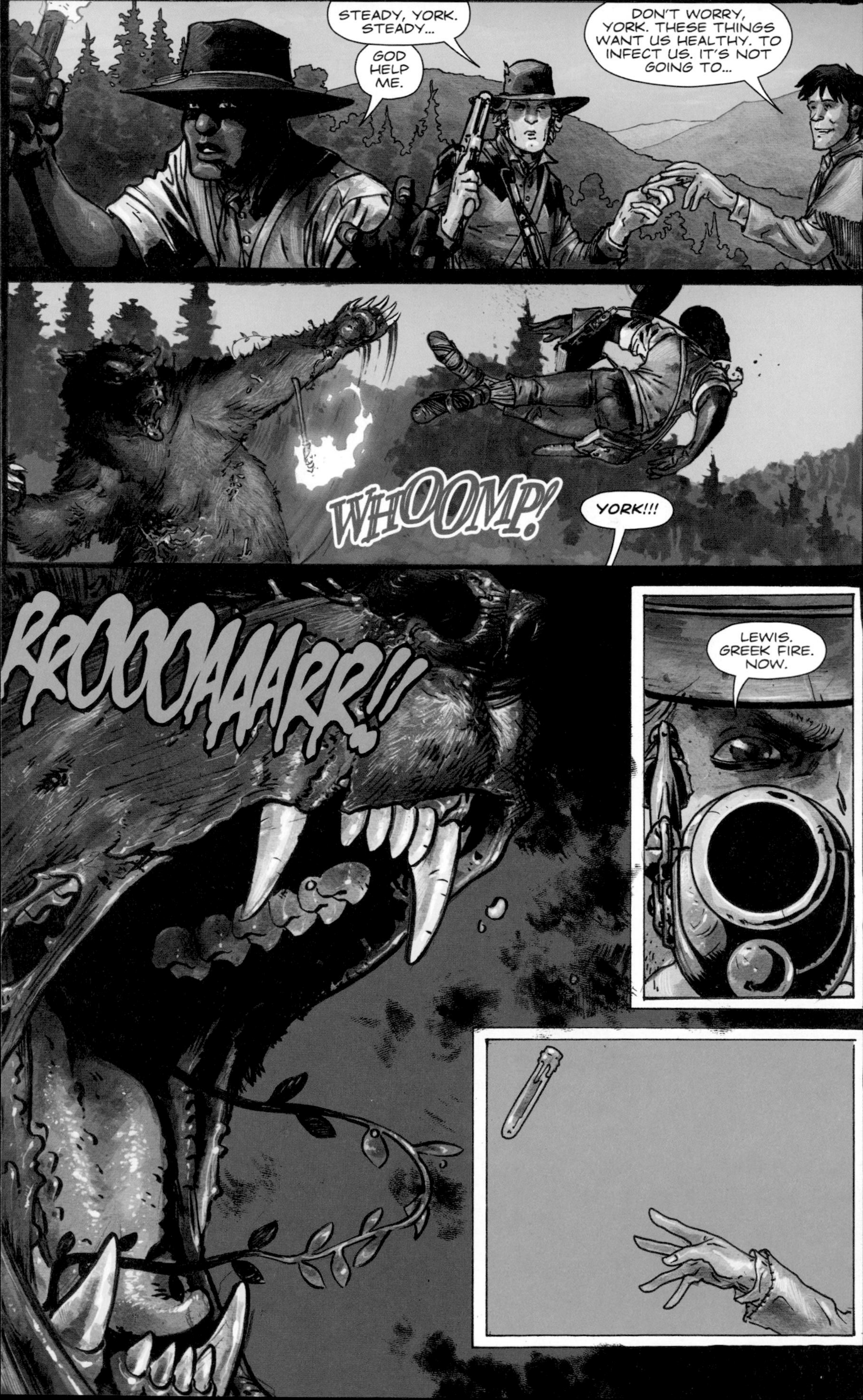
STEADY, YORK. STEADY...
GOD HELP ME.
DON'T WORRY, YORK. THESE THINGS WANT US HEALTHY. TO INFECT US. IT'S NOT GOING TO...
WHOOOMP!
YORK!!!
RROOOAAARR!!
LEWIS. GREEK FIRE. NOW.

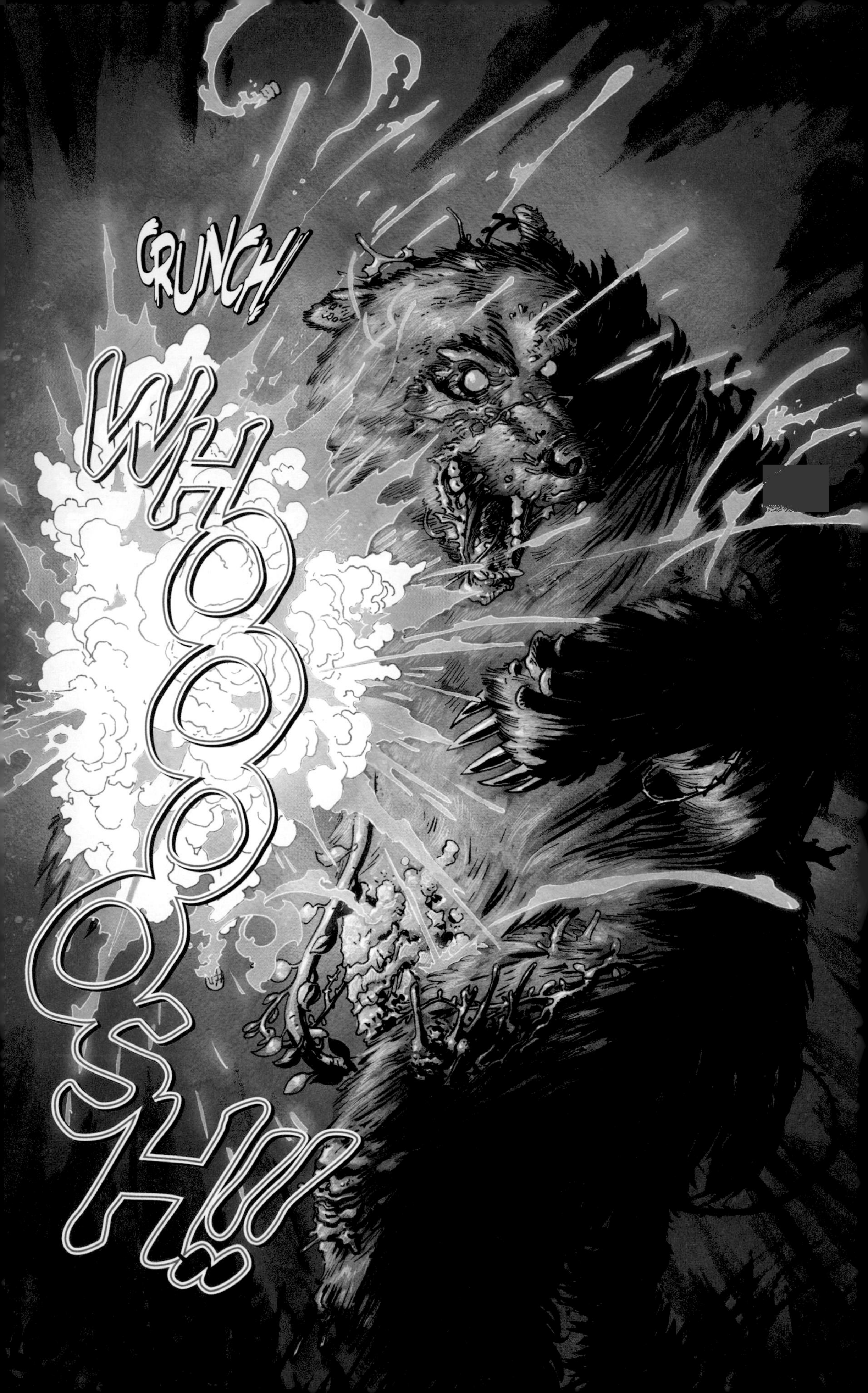
CRUNCH!
WHOOOOSH!!

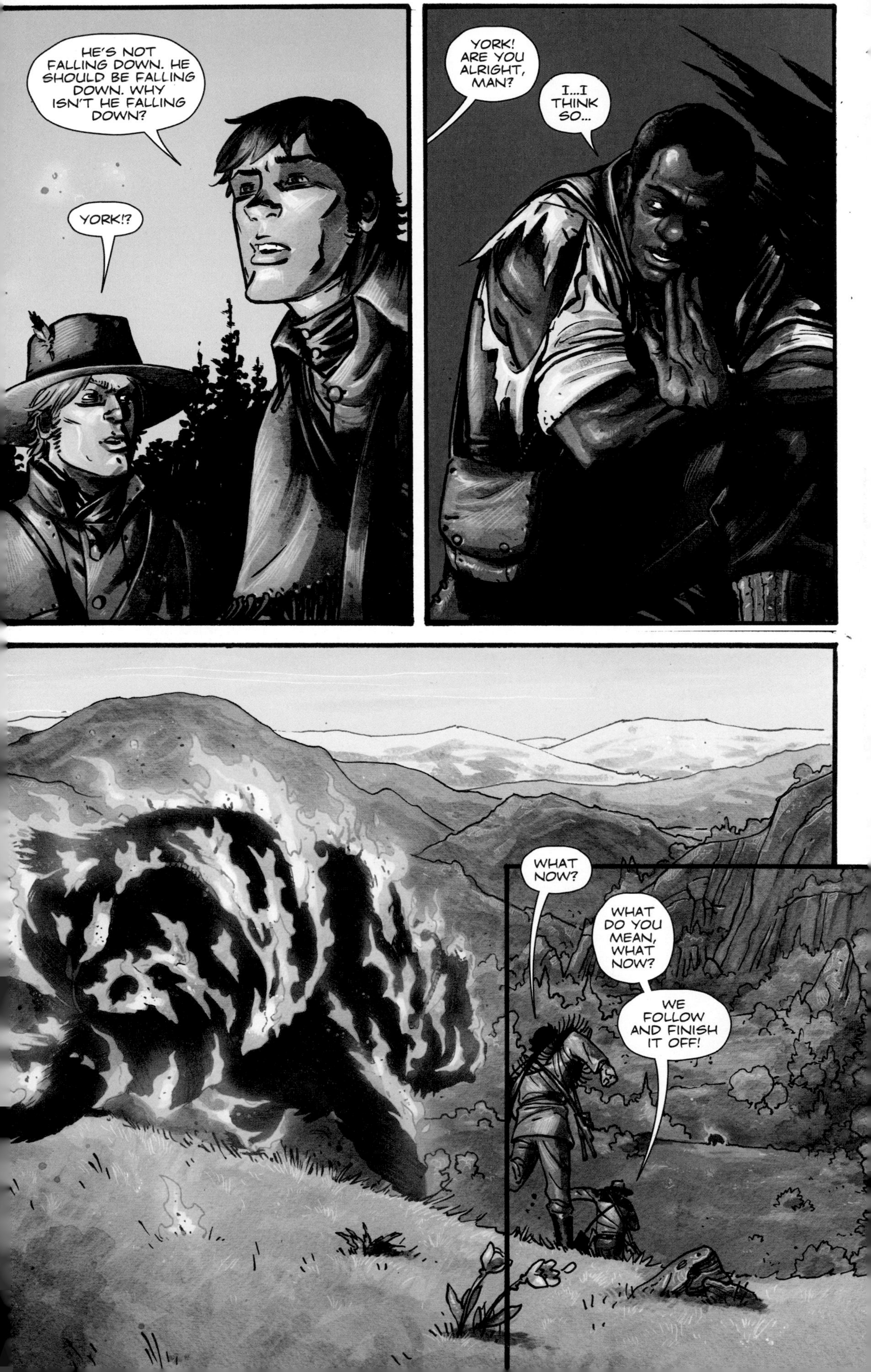

HE'S NOT FALLING DOWN. HE SHOULD BE FALLING DOWN. WHY ISN'T HE FALLING DOWN?
YORK!?
YORK! ARE YOU ALRIGHT, MAN?
I...I THINK SO...
WHAT NOW?
WHAT DO YOU MEAN, WHAT NOW?
WE FOLLOW AND FINISH IT OFF!

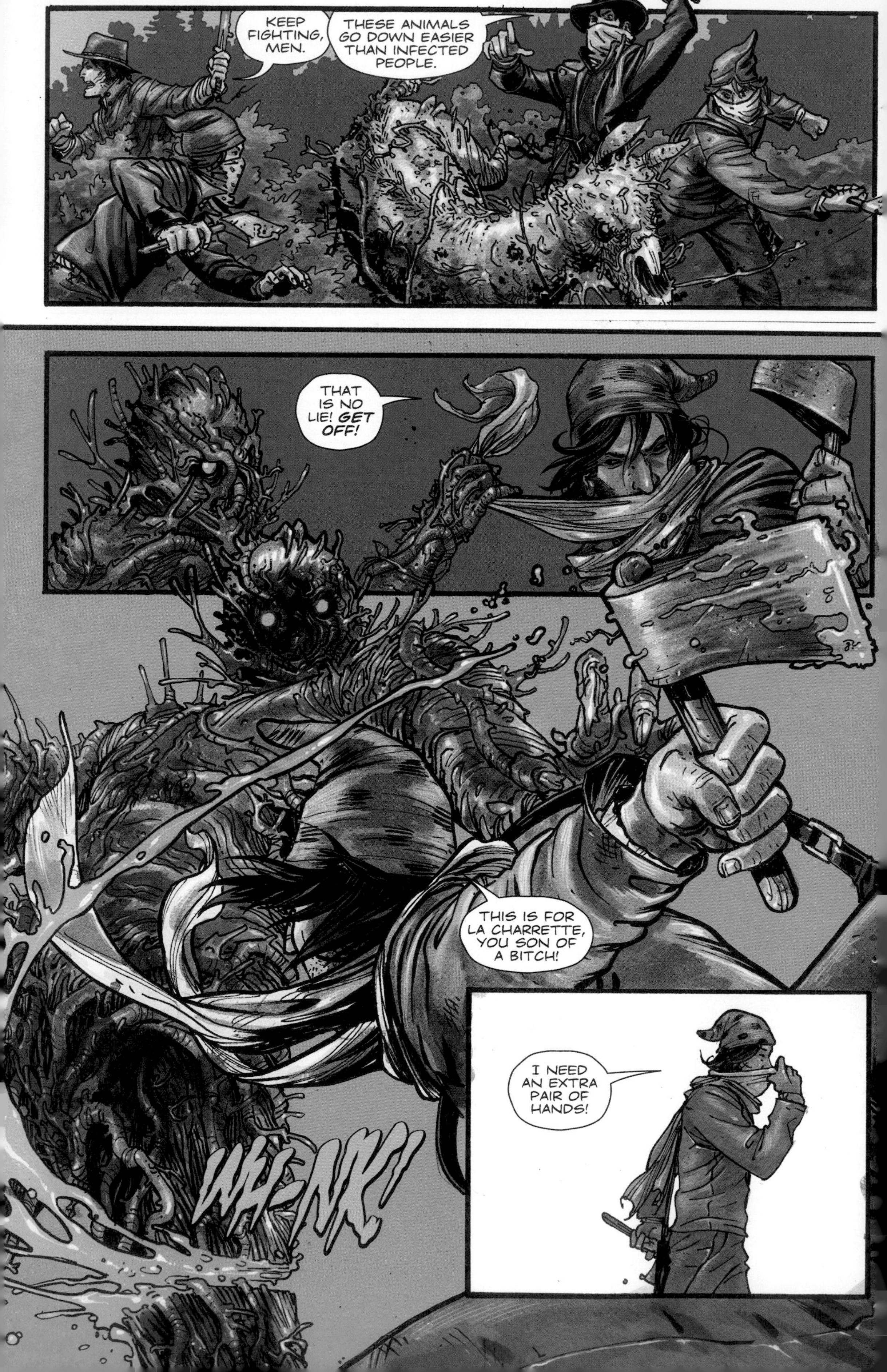
KEEP FIGHTING, MEN.
THESE ANIMALS GO DOWN EASIER THAN INFECTED PEOPLE.
THAT IS NO LIE! GET OFF!
THIS IS FOR LA CHARRETTE, YOU SON OF A BITCH!
WH-NK!
I NEED AN EXTRA PAIR OF HANDS!

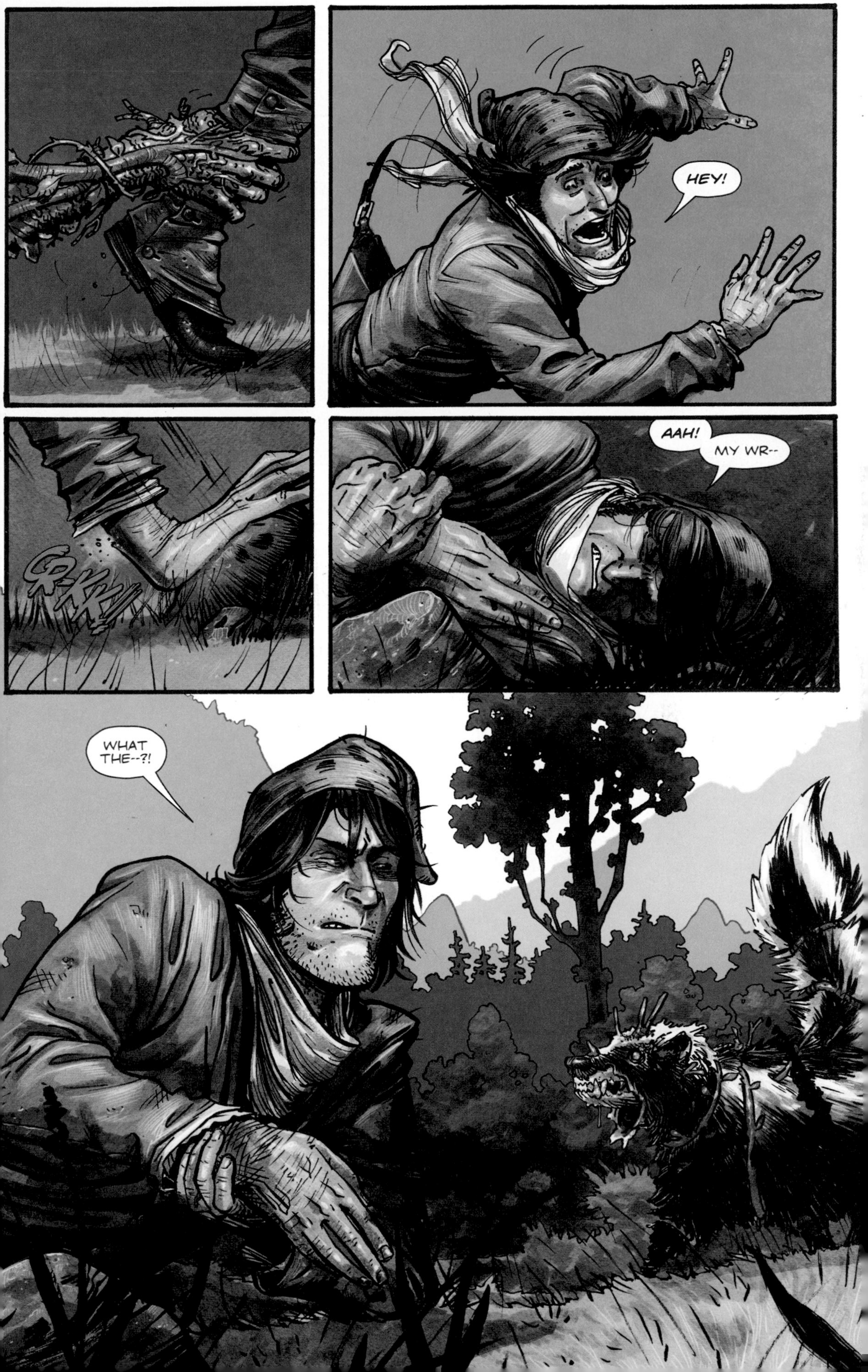
HEY!
GR-KK!
AAH!
MY WR--
WHAT THE--?!

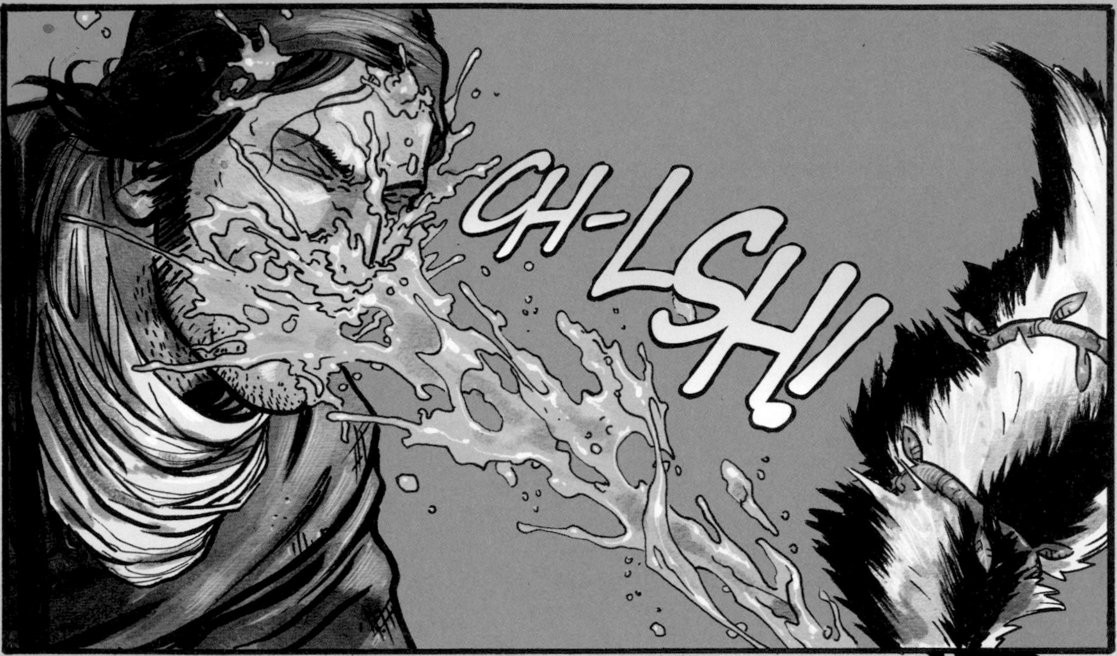
CH-LSH!

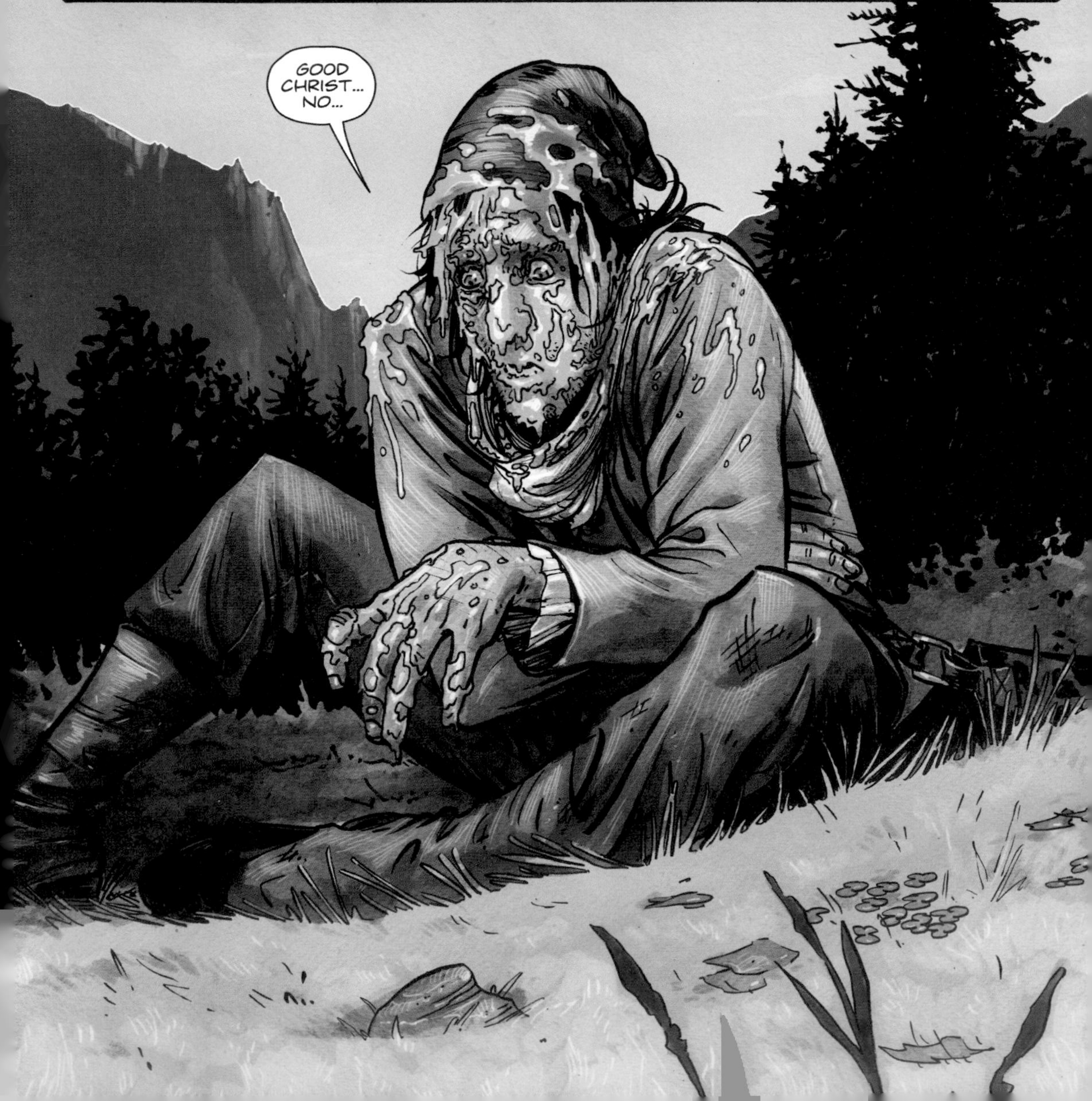
GOOD CHRIST... NO...

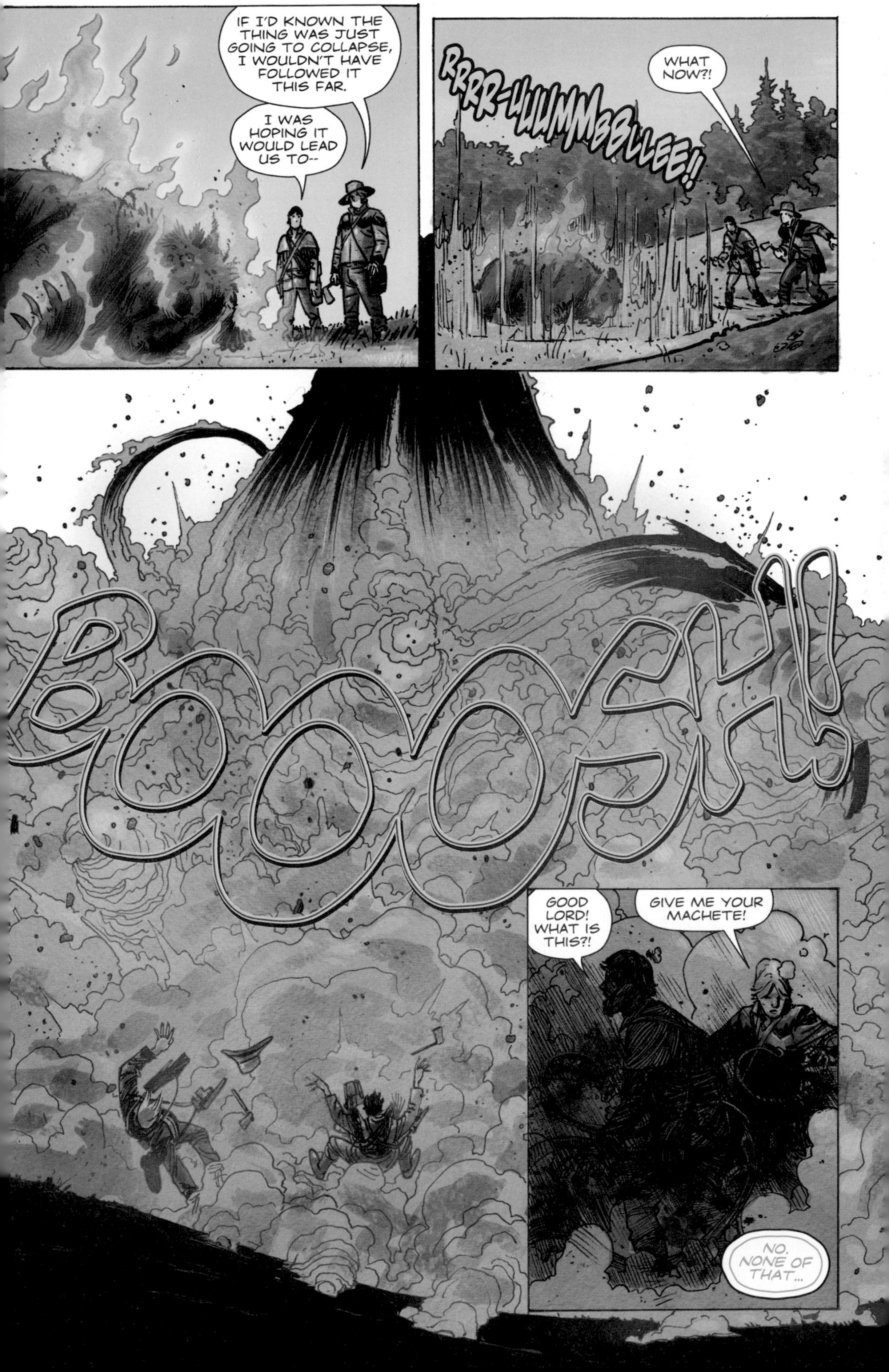
IF I'D KNOWN THE THING WAS JUST GOING TO COLLAPSE, I WOULDN'T HAVE FOLLOWED IT THIS FAR.
I WAS HOPING IT WOULD LEAD US TO--
RRRR-UUUMMBBLLEE!!
WHAT NOW?!
BOOOOSH!!
GOOD LORD! WHAT IS THIS?!
GIVE ME YOUR MACHETE!
NO. NONE OF THAT...

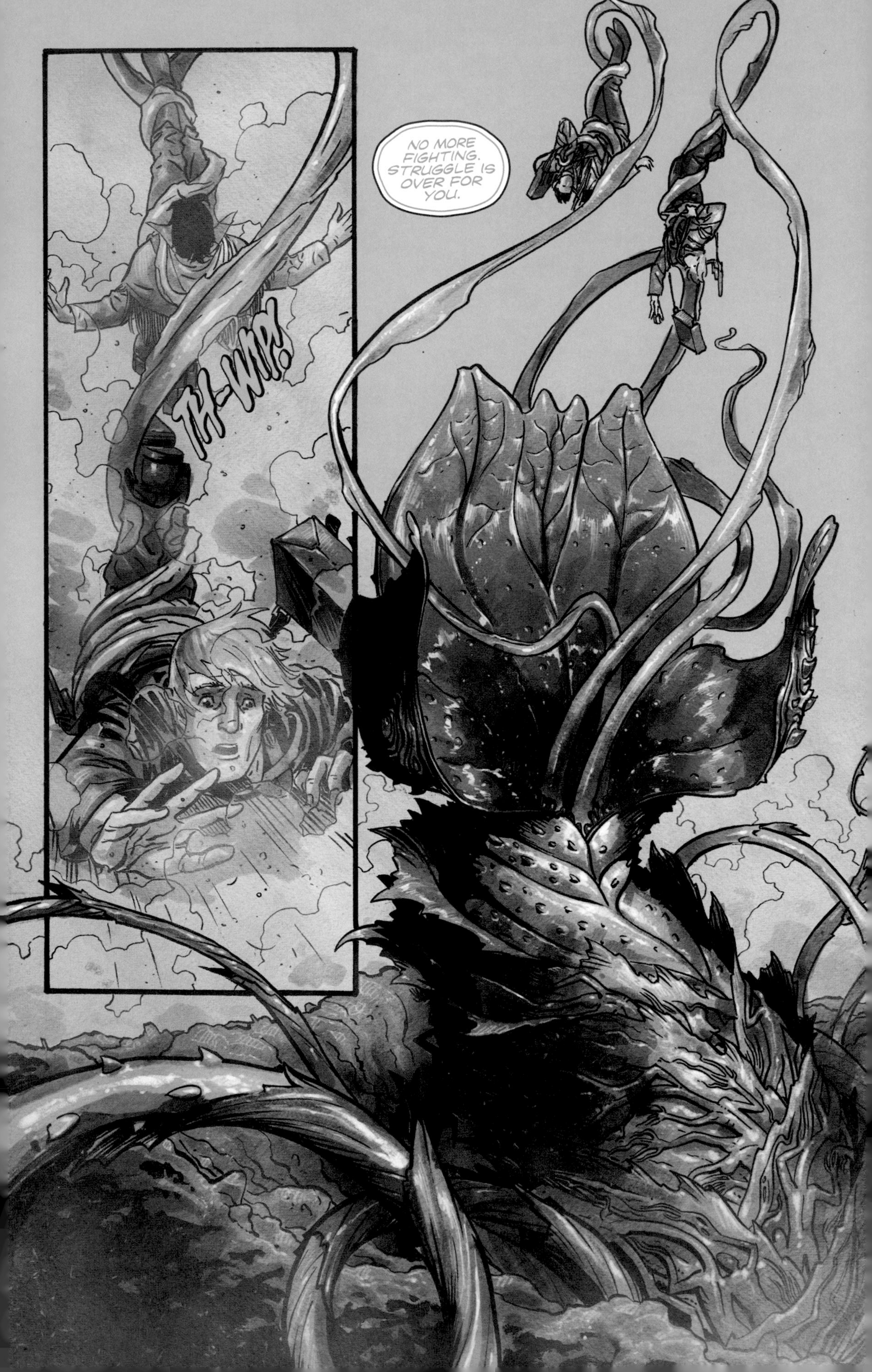
TH-WIP!
NO MORE FIGHTING. STRUGGLE IS OVER FOR YOU.

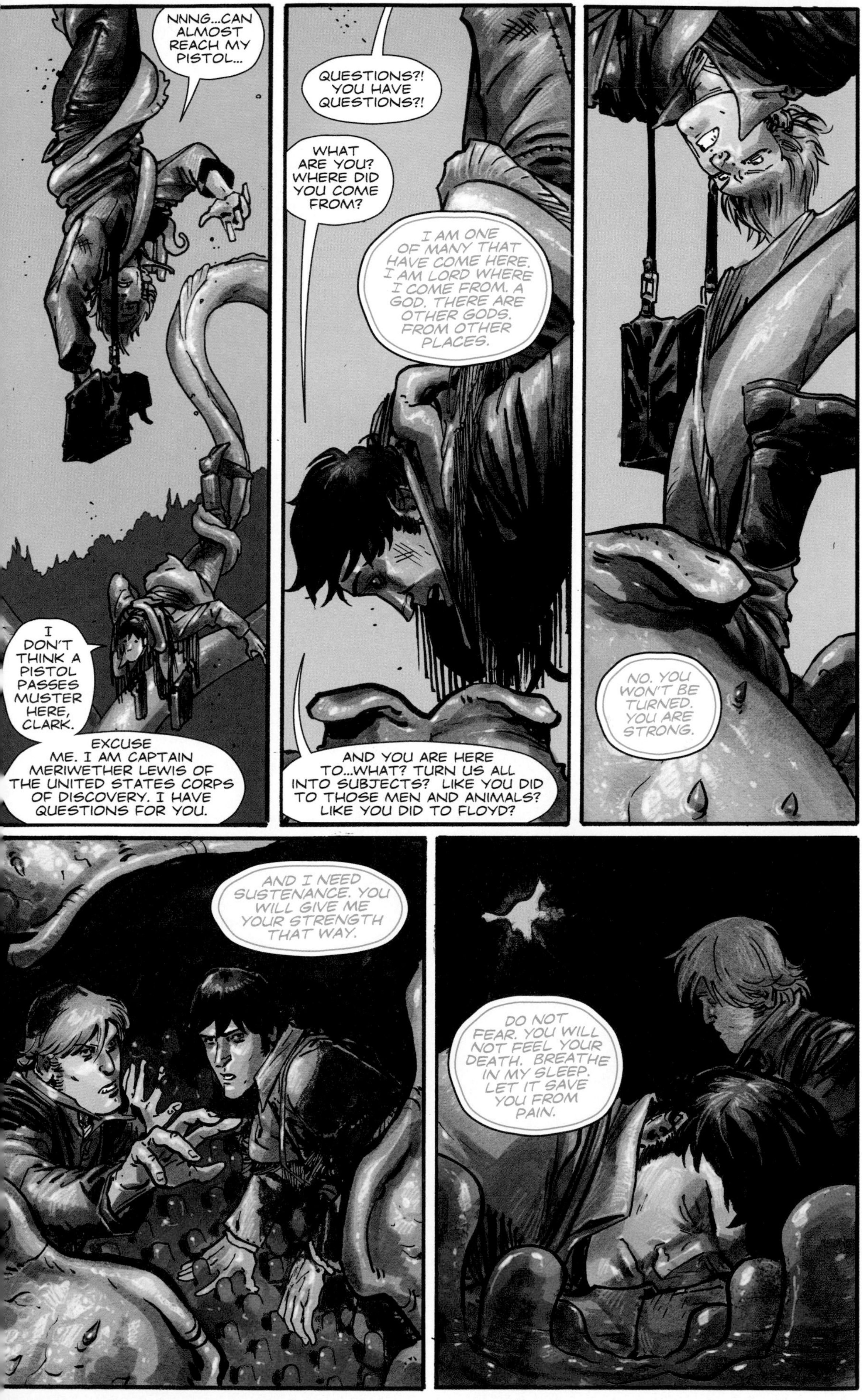
NNNG...CAN ALMOST REACH MY PISTOL...
I DON'T THINK A PISTOL PASSES MUSTER HERE, CLARK.
EXCUSE ME. I AM CAPTAIN MERIWETHER LEWIS OF THE UNITED STATES CORPS OF DISCOVERY. I HAVE QUESTIONS FOR YOU.
QUESTIONS?! YOU HAVE QUESTIONS?!
WHAT ARE YOU? WHERE DID YOU COME FROM?
I AM ONE OF MANY THAT HAVE COME HERE. I AM LORD WHERE I COME FROM. A GOD. THERE ARE OTHER GODS. FROM OTHER PLACES.
AND YOU ARE HERE TO...WHAT? TURN US ALL INTO SUBJECTS? LIKE YOU DID TO THOSE MEN AND ANIMALS? LIKE YOU DID TO FLOYD?
NO. YOU WON'T BE TURNED. YOU ARE STRONG.
AND I NEED SUSTENANCE. YOU WILL GIVE ME YOUR STRENGTH THAT WAY.
DO NOT FEAR. YOU WILL NOT FEEL YOUR DEATH. BREATHE IN MY SLEEP. LET IT SAVE YOU FROM PAIN.

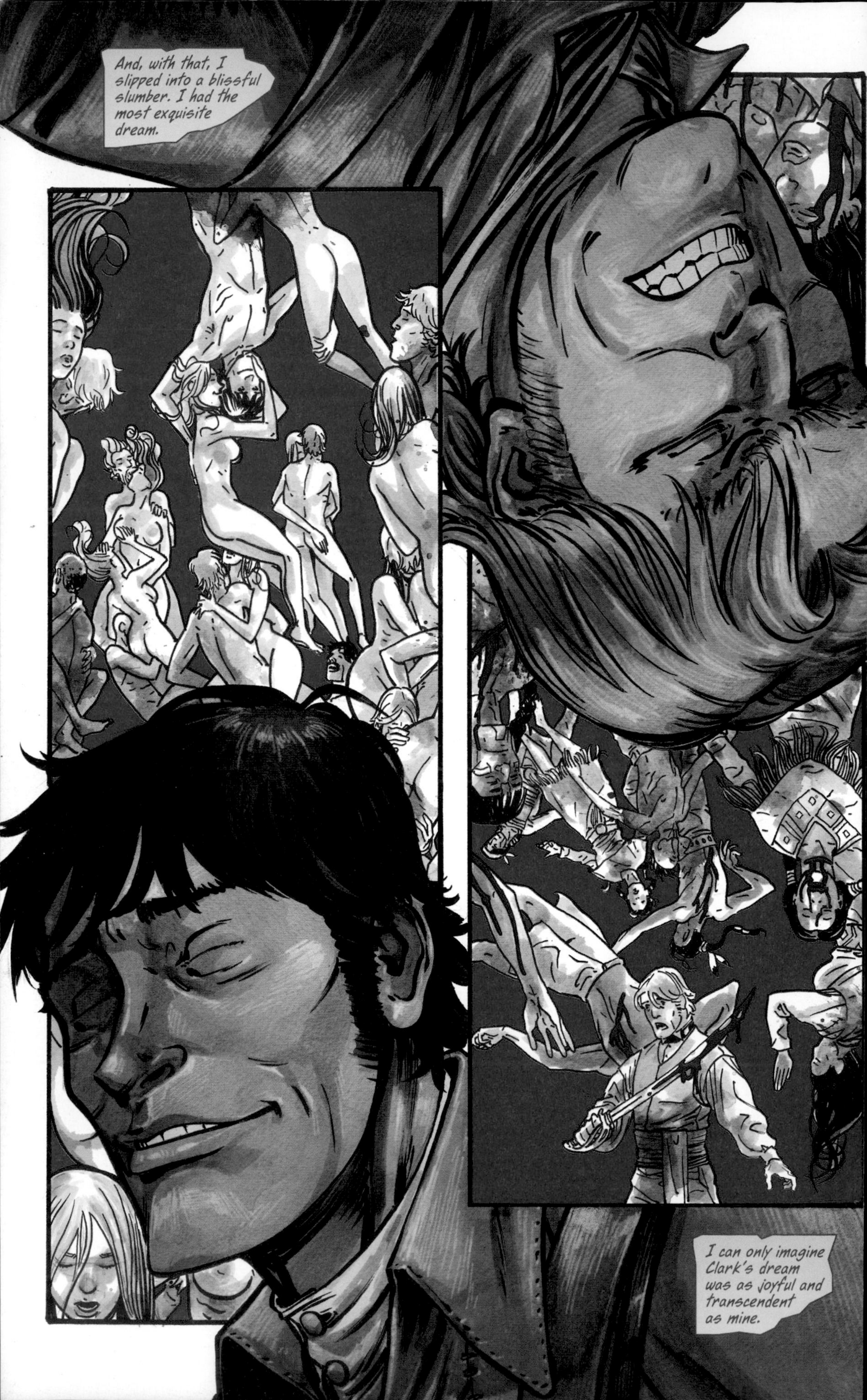
And, with that, I slipped into a blissful slumber. I had the most exquisite dream.
I can only imagine Clark's dream was as joyful and transcendent as mine.

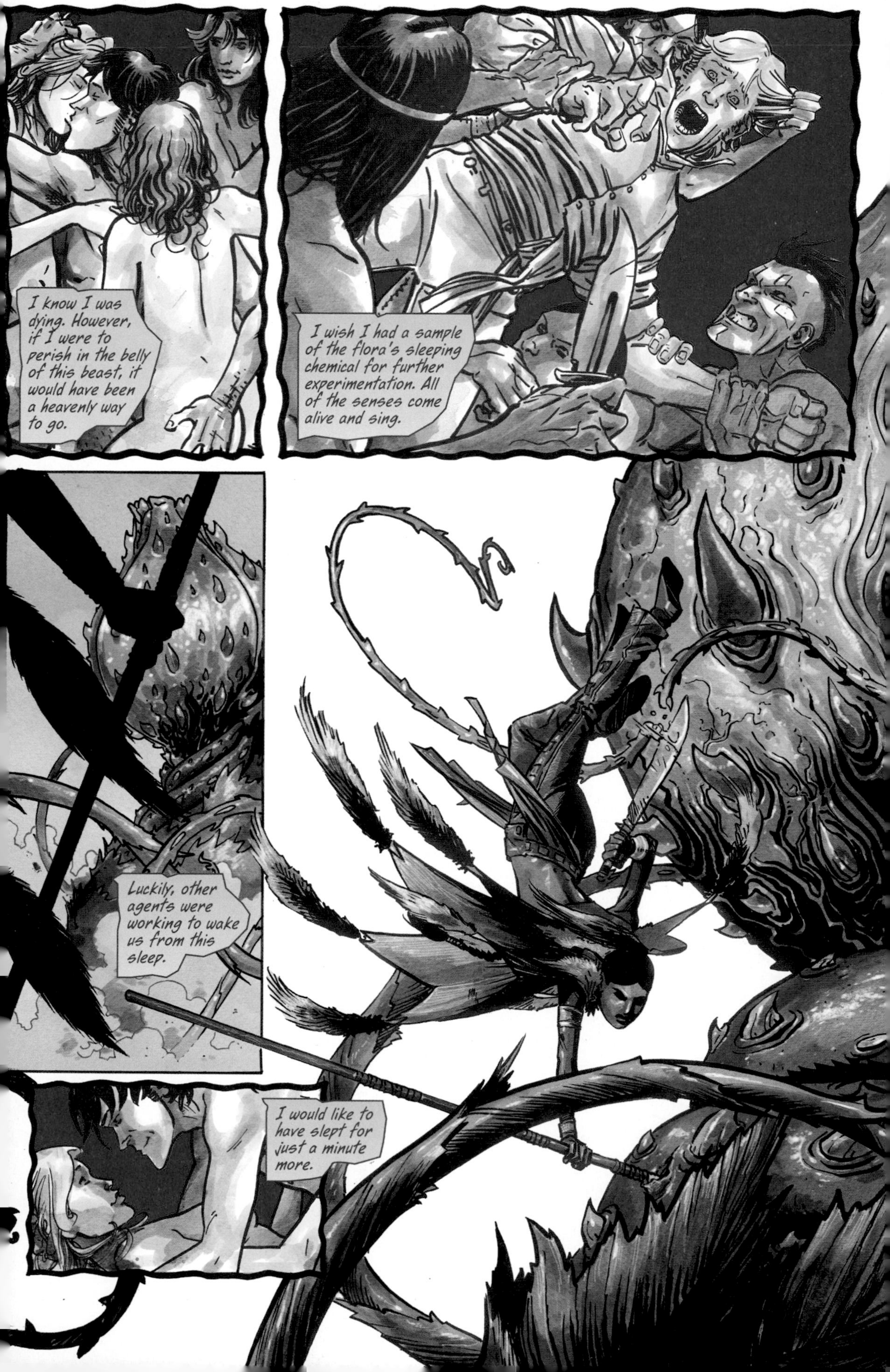
I know I was dying. However, if I were to perish in the belly of this beast, it would have been a heavenly way to go.
I wish I had a sample of the flora's sleeping chemical for further experimentation. All of the senses come alive and sing.
Luckily, other agents were working to wake us from this sleep.
I would like to have slept for just a minute more.

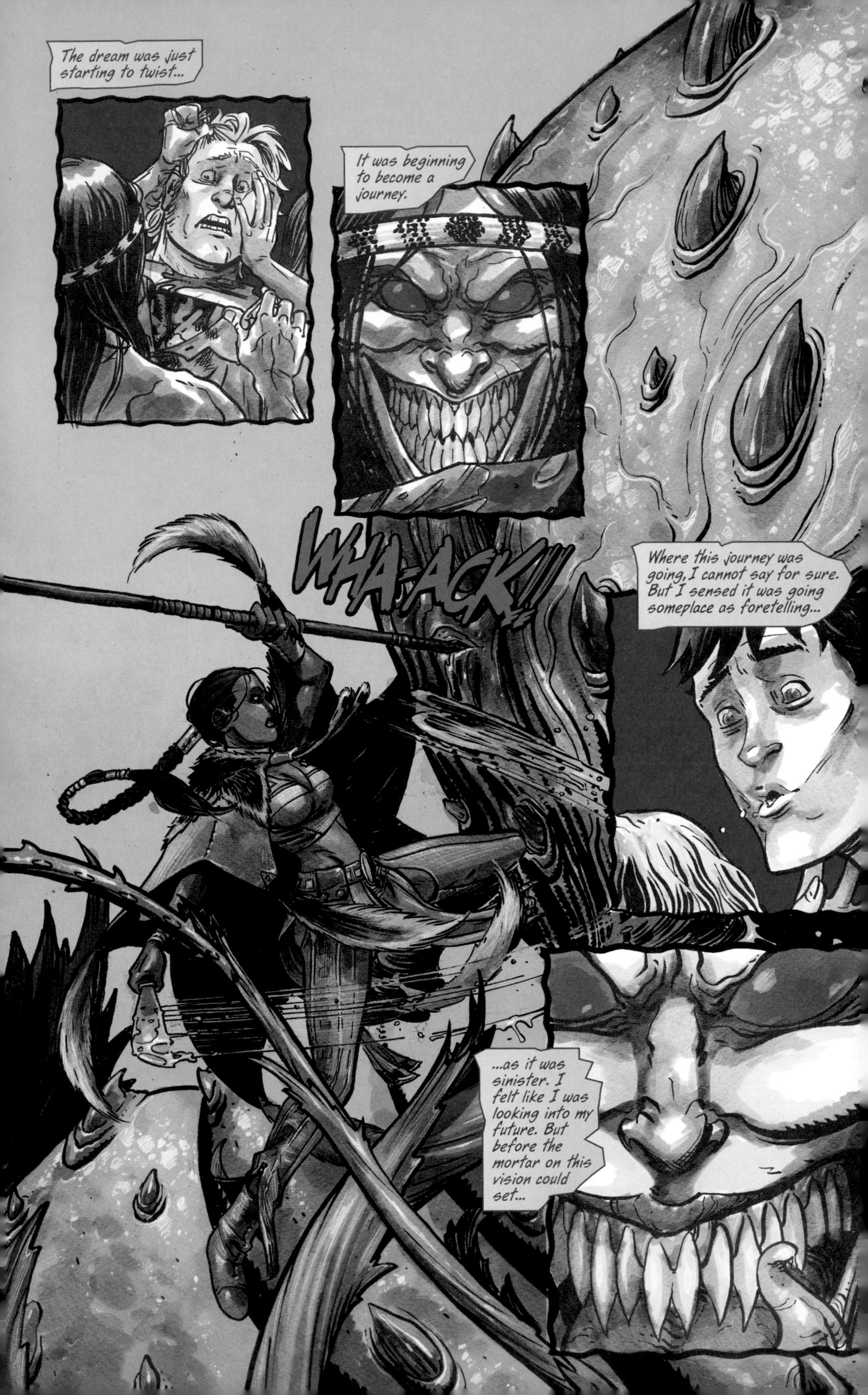
The dream was just starting to twist...
It was beginning to become a journey.
WHA-ACK!!
Where this journey was going, I cannot say for sure. But I sensed it was going someplace as foretelling...
...as it was sinister. I felt like I was looking into my future. But before the mortar on this vision could set...

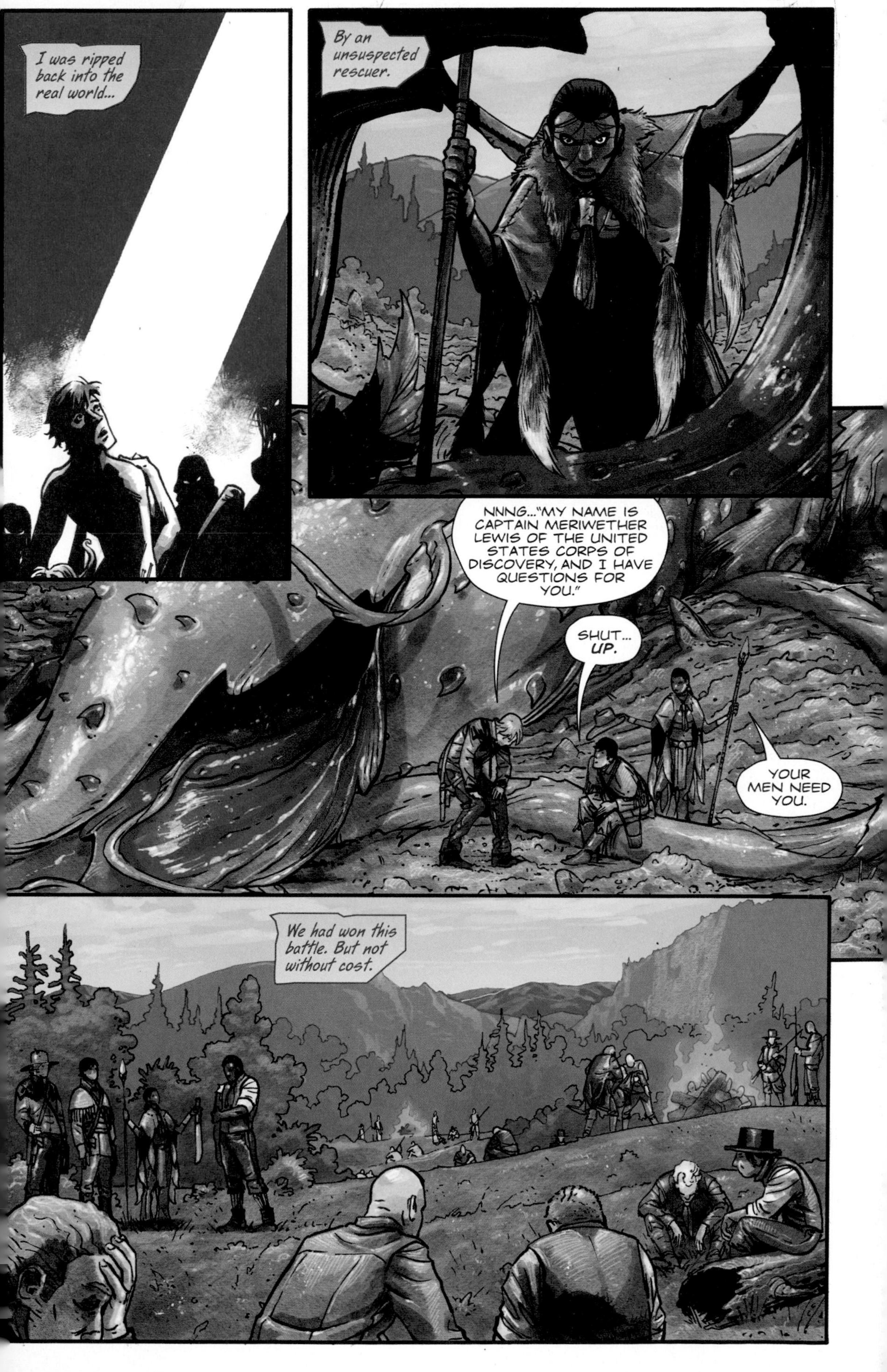
I was ripped back into the real world...
By an unsuspected rescuer.
NNNG..."MY NAME IS CAPTAIN MERIWETHER LEWIS OF THE UNITED STATES CORPS OF DISCOVERY, AND I HAVE QUESTIONS FOR YOU."
SHUT... UP.
YOUR MEN NEED YOU.
We had won this battle. But not without cost.

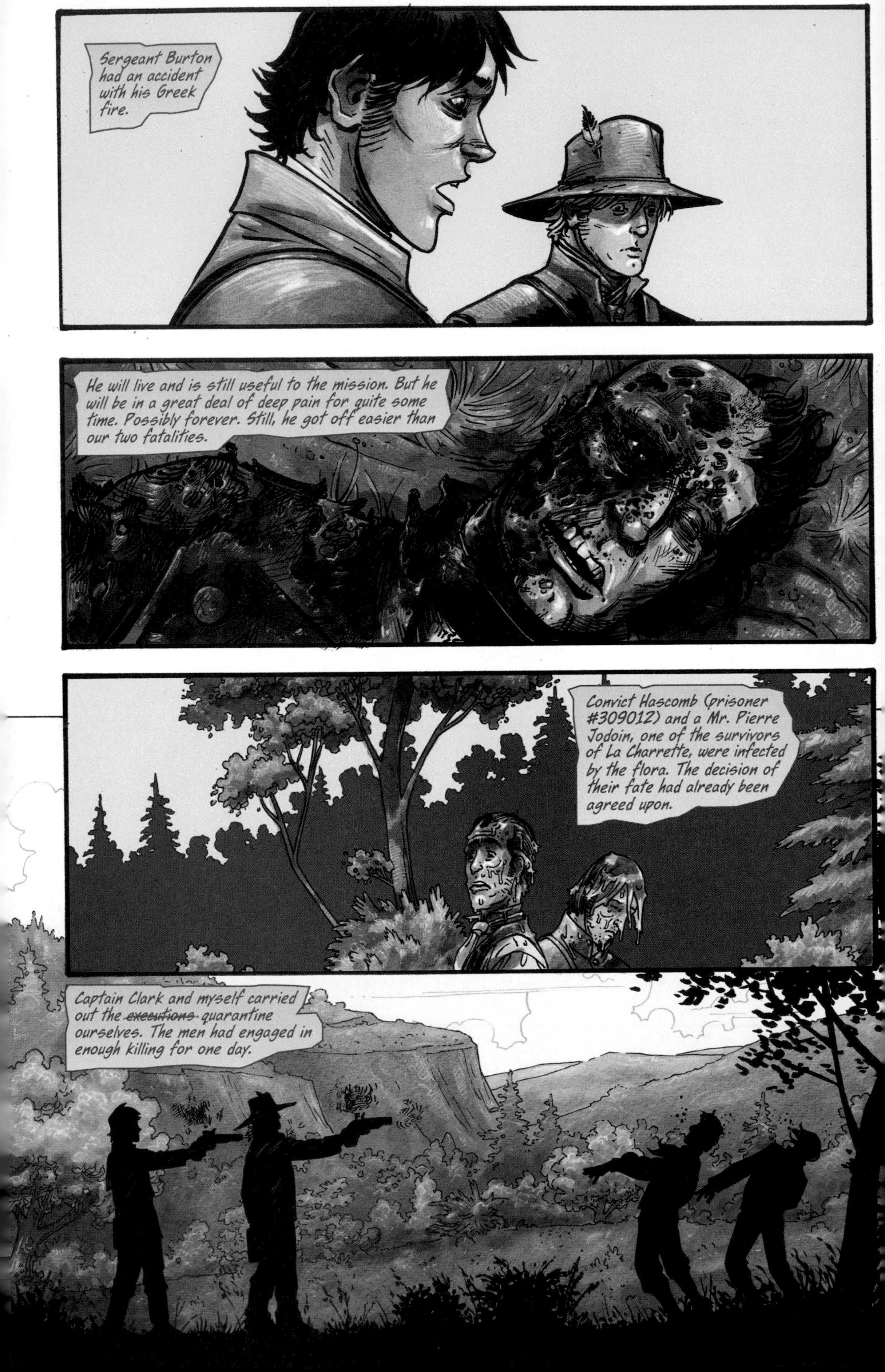
Sergeant Burton had an accident with his Greek fire.
He will live and is still useful to the mission. But he will be in a great deal of deep pain for quite some time. Possibly forever. Still, he got off easier than our two fatalities.
Convict Hascomb (prisoner #309012) and a Mr. Pierre Jodoin, one of the survivors of La Charrette, were infected by the flora. The decision of their fate had already been agreed upon.
Captain Clark and myself carried out the ~~executions~~ quarantine ourselves. The men had engaged in enough killing for one day.

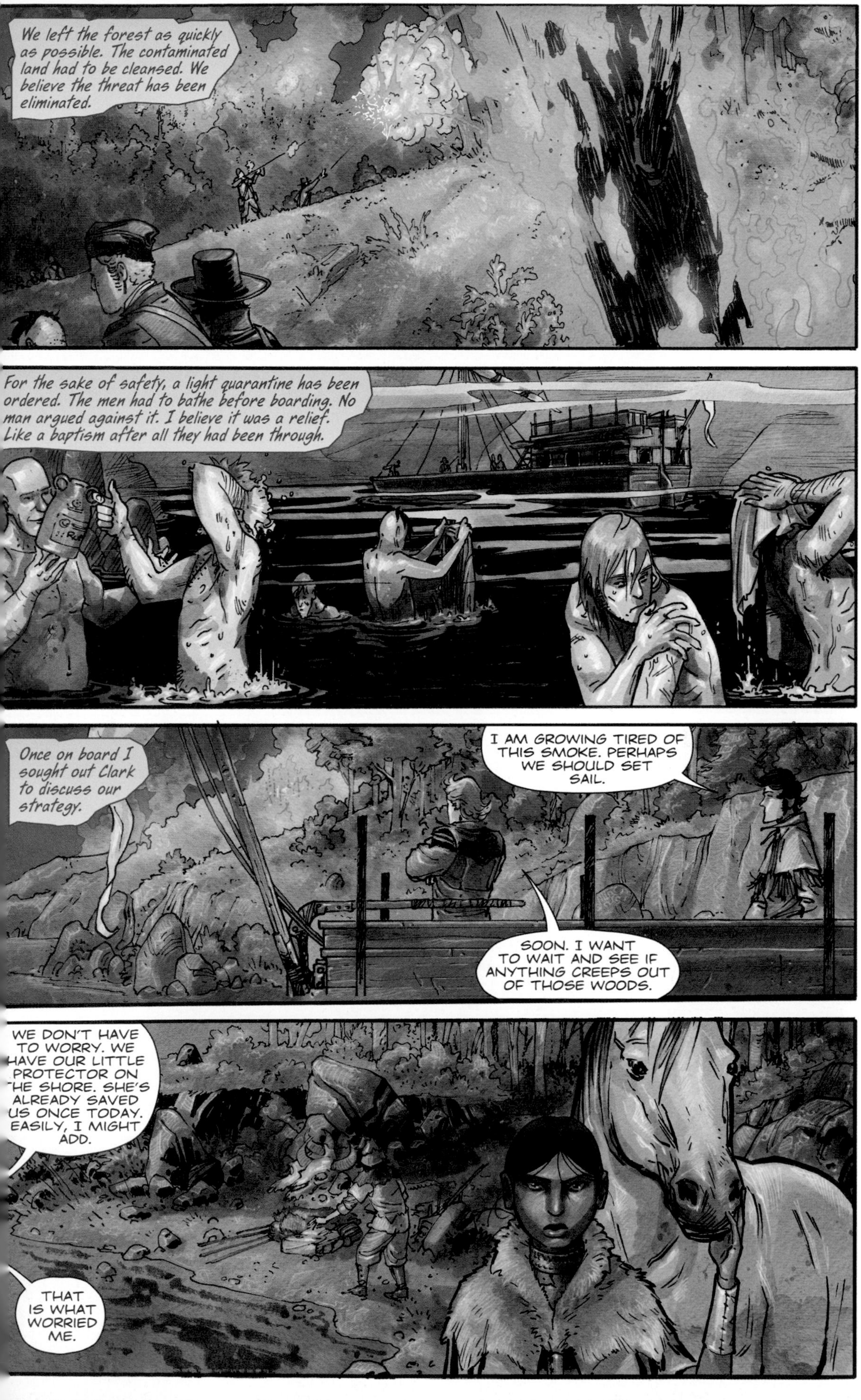
We left the forest as quickly as possible. The contaminated land had to be cleansed. We believe the threat has been eliminated.
For the sake of safety, a light quarantine has been ordered. The men had to bathe before boarding. No man argued against it. I believe it was a relief. Like a baptism after all they had been through.
Once on board I sought out Clark to discuss our strategy.
I AM GROWING TIRED OF THIS SMOKE. PERHAPS WE SHOULD SET SAIL.
SOON. I WANT TO WAIT AND SEE IF ANYTHING CREEPS OUT OF THOSE WOODS.
WE DON'T HAVE TO WORRY. WE HAVE OUR LITTLE PROTECTOR ON THE SHORE. SHE'S ALREADY SAVED US ONCE TODAY. EASILY, I MIGHT ADD.
THAT IS WHAT WORRIED ME.

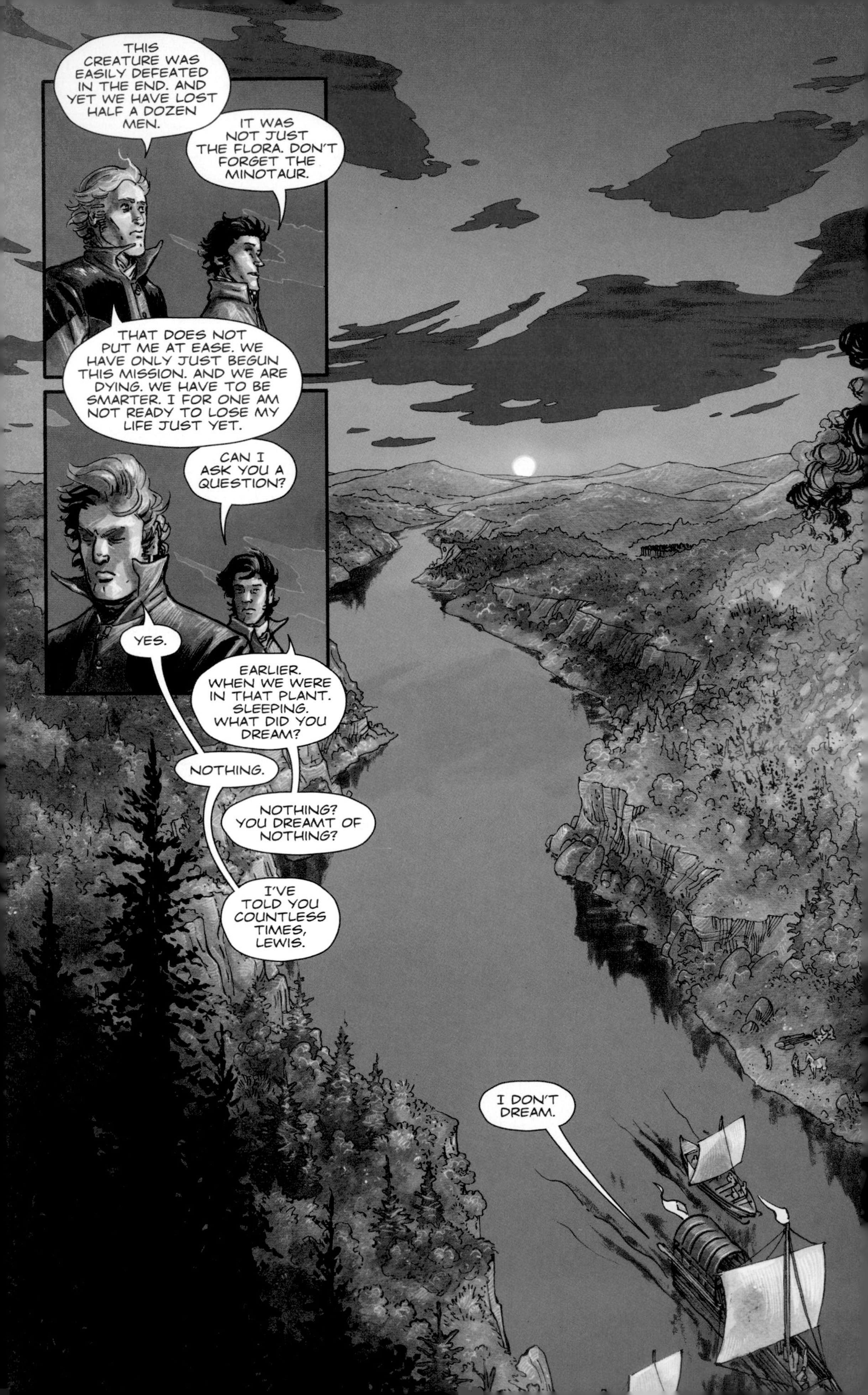
THIS CREATURE WAS EASILY DEFEATED IN THE END. AND YET WE HAVE LOST HALF A DOZEN MEN.
IT WAS NOT JUST THE FLORA. DON'T FORGET THE MINOTAUR.
THAT DOES NOT PUT ME AT EASE. WE HAVE ONLY JUST BEGUN THIS MISSION. AND WE ARE DYING. WE HAVE TO BE SMARTER. I FOR ONE AM NOT READY TO LOSE MY LIFE JUST YET.
CAN I ASK YOU A QUESTION?
YES.
EARLIER. WHEN WE WERE IN THAT PLANT. SLEEPING. WHAT DID YOU DREAM?
NOTHING.
NOTHING? YOU DREAMT OF NOTHING?
I'VE TOLD YOU COUNTLESS TIMES, LEWIS.
I DON'T DREAM.

To be continued...

For more tales from Robert Kirkman and Skybound

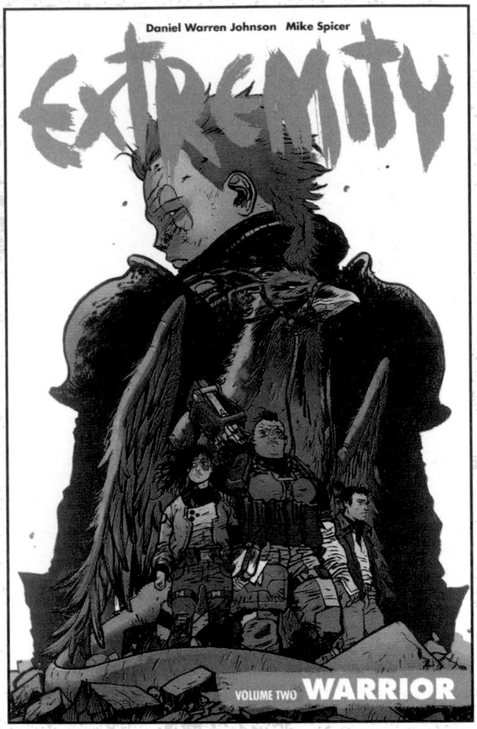
Daniel Warren Johnson Mike Spicer
EXTREMITY
VOLUME TWO WARRIOR

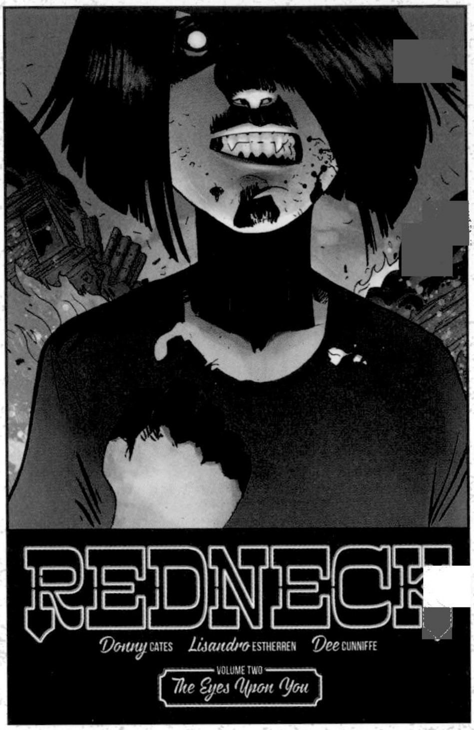
REDNECK
Donny CATES Lisandro ESTHERREN Dee CUNNIFFE
VOLUME TWO
The Eyes Upon You

VOL. 1: ARTIST TP
ISBN: 978-1-5343-0242-6
$16.99

VOL. 2: WARRIOR TP
ISBN: 978-1-5343-0649-3
$16.99

VOL. 1: DEEP IN THE HEART TP
ISBN: 978-1-5343-0331-7
$16.99

VOL. 2: THE EYES UPON YOU TP
ISBN: 978-1-5343-0665-3
$16.99

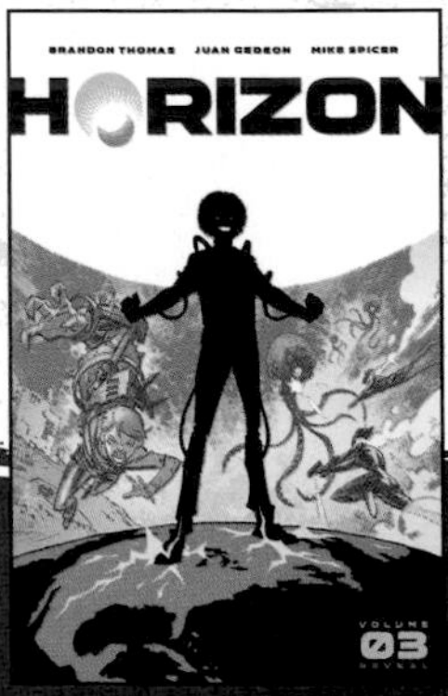
HORIZON
03

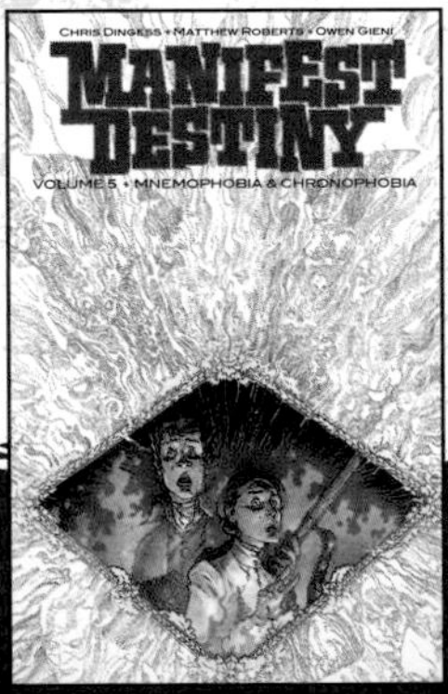
MANIFEST DESTINY
VOLUME 5 • MNEMOPHOBIA & CHRONOPHOBIA

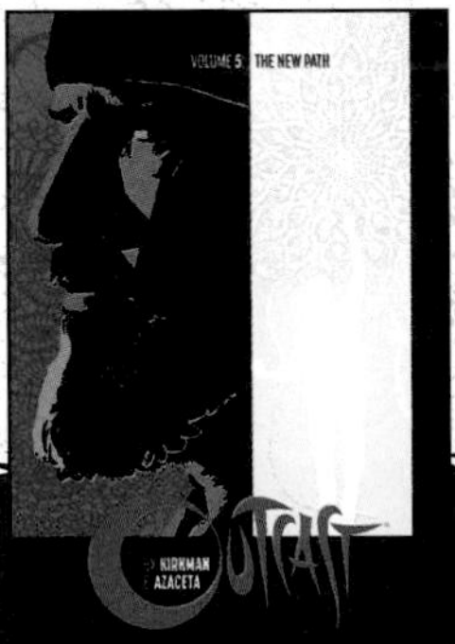
VOLUME 5 THE NEW PATH
KIRKMAN AZACETA
OUTCAST

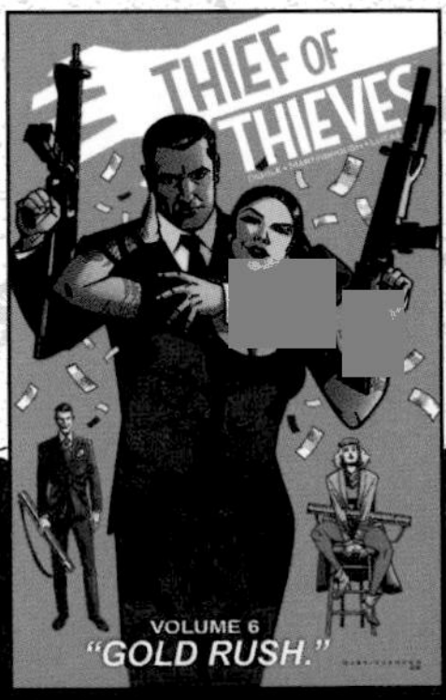
THIEF OF THIEVES
VOLUME 6
"GOLD RUSH."

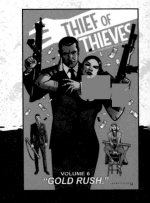

VOL. 1: REPRISAL TP
ISBN: 978-1-5343-0047-7
$9.99

VOL. 2: REMNANT TP
ISBN: 978-1-5343-0227-3
$12.99

VOL. 3: REVEAL TP
ISBN: 978-1-5343-0487-1
$16.99

VOL. 1: FLORA & FAUNA TP
ISBN: 978-1-60706-982-9
$9.99

VOL. 2: AMPHIBIA & INSECTA TP
ISBN: 978-1-63215-052-3
$14.99

VOL. 3: CHIROPTERA & CARNIFORMAVES TP
ISBN: 978-1-63215-397-5
$14.99

VOL. 4: SASQUATCH TP
ISBN: 978-1-63215-890-1
$14.99

VOL. 5: MNEMOPHOBIA & CHRONOPHOBIA TP
ISBN: 978-1-5343-0230-3
$16.99

VOL. 1: A DARKNESS SURROUNDS HIM TP
ISBN: 978-1-63215-053-0
$9.99

VOL. 2: A VAST AND UNENDING RUIN TP
ISBN: 978-1-63215-448-4
$14.99

VOL. 3: THIS LITTLE LIGHT TP
ISBN: 978-1-63215-693-8
$14.99

VOL. 4: UNDER DEVIL'S WING TP
ISBN: 978-1-5343-0050-7
$14.99

VOL. 5: THE NEW PATH TP
ISBN: 978-1-5343-0249-5
$16.99

VOL. 1: "I QUIT."
ISBN: 978-1-60706-592-0
$14.99

VOL. 2: "HELP ME."
ISBN: 978-1-60706-676-7
$14.99

VOL. 3: "VENICE."
ISBN: 978-1-60706-844-0
$14.99

VOL. 4: "THE HIT LIST."
ISBN: 978-1-63215-037-0
$14.99

VOL. 5: "TAKE ME."
ISBN: 978-1-63215-401-9
$14.99

VOL. 6: "GOLD RUSH."
ISBN: 978-1-53430-037-8
$14.99